D1403239

DRIVE-BY

ALSO BY GARY RIVLIN

Fire on the Prairie:
Chicago's Harold Washington and the Politics of Race

DRIVE-BY

GARY RIVLIN

DISCARDED

HENRY HOLT AND COMPANY/NEW YORK

Henry Holt and Company, Inc.
Publishers since 1866
115 West 18th Street
New York, New York 10011

Henry Holt® is a registered
trademark of Henry Holt and Company, Inc.

Copyright © 1995 by Gary Rivlin
All rights reserved.
Published in Canada by Fitzhenry & Whiteside Ltd.,
195 Allstate Parkway, Markham, Ontario L3R 4T8.

Library of Congress Cataloging-in-Publication Data
Rivlin, Gary.
Drive-by / Gary Rivlin—1st ed.
p.   cm.
1. Homicide—California—Oakland.   2. Violence—California—
Oakland.   3. Violence in children—California—Oakland.   4. Oakland
(Calif.)—Social conditions.   I. Title.
HV6534.023R59   1995   95-6390
364.1'523'0979466—dc20   CIP

ISBN 0-8050-2921-4

Henry Holt books are available for special
promotions and premiums. For details contact:
Director, Special Markets.

First Edition—1995

Designed by Katy Riegel

Printed in the United States of America
All first editions are printed on acid-free paper. ∞

1 3 5 7 9 10 8 6 4 2

WINONA PUBLIC LIBRARY
151 WEST 5TH STREET
P. O. BOX 1247
WINONA, MN. 55987

To Denny

CONTENTS

Part Three: Two Years Later

PROLOGUE

Aaron was fifteen when he sat in the idling car listening to two friends prepare for a showdown with some boys they feared had a gun. "Whaddaya wanna do?" he asked. He was behind the wheel of a four-door 1967 Chrysler Newport he had bought for two hundred dollars two weeks earlier, waiting.

"I want to pop them fools!" said a sixteen-year-old kid they called Junebug. An awkward pause followed. Then the third kid in the car, Fat 'Tone, said, "I ain't fit to kill nobody."

PART ONE
THE FAMILIES

VERA

On a summer night several decades ago, in a home long since destroyed by the urban renewal wrecking ball, a half dozen people sat around a metal-legged kitchen table playing cards. A bottle of whiskey stood open on the Formica tabletop. Later, in court, several players would testify that everyone remained relatively sober throughout the two hours they played that night. Only O. D. Clay's clan would claim that the drinking was anything but moderate. What other possible explanation was there for all that followed the abrupt end to their game?

They were playing in the kitchen of a pale yellow Victorian on Fifth Street, in West Oakland, a part of town that had seen better days. The year was 1957. The great world war that had drawn tens of thousands of blacks to Oakland for jobs in the shipyards and munitions plants had ended a dozen years earlier, and this neighborhood, which had once bustled with an around-the-clock fervor, was home to people hustling for whatever work they could find. Poverty and the passing of decades had taken their toll on the wooden housing stock, built on the cheap during the city's previous big boom more than a hundred years earlier, when Oakland (and not San Francisco) had been designated the western spur of the transcontinental railroad.

In the name of progress and supposedly on behalf of the poor, the city fathers launched a "blight removal" program in 1955, a series of government-funded projects that—according to the city's own reports—destroyed many more sturdy structures than dilapidated, uninhabitable ones. Everyone but the residents of West Oakland seemed to benefit from the projects built in place of the destroyed homes, including a double-decker freeway (connecting San Francisco to the southern suburbs) that gouged the neighborhood like a vast wound and a new commuter train line, which was like another slicing. The final insult was the razing of Seventh Street, a bustling strip that was once home to the likes of Slim Jenkin's Place and the Creole Club. A forbidding and uninviting high-rise housing project was erected in its place.

The yellow Victorian on Fifth Street was destroyed in the sixties to make way for the city's new central post office. "The guv'ment took it like they always do in a minority community," said Jasper Newton, O. D. Clay's nephew and a resident of the house in 1957. "They knocked on the door one day and said something about imminent domain, and that was that. What can you do? You know they're going to bulldoze anyway, so you take their check.

"People talk about communist countries but far as I'm concerned, that's communism right there, the guv'ment ordering you out of your house like that."

Jasper recalled his uncle O.D. as a fun-loving man whose great flaw was his fiery temper. It flared up suddenly and violently, like the brawls in the bars lining the bay along the city's western edge, jammed with dockhands, steelworkers, and the unemployed. O. D. Clay was a stocky man, short and wide. He was born in a tiny town on the Louisiana-Arkansas border and served in the army during World War II. He moved to Oakland after the war, no longer wanting any part of the rural South.

He was the kind of man who worked hard at the same job for years—always blue-collar, unskilled work—then quit capriciously, without so much as giving notice. He gambled, he drank, he frequented the dancing clubs that once lined Seventh Street. His friends knew him to be an easygoing, good-time Charlie—so long as you didn't cross some imaginary line of betrayal and disrespect. Then you were wisest to steer clear of him as best you could.

In 1957, O.D. was thirty-one years old, married, and the father of three. His wife, Vera, was twenty-one. O.D. always suspected the worst of his young bride, at least where men were concerned. She was friendly and outgoing in a manner that O.D. was inclined to see as flirtatious. By the night of that fateful card game, Vera was at home swollen and sore, eight months pregnant with their fourth child. "Ain't no *time* for messing around, with three small ones at home and a fourth in my belly," Vera would plead. But sometimes there was no reasoning with O.D., especially when he was full of drink.

When he wasn't out carousing at clubs, O.D. usually could be found playing cards at the yellow Victorian on Fifth Street. O.D.'s sister Rosie owned the house. Though Rosie never much cared for cards herself, there always seemed to be a game going on at her place. Her pleasure came in the small percentage she took out of every pot.

Vernest Parker—"Parker," even to those who knew him well—was the first to arrive on that September night in 1957. Parker lived a few doors down from Rosie, but he was no regular. He was a quiet and modest man who worked the late shift at the Ambassador Laundry Service and mainly kept to himself. But his car was on the blink and his buddy Jimmy King had promised him a ride to work. Jimmy, a regular at Rosie's, suggested that they meet there. It'd be a friendly neighborhood game, Jimmy told him, just some of Parker's neighbor's family and some of their friends. Parker took him up on the offer.

Jimmy drove a bus at a nearby military base. He was a large man whose bulk was matched by an oversize personality. He was six feet one, if not taller, and large around the chest. He towered over O.D. Jimmy was more easygoing than O.D., but he was loud and blustery and a real talker just the same. Jimmy knew Vera—enjoyed flirting with her, if the truth be known, just as he enjoyed flirting with any number of pretty young women around the neighborhood. O.D. figured Jimmy to be one of those no-good bastards sniffing around his wife—and not without cause, at least according to his nephew Jasper. O.D. didn't really know Parker, but he immediately disliked him anyway, if for no other reason than the company he kept.

On that late summer night, the willowy palm trees that once lent Fifth Street a regal air would have been bristling with a slight, warm breeze off the bay. People around the neighborhood would have been sitting out on stoops and on front porches, soaking in the delight of something resembling a summer night back home in the South. The Bay Area doesn't have Indian summers so much as mild, sometimes chilly Julys and Augusts followed by hot September and October days that end in evenings so delightfully pleasant they take your breath away.

The preferred game at Rosie's was blackjack. O.D. was dealing when Parker decided to split a pair of fours. His play was a foolhardy one, but O.D. busted and ended up owing him double his wager. O.D. paid Parker off, but not without first telling him what a stupid ass fool he thought him to be. And just like that, it seemed as if a fuse inside O.D. had been lit, an explosion inevitable.

"None of you black ass niggers mean shit to me," O. D. Clay told the table.

"I'm too intelligent a person to be spoken to like that," Parker responded, "and you're too intelligent a person to be using them words." Rosie immediately stepped in. She knew her brother's temper. She ordered him out of her house. O.D. started cursing his sister, so his brother-in-law grabbed him by the elbow and steered him outside. There, just outside the house, he still stood when Parker and Jimmy King left a short time later.

In O.D.'s hand was a small, pearl-handled .22 that his nephew Jasper had pawned a few days earlier. O.D. had lifted the pawn ticket and redeemed the gun without Jasper's knowledge. O.D. raised the gun to fire; his brother-in-law tried knocking the weapon from his hand. Presumably O.D. was aiming at Jimmy King, the true object of his ire, but the first shot struck Parker square in the chest.

"Now why'd you go and shoot that boy for?" Jimmy asked O.D., plain and calm as could be, as if they were still sitting around the table and Jimmy was asking him to hit him with another card. "That boy ain't done nothing to you."

"I'll give you more of the same," O.D. said. He fired the pistol five more times. Jimmy was struck three times in the gut, once in the arm, and once in the face. Parker survived the shooting, but Jimmy was pronounced dead on arrival at the hospital.

O.D. was drunk when later that night he turned himself in to the police. He first told the cops that he had been outside, sure, but some unknown assailant had been standing behind him. Then he confessed to the double shooting, but he claimed that he fired the gun in self-defense, that Parker and King had each pulled out a knife. But witnesses standing outside that night—including O.D.'s own people—contradicted his version of events. O.D., everyone agreed, had started shooting without so much as a word or an action by anyone else. He was found guilty of second-degree murder and sent to the state penitentiary, leaving Vera and the kids to fend for themselves.

Vera Mae Clay was a strong woman, compact and sturdy. She worked a series of backbreaking, low-wage jobs while O.D. served his time. She worked as a domestic in the homes of well-off white ladies; she mopped up after hours in a nearby bar; she worked as a janitor in a nursing home. Her biggest headache was her third child, Carol, the baby of the family when O.D. killed Jimmy King. One could say Carol's problem was her father's hot blood coursing through her veins, but the truth was Vera had been no angel herself. She had taken a serious misstep or two in her life, disappointing her own mother just as Carol would disappoint her.

Vera was born in the backwoods of Arkansas, the youngest girl among five children. She was still a small child when, in the early 1940s, her parents shuffled her off to kin so they could work war-related factory jobs in Saint Louis. When a man came to their factory offering free one-way train tickets to anyone wanting work at the Mare Island Naval Shipyard in California, her parents seized the chance. They moved the entire family west to Oakland when Vera was around seven years old.

Her father worked as a welder; her mother was assigned to a clean-up crew at Mare Island. The clean-up crew didn't offer much, but Vera's mother felt like she had reached the promised land. West Oakland was like a small slice of heaven then, alive and friendly with people aspiring to something beyond day-to-day survival. Even after the shipyard laid off the two of them after the war and her husband left her, she looked on Oakland as far superior to what she had left behind in the South. There was less overt prejudice, more opportunities. Vera's mother found a job as a psychiatric technician at the county's public hospital. She heard the scuttlebutt about the menace creeping through West Oakland, but she never witnessed any signs of it herself. She was a devout Pentecostal who spent her days working at the hospital and her nights attending one church function or another. She lived in a cocoon with other middle-aged black southern expatriates for whom the year's highlight was the church's national revival meeting.

Vera was a short and scrawny kid, hardheaded and strong-willed. But she was outgoing and friendly and also a good student who seemed to enjoy school—until she reached the tenth grade. Then Vera suddenly lost interest. She pleaded with her mother to allow her to drop out. Her grades slid. Only months later did her mother learn that the real problem was that Vera was pregnant.

Vera dropped out of school at fifteen. Her mother treated her as if she had been bitten by Satan himself. O.D. seemed nice enough, even charming when he wanted to be, but Vera's mother saw him as the kind of man no decent woman should be seen talking to. He drank and cussed and seemed more interested in raising Cain than in providing for a family. He was a grown man and her baby just a little girl. By the time O.D. murdered a man, she couldn't say she would be surprised by anything that no-good man did.

O.D. was released from prison after serving only four years. By then Vera had moved away from West Oakland, distancing herself from the bad memories and any lingering bad blood. Besides, affordable places were increasingly hard to come by in West Oakland. In Oakland there are the flatlands and there are the hills. The hills were off-limits to the Clays, because of both race and economics. The hills were for those with enough money to buy a little bit of paradise, and they were almost exclusively white. The city's working class and its poor lived in the flatlands, divided into west, east, and north. Those displaced from West Oakland tended to move east—like Vera, her kids, and O.D.—joining the swelling legions of former West Oaklanders making a home in East Oakland.

They tried rebuilding the life that O.D.'s temper had shattered. Through a brother-in-law, O.D. got a job driving a forklift. Vera worked when she could, but that proved difficult with her expanding family. She and O.D. had four more kids to match the four they'd had before his incarceration.

Their marriage was no better than it had been before. There were several breakups over infidelities, real or imagined. According to Vera's best friend, a woman named Bobbie who became like a sister to her in the years O.D. was away, O.D. regularly hit Vera. Eventually Vera walked out on O.D. for good, in no small part because of Bobbie's support. She didn't mince any words when speaking with Vera: "He's a good man, honey, but he's a drunk. And when he drinks, he's got himself a temper." Vera would talk about how hard life was when he was away, but Bobbie always offered the same rejoinder: at least no one hits you. Bobbie, who knew troubles of her own, planned a trip downtown to place her name on the waiting list for public housing. She convinced Vera to do the same.

In November 1966 the voters of Oakland, for the third time in two years, rejected a proposed hike in the city's school tax, burdening future generations of kids with a system that by 1990 would be described by the state's auditor general as the worst he'd seen in fifteen years on the job. On that same ballot, voters approved a bond initiative proposing that scores of "turnkey" housing units be built around the flatlands. The turnkeys were Oakland's approach to scattered site public housing. They were four-, five-, or six-unit buildings, funded by the government but built by private developers who then turned the keys over to the Oakland Housing Authority upon completion.

The appeal of the turnkey plan, pushed by the white Republican regime that ran the city through the mid-1970s, was that it removed government from the construction phase of public housing. But the plan had inherent flaws. The units were built on the cheap by people who knew that any calamities down the road weren't theirs, but government's. Countless corners were cut by private developers eager to maximize profits.

The other major flaw was in the design. There, among neighborhoods of modest-size single-family homes, were scattered these unsightly anomalies that looked like shrunken versions of a 1960s-era, two-story motel. Yet, no matter how regrettable, the turnkeys offered salvation, a cheap new place to live in a city in which affordable housing had grown increasingly precious.

Vera's name reached the top of Housing's waiting list in 1969, around seven years after O.D.'s release from prison. That's when she decided to walk out on her husband for good. Vera and her friend Bobbie walked through East Oakland looking at the available units, which is how Vera and her kids came to be the first residents of the new turnkey built on Ninety-second Avenue near Holly Street, a three-bedroom apartment that struck Vera as maybe the nicest place in which she had ever lived. She was, for the moment at least, overjoyed.

2

ANN

There was nothing remotely resembling joy the day Ann Benjamin moved into that same turnkey on Ninety-second Avenue near Holly. The dense gray air on that ominous day in February of 1980 matched the feeling that lay heavy on her slight frame. Ann had been bad with dates her entire life, but the month and year she became a tenant of the Oakland Housing Authority she would recall forever, just as a prisoner would remember the day a judge pronounced her ten-year sentence.

She was twenty-three years old, with two little ones and a third on the way. That depressed her more than anything else, the thought of her children growing up on Ninety-second Avenue, only a block from the lures and dangers of East Fourteenth Street. East Fourteenth was one of the two main arteries running the length of East Oakland, a river of addicts, prostitutes, and down-and-outers drifting by the good people of the community who called the area home. She asked herself for maybe the thousandth time whether she was doing the right thing, whether she should have waited to see if Housing could come up with something better. But at the same time she knew it was either there or someplace worse or nothing at all. It hurt even to think about it.

The turnkey was a two-story, five-unit stucco building surrounded by cement, presumably because concrete was easier for Housing to maintain than grass. The apartment Ann was assigned—on the ground floor and in the front of the building, maximizing her exposure to the streets—had pale brown linoleum floors marred by a huge slash, as if someone had taken a knife to it in rage. The walls were painted a luster-less yellow. Chunks of plaster had been gouged from the walls.

Thick boards covered the windows the day she moved in. The man from Housing had promised her that the boards would be down by moving day, but that would be only the first of this foul man's broken promises. With a sigh, she called a friend to ask for his help. She was only twenty-three, but already she understood that doing things herself would be far more efficient than waiting for Housing to send someone out.

The electricity hadn't been turned on yet, so that first night Ann and the children sat around a packing box eating take-out chicken by candlelight. It was a chilly February night, so the three of them slept on blankets and pillows sprawled across the living room floor. Like she had done many nights before, she fell asleep dreaming of life in the South. Her life as a girl in Louisiana had hardly been perfect, but it glowed in her mind like a far-off beacon, a reminder of how much simpler her life had been prior to the long and tortuous journey that had landed her on Ninety-second Avenue.

Ann Benjamin grew up in a log cabin in the tiny town of Pine Grove, Louisiana. Pine Grove, the locals liked to joke, was more a widening in the road than a town. To get there, you turned off a highway onto a road that seemed to lead nowhere except deep into a forest. The nearest store—at least when Ann was a girl, in the 1960s and early 1970s—was miles away. Most everything that people needed they grew in their back-yards or bartered for with neighbors.

Her family had no telephone, no running water, no electricity. To take a bath, you first had to fetch the water from a well and heat it on the stove. You then sat in a tin tub outside, not far from the outhouse. Almost everyone living in the black section of town earned their keep picking beans or cotton, depending on the season. As far back as she can recall, Ann was picking one or another for the coins the growers paid for a sack of cotton or a hamper of beans. She was the second youngest in a family of eight children.

Ann was around two years old when her parents split up. Her mother took the two oldest and the two youngest; her father took the middle four and moved back to northern Louisiana, where his people lived. When Ann was about thirteen years old, a man she didn't recognize asked her, "You know who I am?" He was angry when she truthfully said no. He asked her how a girl could not recognize her own father.

Ann's mother was rigidly devout, a Pentecostal for whom the church wasn't Sundays-only but a twenty-four-hour-a-day, seven-day-a-week commitment. God, as Ann envisioned him, was a deity to be feared, not a benevolent and kindly presence to be loved and praised. Religion was more a list of don'ts than a set of deeply held beliefs. Don't paint your nails. Don't wear makeup. Don't wear pants. No dancing. No music.

More than once the white sheriff came to fetch her mother during one of her mother's "spells." Only later, after they had moved to Oakland, would a city doctor diagnose her mother to be a schizophrenic. In Ann's youth, her mother would be a wonderful and loving woman one moment, an out-of-control tyrant the next. Ann never knew from moment to moment which mother she'd be.

Pine Grove was predominantly black, but its schools admitted only whites. The black children were bused to schools in the town of Montpelier. Ann swears that the signs indicating black-only and white-only toilets and drinking fountains were never removed while she still lived in Pine Grove. It was as if the civil rights gains of the sixties and early seventies passed right over the town.

When she was fourteen, Ann, her mother, and her baby brother moved to Oakland. Ann hated the city almost from the moment they arrived. The other kids teased her about her demure, countryish ways, while inside she wondered about this strange breed of people she found herself among. People were mistrustful almost as a reflex; kindness was taken as weakness, sweet thoughts seen as ignorance. It may have been that a bit of straw fell out of her hair every time she opened her mouth, but the opposite was true as well: a bit of grease seemed to flick off the treated hair of the city slickers, who baffled her just as surely as she confused them.

She was by nature shy and quiet, traits Oakland exacerbated. She had a few close friends, but mainly she kept to herself. She didn't touch drugs, she didn't drink, she didn't swear. Her girlfriends would ask her to repeat a line from a particular song, hoping to trick her into saying a curse word, but she wouldn't or couldn't repeat the offending phrase, unable to utter a blasphemous word.

With time Ann learned to fit in. She stopped playing everyone's fool, learned the rules for safely negotiating the streets. She even began wearing makeup and caring more about her appearance. Yet at sixteen she was hardly sophisticated, and she certainly was not ready to live on her own.

Ann's mother met a woman from the church who convinced her that her children were possessed by the devil and thus should be banished from the house. Neither Ann nor her younger brother attended church any longer; both had, in their mother's eyes, chosen the path of the damned. Ann had lived in Oakland for barely two years, yet she was out on the street with no idea where or to whom to turn.

There was a boy at school, John Jones, Jr., who lived in a garage behind his family's home. They had barely started socializing with each other outside of school when John invited her to stay in the room he had set up for himself. It wasn't like she had any other offers, so she moved her stuff in, thinking that she wouldn't need to spend more than a week or two on his floor. Her mother would regain her senses, she told herself. Only after two weeks became two months, with no hope of reconciliation with her mother, did Ann realize that the Joneses, complete strangers only a few weeks earlier, were now the only thing she had resembling a family.

She had never encountered a clan quite like them, the way they spoke to one another. John's mother was the worst. Words came out of her mouth like Ann had never heard before. She'd get drunk and call her daughters bitches, whores, and sluts. She'd accuse them of trying to steal her boyfriend. Ann tried to remain as inconspicuous as possible. If she talked to her own daughters like that, Ann figured, Lord knew what she'd say about her if given half a chance.

When John was around, everybody treated her OK, but when he wasn't there, she felt like cowering in the corner. His siblings treated her like she was an intruder, his mother like she was a leech taking advan-

tage of her sweetness and goodwill. She had turned her back on organized religion, but she prayed to God just the same. "Lord, I want out of
this house," she'd say when she was alone, but the problem was figuring
out where else to go.

No one had ever explained to Ann about sex and its consequences. The
words would never cross her mother's lips and she wasn't about to ask
this woman who was the closest thing available to a surrogate mother.
Ann was already carrying a baby by the time she learned that you need
to use birth control to avoid getting pregnant. She was still a junior in
high school.

Ann dreaded the day she'd have to knock on her mother's door to
break the news to her. Secretly she was hoping that maybe her mother
would allow her to move back home. When the day came, however, her
mother didn't offer anything in the way of consolation. She didn't share
in the blame; she didn't even raise her voice in anger. She just said, "Better not get rid of it," and left it at that. Ann was on her own.

The bathroom at the Jones house had always been a problem. There
was only the one inside the house. The rest of the family seemed to view
her need to use the privy as yet another annoyance she was intent on
putting them through. "Go to your mother's house if you gotta use the
can," John's brother would snap if he happened to be in a bad mood.
With a baby weighing on her bladder, she decided to skip going inside
the house altogether. It seemed a lot easier to squat in the backyard.

Her first child was born when Ann was still sixteen, in March 1974.
She named him John Jones III. "Junebug," everyone called him to avoid
the confusion of two Johns around the house.

The first time Ann had gone to see about birth control, the doctor
had asked her a lot of questions about sex that she couldn't answer. With
all she didn't know about sex, she had no business even asking about
birth control, the doctor lectured, but the woman did write out a pre-
scription for the pill. The doctor phoned a few days later to say that the
pills were unnecessary because Ann was already pregnant.

Ann started taking the pill after Junebug was born. Almost immediately she began feeling sick. It got to the point were she was incapaci-

tated, the pills made her so ill. She couldn't stand the thought of returning to the doctor who had prescribed them to her, and she couldn't talk
with her own mother. So she turned to the Joneses.

"If the pills make you sick, stop taking the damn things," they counseled her. Not three months later, she was pregnant again. She considered an abortion, even made an appointment at a clinic, but she
couldn't go through with it. In April 1975 she gave birth to a baby girl
she named Lakeisha, or Keisha, for short.

John Jones, Jr., had perhaps been a high schooler who saw an opportunity
when he offered a safe haven to this attractive girl with a sugary, down-
home southern accent. It may have been a masterful play for getting the
girl, yet two years later he was still a teen and the father of two. Not surprisingly, theirs was not the most blissful of romantic arrangements.

Ann would sometimes stalk angrily out of their room, forgetting for
the moment that she didn't have anyplace else to go. A couple of times
she knocked on her mother's door, but her mother would never let her
in, no matter how much she pleaded. So she'd walk back to John's place
with her tail between her legs. "You wouldn't survive a day without me,"
she remembers him yelling at her. Back then she was inclined to think
he was right.

After a time they got a place of their own, but John seemed to treat
their new apartment like it was his, not theirs. More than once he got
drunk and put her and the children out. Sometimes she'd impose on
one of her brothers, who lived in a small studio apartment in Oakland.
During one particularly rocky spell, she and the kids lived for about two
months with an older brother who had also moved to Oakland. He slept
on the floor, giving Ann and the kids his bed. She tried not to be a burden, though. If she had money in her pocket, she'd splurge on a motel
room for the night.

Once after they had checked themselves into a motel, Keisha asked
Ann, "Mommy, why don't you leave Daddy if he's so mean?" Keisha
was only about four at the time, a sweet pixie of a girl whose hair was in
pigtails, but the question sent shivers up Ann's spine. Not long afterward, Ann put her name on the waiting list for public housing. She

began to realize that she was feeling trapped when she should have been feeling angry.

Ann wasn't thirty seconds into her story when the Housing Authority clerk cut her short. "Fill out this form and we'll let you know when there's an opening," she told her. She asked the woman behind the counter for options in the meantime. If the clerk said anything other than "Next!" Ann doesn't remember. Two years passed before her name reached the top of Housing's waiting list, in the winter of 1980.

The opening was in the San Antonio Villa, an East Oakland project of considerable infamy. San Antonio was then home base to a heroin dealer named Felix Mitchell. From the mid-1970s through 1984, Mitchell and his Sixty-ninth Avenue Mob had turned this complex of three-story, bunkerlike buildings into an assembly line plant for selling heroin. Paid sentries patrolled the rooftops with walkie-talkies, watching for cops along the only two roads in or out of the complex. As one of many security precautions, customers were first patted down and examined for needle marks (to reduce the risk of a police undercover buy). In abandoned units taken over by the Mob, salaried workers punching a time clock cut heroin shipped directly from Mexico and broke it down into dime bags.

Terror was the Mob's most effective weapon. Whether true or not, the word on the streets was that the Mitchell gang would chop off a person's hand if they were caught stealing even one extra dime (ten dollars' worth) of dope. One tenant was told she could no longer use the back stairs to empty her trash because they needed her strategically placed back porch. Instead she had to walk around the building, two blocks in all. One day she used the back stairs anyway; she was beaten so badly she lost an eye.

The Housing Authority manager who phoned gave Ann a street address instead of mentioning San Antonio Villa by name, but an address for a housing project on Sixty-ninth Avenue was all Ann needed to hear. The manager tried reassuring her. "You won't be there long," he told her. "We're remodeling soon, we'll be moving people out in a matter of months." (As it turns out, "a matter of months" would have been more like ten years, which is how long it took the Housing Authority to secure funds for the proposed rehab project.)

Ann refused even to take a look. "If you're really so desperate for a place like you say," he challenged her, "you'd move in." He told her it might very well be San Antonio or nothing—she should take it or risk remaining on the waiting list for another couple of years. His hard sell weakened her resolve, but she stood her ground.

Despite his threats, this same manager was on the phone a couple of weeks later. He told her about an opening in a small building on Ninety-second Avenue. Ann felt like hanging up the phone without a word; she had heard too many frightening tales about East Oakland above Ninetieth Avenue. ("Don't go to West Oakland at all," people advised her when she first moved to the area; "East Oakland is OK so long as you stay away from the nineties.") "I can't live there," she told him. But even as she was saying the words, she knew she had no choice but to accept. It would be Ninety-second Avenue because the only alternative was San Antonio Villa. At least it would be a place of her own, with her name on the lease, she told herself between the tears.

3

THE REED CLAN

A dozen blocks from the turnkey at Ninety-second and Holly, behind the ball fields of Castlemont High, stood a modest-size bungalow of a kind people all over East Oakland were abandoning throughout the sixties and seventies. "A real fixer-upper," a classified ad might have said of the house on Auseon Avenue, near Eighty-seventh Avenue and Dowling; a small "dream house" that could be had for a song. By 1975, when Annette and Donald Reed scrimped together what they needed to qualify for a mortgage, the house had sat abandoned for several years. The seller was the U.S. Department of Housing and Urban Development. Throughout the neighborhood, hundreds of houses were unoccupied and for sale by one government agency or another.

Blacks had been migrating to East Oakland gradually prior to the city's grand designs for West Oakland. But this deluge of people from the so-called bad part of town throughout the 1960s upset some kind of delicate balance, causing a great many white working-class East Oaklanders to flee to the hills or the suburbs. Elmhurst—that part of East Oakland south of Seventy-third Avenue—fell from four-fifths white in 1960 to one-third white in 1970. By 1980 the neighborhood was less than one-tenth white. The wrecking balls and bulldozers that claimed wide swatches of West Oakland, it seemed, had not only destroyed much of that part of the city but indelibly changed East Oakland as well.

Yet, for all the turmoil around them, Annette and Donald Reed were happy to have a home they could call their own, even if it meant a snug fit with five kids. For years they had moved from apartment to apartment, an odyssey that included a recent escape from a public housing project in West Oakland. But now they owned a house, and their past, marred not only by too many moves but by drug addiction and jail time, seemed behind them for good.

Curtis Reed was around thirty-three years old, his son Donald maybe ten, when he received a sign from God that he should open a storefront Pentecostal church on Twelfth Street, not far from downtown. The elder Reed was a former prize fighter, a whip of a welterweight whose career had been ended by a detached retina. He dreamed of big money, but he was, in the end, a practical man. He hedged his bets, enrolling in a school that taught him to become a welder. He ended up working as an aircraft mechanic at the Alameda Naval Air Station for twenty-seven years.

He was born in Texas, but he had been stationed at Alameda during World War II. He hated the "yassuh, nossuh" essential to surviving the South, and Oakland seemed as good a place as any to make a new life for himself. He was a fun-loving sinner who one night found himself on his knees, scared and humble, pleading to God for another chance, vowing to live a more righteous life. Soon afterward he started up the Glory Temple Church of God in Christ. By day he worked as a welder at the base; in his free time he tended to the church, leading twice-a-week church services among a congregation of maybe twenty, including his own kin.

At around the same time as he opened his church, the reverend and his wife bought a home in East Oakland not two blocks west of where his son Donald and Annette would eventually buy theirs. They were the fourth or maybe the fifth black family on the block when they moved to Elmhurst in 1962. Later, after panic seized the area, he'd feel a bitterness toward the people who had lived around him. But his early days on Auseon Avenue went as smoothly as he had hoped, at least in terms of his relations with his neighbors. His relationship with his wife was another matter, as were his dealings with his eldest son, Donald.

He tried raising Donald to be a good Christian, to maybe even take up preaching himself, but to his mind, his son respected neither him nor his calling. Donald, he'd tell you, was always messing up. He alone among his six kids failed to graduate high school. He was into drugs; he served a stint in juvenile hall. He spent hard time in a state penitentiary when he was older. "Been in trouble ever since he was old enough to get into it," the reverend would later say.

There were times when the reverend could sympathize with Donald. Donald took the brunt of what his father referred to as "that bad spell" following his first wife's desertion for another man. But the Reverend Curtis W. Reed was first and last a severe and rigid man whose harshest criticisms seemed reserved for his eldest son. "A sorry, sorry boy," he'd say. "A disgrace to my name." He even tried talking Annette out of marrying Donald because, as he told her bluntly, he didn't think his son would ever amount to anything good.

Donald was seventeen when he married the former Annette Bradley, then sixteen. As his father had predicted, the early years of their marriage were indeed rocky. Around the time Annette was pregnant with their first child, Donald was picked up with two others on a purse-snatching charge. He pled guilty and was sentenced to three months in the county jail. Annette could only hope that this one incident would scare Donald straight for good.

Rock bottom—at least prior to 1990, when events would come close to destroying both of their lives—were the two years they spent in public housing in the mid-1970s. By then they had three kids and a fourth on the way. They couldn't afford the rent on a larger apartment, and landlords wouldn't rent them the smaller units that they could afford. Public housing seemed their only alternative.

Annette had grown up in public housing. She had lived at the Camel Village housing project, which for her mother had been a safe haven after escaping both the South and her marriage. Camel Village wasn't so bad in the 1950s. As Annette recalled, people seemed to get along with everyone else. Children respected their elders and minded their manners. "Wild" implied fistfights or experimenting with drugs, not guns or funerals for thirteen-year-old innocents. It was nothing like the complex the Reeds moved into after falling on hard times. There it was "like living with a permanent eerie and unsafe feeling," Annette told anyone who asked about her two years in a housing project just off a main drag in West Oakland.

There was the noise and the grime and the graffiti, and also the neighbors who seemed tragically young to be spending their days with all the enthusiasm of inmates serving life sentences. The lifers baffled Annette and at the same time frightened her, as if warning signs of what too many years stuck in public housing might do to a person.

Another aspect of the nightmare was the local thugs. Coming and going, day and night, Annette and her young family had to run a gauntlet of tough-looking teens who never gave way but instead made you squeeze past. While attending church services one night, the Reeds' front door was smashed open and their television set stolen. Annette couldn't be certain if these local toughs were to blame—until she saw her TV set inside the abandoned apartment they hung out in. A cop came out and filled out a complaint, but that was the last Annette heard about it. It seemed that a break-in hardly drew the notice of the local police, at least when the victims were a poor black family living in the projects.

Her oldest was nine when they moved into public housing. That gave focus to her life: get out before the kids are old enough to fall prey to what lurked just outside the door.

During their stay in public housing, at least as Annette tells it, Donald finally settled into his responsibilities. He found steady work, including a job on the BART—Bay Area Rapid Transit—project that sliced through West Oakland. He even got back into his father's church, joining his wife and kids for Wednesday night and Sunday morning services. Getting back into the reverend's good graces meant that favors were bestowed on them, the first of which was the inside track on an apartment in East Oakland through one of Donald's aunts.

The apartment was smaller than the one they had in public housing, and more expensive. It meant another temporary perch when Annette craved stability. Yet the bottom line was that it allowed them to escape from public housing, and they jumped at the chance.

■ ■ ■

Permanence and stability meant the Reeds owning their own home, but both the down payment and the mortgage seemed out of reach. Even with Donald working, five kids to clothe and feed meant that they still received some public assistance. They had no savings, and they were hardly a bank's idea of ideal candidates for a mortgage. Yet Annette never abandoned faith. "Nothing is impossible with God," she would tell her husband, not always a true believer.

Their prayers were answered by her father-in-law, not three months after they moved out of public housing. The reverend told them about a pretty little home down the street that could be purchased through a Federal Housing Administration program for low-income families. Under the FHA's relaxed lending standards, they needed only six hundred dollars for a down payment. The total price tag on the home was a mere twelve thousand dollars.

To get around the blemishes that would have appeared on Annette and Donald's application, the reverend agreed to put the house in his name. He was only too happy to help his prodigal son rejoin his flock.

With only two bedrooms, the home was too small for their expanding family. The Reeds had five kids and a sixth on the way, leaving them to wonder where everybody would sleep. The house was built on a modest-size lot that was overgrown and unkempt, mostly dirt and weeds. There was barely any room between their house and the one next door, and only a chain-link fence and an asphalt lot separated them from a twenty-nine-unit apartment building, which meant twenty-nine potential problem neighbors. Still, Annette felt something resembling bliss. "Like being on the streets homeless and finding yourself in a nice living situation," she'd tell friends. "Like the feeling someone else would get moving up into the hills." It also meant she might never have to move again.

4

TONY

In 1969, the year she moved into the turnkey on Ninety-second Avenue, Vera Clay was only thirty-four years old. Her legs and back ached from more than ten years of scrubbing floors on her knees. Her diet, typical of a black southerner who grew up poor, was rich in fats and salt; she smoked cigarettes and was overweight. She had developed diabetes. Her blood pressure was so alarmingly high that a doctor qualified her for disability. She was granted a temporary leave of absence from the nursing home where she worked, but she never went back.

Vera had worked hard through the fifties and sixties, especially during those years when O.D. was serving time. After moving to Ninety-second Avenue, she never worked again in her life. Instead she survived on a monthly disability check and whatever money O.D. gave her to help with the kids. Officially she blamed the diabetes and the high blood pressure, though privately she confessed to exhaustion.

People on government aid are widely perceived to be living the life, but Vera's was hardly an enviable existence. As a tenant of public housing, her rent could not exceed 30 percent of the $270 she got a month in disability in 1970. There were the strains of raising eight kids in a declining neighborhood and of dealing with her eldest daughter, Carol. At thirteen, Carol started running with an older, faster crowd that consumed a lot of drugs and got themselves into all sorts of trouble. By the time she was seventeen years old, she was a heroin addict and an expectant mother.

Carol's pregnancy was inevitable, Vera supposed. Equally unavoidable was that Vera would end up caring for her grandchild. "That girl can't take care of herself, let alone no baby," she confided in her friend Bobbie.

Six years earlier, Vera had given birth to her eighth child; several of her kids were still under the age of ten. Another infant meant more diapers and sleepless nights long after she figured she was done with those headaches. She grew weary just thinking about it.

Carol gave birth to a baby boy in the summer of 1971 — Tony Davis. The father was a twenty-eight-year-old named Thomas Rayborn who listed his occupation as "laborer" on Tony's birth certificate. Carol was seventeen.

Vera cared for Tony from the time he was two days old. Three years after Tony was born, Carol gave birth to a second child, Angela. Three years later she'd have another boy, Troy. Vera also cared for Angela and Troy from the moment they came home from the hospital.

After Troy was born, Vera set up an appointment with someone from the county. She wanted to see about placing her grandkids in foster homes. Vera might very well have given them up if not for her youngest daughter. Paula was twelve years old when one day a white man wearing a tie knocked on their door. Paula realized who this man was and why he was there, and in tears, volunteered to feed and bathe Carol's kids, to do whatever she had to do to change Vera's mind. Only seven years separated Paula and Tony, but she vowed to care for the kids like they were her own. Apparently Vera had harbored doubts of her own. She thanked the man for coming and never mentioned foster care again.

Paula's siblings—and of course Vera—pitched in where they could, but Paula, true to her vow, played surrogate mother to her niece and two nephews. In the morning she helped Tony and Angela get ready for school while Vera looked after Troy. Troy was Vera's responsibility while Paula was at school, but after her last class, Paula rushed home to do whatever needed to be done: to grocery shop so her mother could make dinner; to spell her mother by taking Troy for a few hours; to take them clothes shopping or for school supplies. Wherever she went, Tony and Angela walked in tow; sometimes she carried Troy in her arms as well.

Who knew what to think? Was she adorable, this heroic twelve-year-old with her three adopted children? Or was this sight merely depressing, given the odds against these kids making something of themselves since their surrogate mother was only in junior high?

Tony was a chubby little kid who loved to show off and to make everyone laugh. He was showered with attention growing up inside an apartment crowded with aunts and uncles. They'd pick him up and give him a ride and let him have whatever he wanted to make him stop crying. It seemed like Vera was always saying, "Y'all better stop, or you'll spoil that boy rotten."

Tony met his father for the first time when he was around eight years old; all told, he saw him maybe five times. There were no baseball outings, no fishing trips to the estuary, no heart-to-hearts. It was just, "Hey, boy, how y'all doing?" Tony was always quick to forgive his mother's frequent transgressions, but he hated his father. Through much of his childhood, when he thought of his father at all, he fantasized about killing him.

Tony and his siblings would go months without seeing their mother. Sometimes she was off on an extended binge, other times she was serving time—on a drug charge, for burglary, for battery, for petty theft. When she did come by, often she was high. Sober, Carol could be good-hearted and full of life, but lit up on heroin, she invariably sparked a blowout that left everyone feeling torn up inside.

Carol raged with bitterness. She resented her children calling Paula "Mama." They heeded Paula or Vera more than they minded her. "All you did was have 'em and leave 'em," Paula would say in the fashion of a righteous teenager.

"You trying to take my kids from me," Carol would counter accusingly.

"If you did your job the way you s'posed to, no one would be messing with 'em in the first place." Paula always had a quick comeback.

If anything, the fights between Carol and Vera were worse. Family members used to say that Carol loved her mother when she was straight but hated her when high. Vera loved her daughter either way. She never gave up hope that Carol would kick the heroin and take her kids back, but then Carol would come around high and Vera would launch into yet another lecture or slip in an offhand comment. And Carol would explode.

Invariably the apartment would be crowded when Vera and Carol had one of their rows. The room would boil over with emotions. "Watch Mama's blood pressure." "You're worrying Mama sick." Everyone would talk and yell at once, trying to calm Carol down or soothe Vera.

When Vera caught Carol stealing from the family, all hell would break loose. One of those times, according to Vera's friend Bobbie, Carol ended up biting Vera in the face. She knows, Bobbie said, because she drove her friend to the hospital to have the gash in her cheek stitched closed.

If Tony and Angela weren't in the room during Carol and Vera's fights, they heard the screaming in the next room just the same. The children would curl up on a bed and hug each other tight. Angela would cry and Tony would try soothing her. "Mama don't mean what she saying," he'd tell her. Or, "Mama's probably just mad because she don't have no money right now."

Tony would ask Paula, "Why Mama have to act like that?" Paula never knew what to say. She didn't want to say anything to further alienate Tony from his mother. Still, she felt angry at her sister. No doubt some of that spilled out no matter how hard Paula tried to shield the children from her true feelings.

Vera recognized that growing up without your real mother or father would take its toll, but she was at a loss for solutions. She was struggling to keep food in the house and a roof over their heads while simultaneously looking after a newborn. She avoided talking to Tony about Carol or about his father because she didn't know what to say. How do you explain addiction or abandonment to a child? Tony would look lonely and sad, but she couldn't determine if that was just the stuff of childhood or a kid suffering through a mother who didn't seem to care about him. She never knew what was going on in that mind of his.

Tony struck those around him as an even-keeled kid, but secretly he felt overwhelmed by roiling emotions and deep resentments. It took people by surprise when occasionally he would explode in a fury of feelings. At times he could seem the saddest of children.

Paula would ignore Tony when he was moody and sullen—what she would call being in "one of his snits." She parroted Vera's line: cater to his moods and you'll only spoil him further.

Tony shared a room with Troy and two uncles, yet he frequently felt all alone in the world as a kid. He had love, but missing were the guiding lights to help him through childhood. Paula and Vera made sure he went to school and minded his manners, but there was no one around to patiently explain things to him or to probe to see what was going on in his head. Paula tried, but she was a teenager. She continued to do her chores and look after Tony and his siblings, but she also liked to hang out with her smart-mouth friends and goof off. Teenagers tend to embrace a black-and-white morality, yet they're hardly the best choice for teaching children right from wrong.

With Vera, Tony felt an enormous and insurmountable generation gap. His earliest recollections of his grandmother were of a sweet woman who had her Bible, her bingo, her cigarettes, her television, and little else. She was always after him about his swearing, even when it was something innocuous, like "swear to God." Yet his most vivid memory of her was of a woman forever tired, as if God had granted her a finite reserve of energy that she had exhausted completely by the time he came along. He worked at not being a burden on this woman who he understood had been stuck caring for three kids not her own.

Carol had been living here and there for so many years that taking the kids was never really an issue. But then she landed an apartment in the San Antonio Villa—the projects that Felix Mitchell had turned into an assembly line for selling heroin. She demanded custody of Tony and Angela, but not Troy, because he was still a toddler. Vera suspected that Carol had cooked up the whole scheme to qualify for welfare, but legally Vera had no standing. In the eyes of the law, the children belonged to their mother.

"I ain't gonna fight you no more," Vera told Carol. "You want to take care of them kids, take care of 'em." Tony was eleven, Angela eight.

Angela didn't last a month with her mother. The few weeks she lived there might have been the most frightening of her life. Outside, Mitchell's snipers sat on rooftops, rifles in hand. Junkies paraded through the complex day and night. Things inside the apartment were no calmer. Carol and her boyfriend—Angela and Troy's father—were high much of the time. They were constantly fighting. He beat Carol and didn't really pay attention to his daughter, which might have been just as well.

Tony didn't like life inside the Villa any more than Angela, but he desperately wanted to make a go of it with his mother. The beatings made him crazy with rage. The walls were so thin it was like his mother was there in the room, pleading with her boyfriend to stop. Tony winced with every blow, with every loud sob. He fantasized about protecting his mother but, though enormous for his age, he was still just a pudgy kid.

Tony missed the crowd at Vera's and longed for the security of the life he had known on Ninety-second Avenue. The other kids told tales about Mitchell and his gang, some of them apocryphal and some true, but all of them frightening to an eleven-year-old. Tony never actually witnessed a shooting, but he heard gunfire often enough to be scared when he was outside.

Paula and one of her sisters stopped by every few weeks to check on Tony and also to spy on Carol. Carol never let the apartment deteriorate into a sty, as some addicts are said to do. She was usually lucid enough to fix Tony something to eat. But there were also those nights when she'd ask, "You eaten, baby?" even though it was already nine o'clock and Tony had hours earlier resorted to a bowl of cereal.

Paula was always sure to repeat what she had seen to her mother. Sometimes there were needles or other drug paraphernalia lying around. Dirty dishes would be scattered everywhere and the kitchen would be without food. Tony would have no clean clothes in his drawers.

Eventually Vera couldn't stand the stories any longer. She showed up at Carol's apartment to fetch Tony, then filed the necessary papers to gain legal custody of all three of Carol's kids.

■   ■   ■

Tony had survived San Antonio Villa by keeping pretty much to himself. About the only real friend he made was a kid from his building named James. James worked as a lookout for the Mitchell gang, watching for the cops. He was paid around fifty dollars a day and probably considered himself lucky. The gang tended to hire lonely kids whose mothers were off working all day or high on heroin inside an apartment. A lot of these kids considered themselves nobodies, but in the Mitchell gang they were somebodies.

During his one summer living at the Villa, Tony would tag along when James went to learn his morning assignment. Often he'd keep James company all day. One morning shortly before the start of school, one of Mitchell's men asked Tony, "Why don't we hook you up on your own?" He readily said yes.

Tony was drawn to the Mitchell gang—Mitchell especially—yet at the same time he couldn't fathom these people for whom killing somebody seemed second nature. He stared in wonder at the sentries with their rifles. Yet like almost every kid living there, he gawked with delight on those rare occasions when he caught Mitchell driving through the projects in a Rolls. In 1985 Mitchell would be sentenced to life in prison and then killed in Leavenworth less than a year later (over a ten-dollar drug deal gone bad), but back then Tony figured Mitchell had it made.

Tony had it all figured out. He'd earn enough money so that his mother wouldn't have to steal anymore and his grandmother could move to someplace nice. His pockets would be stuffed with cash so that he'd never have to bother anyone—not his grandmother, not Paula, not his mother—about money ever again.

Tony's tenure in the Mitchell gang didn't last two weeks before he moved out of his mother's place. Despite his dreams, however, he felt nothing but joy the day Vera showed up at the Villa to bring him back home.

School was always torture for Tony. He was a decent enough reader, but that was his only good subject. He was always bigger than just about everyone else in his class, but he was also among the slowest learners.

Sometimes he'd try concentrating so hard he was afraid his brain would explode.

He easily grew frustrated. "I'm never gonna do good in school," he'd cry to his aunt Paula. "I'm not smart enough to learn." Concerned elementary school teachers would call the apartment asking for Tony's mother, and Paula would get on the phone though she was still in high school.

In the fifth grade, Tony was placed in a class for slower learners. "Special ed," the district called the program, but the other kids called them the "stupid" classes. He was big, so no one dared tease him to his face, but he knew they were making fun of him just the same. He remembered one terrific teacher, who had taken him and a few other boys on a Saturday outing to the zoo in a fancy red sports car, but except for that one year, Tony never liked school. Once he was tracked into special ed, he hated it. He felt relieved a few months later when he moved in with his mother, because at his new school he was back in a regular class.

Tony was around twelve when he started suffering headaches so severe that Vera brought him to the local public hospital to see a doctor. The doctor offered no definitive diagnosis, but his best guess was stress. More troubling still was Tony's blood pressure, very high for a kid his age. His weight and heredity were two likely factors, but the doctor allowed that a third might be tension. He asked Tony if he was going through any hard times, but Tony just said, "No, not really."

He knew he should have told the doctor the truth about school and about his mother, but he felt too embarrassed by either subject to discuss it with a stranger. The truth was he was entertaining suicide, but he couldn't talk about that with Paula or Vera, let alone some white doctor at a busy public hospital who could give him maybe ten minutes.

Junior high, say the experts, represents the critical transition phase for most students. Those who've dissected the failures of the country's inner-city schools say it's in the middle grades that so many kids are infected with the attitudes that ensure they'll drop out before reaching high school.

Tony's middle school years got off to a dubious start. He was still living with his mother in the Villa when he began the seventh grade, so he was assigned to Havenscourt Junior High. The school year began much the way the previous one had ended, with Tony feeling frustrated, ashamed, and stupid. Somehow he had ended up back in a special ed class. He stopped going to school after a week because no one seemed to notice whether he went or not.

When he moved back to Vera's a couple of weeks later, he transferred to Elmhurst Middle School. He didn't feel quite so isolated as he had at Havenscourt, but familiarity bred its own problems. He was popular there, the class clown who was always ready with a funny quip. He began running with a fast crowd. They'd cut school, they'd get into fights, they'd steal candy, soda, and other small things from the local stores. Tony rationalized that his thievery meant he wouldn't have to impose on Vera or Paula.

Several times Tony was hauled before the principal after a fight. He may have started a fight or two, but his adversaries were mainly kids his age who would pick a fight with him to prove their own toughness. Some kid would incite him to fight, saying something like, "You think you so tough, doughboy," and the next thing he knew, a teacher was pulling him off the kid to bring him to the principal's office. There were also those fights he would get into protecting a smaller friend against a bigger adversary.

Vera warned him, "Don't be going with them boys when they come and get you for a fight," but he'd serve as their guardian angel just the same.

The more of a behavior problem he was at school, the less likely a teacher was to take an interest in helping him. No longer did a concerned teacher phone Vera's place. By the eighth grade, Tony already seemed trapped in a downward spiral. Just as certainly as the school system decided he was a slow learner, so, too, did Tony believe he possessed little or no scholastic potential. Eventually he was kicked out of Elmhurst and transferred to Frick Junior High. By reputation and as measured by standardized test scores, one school was as subpar as the other; but now, of course, Tony would be Frick's headache and not Elmhurst's.

5

FROM OUT
OF THE PAVEMENT

When Annette and Donald Reed first bought their small bungalow on Auseon near Dowling Street in 1975, locals were still drawing important distinctions between East and West Oakland. The homes were nicer, the neighborhood safer, the schools superior. There were exceptions, like San Antonio Villa, but to people's minds East Oakland was still the sort of place where you might think of raising a family and West Oakland was a place people suggested you avoid.

You'd hear about a murder and immediately you'd guess West Oakland. More often than not you were right. West Oakland was where a great many southern expatriates ended up if they brought with them little more than their dreams and a few suitcases of possessions. East Oakland was where most moved to if they could.

By the mid-1980s, however, the distinction would seem a dim memory. By then people were describing East Oakland in the terms they had in the past reserved for West Oakland. What changed the situation was the rise of crack.

Crack—or rock cocaine, as it was called when it first hit Oakland in late 1983—is a cooked-down version of powdered cocaine smoked in a pipe. It's cheaper than powdered coke, and more potent. Powdered coke snorted through the nose dissolves through the membranes of one's nostrils, enters the bloodstream, and then heads for the brain. By contrast, smoking crack allows one to feel the high almost instantly. The vapors are inhaled into the lungs, which supply blood directly to the brain.

Before crack, obtaining a smokable form of cocaine required that the user mix cocaine with either ammonia or ether—both highly flammable chemicals. "Freebasing" was a dangerous proposition. People burned themselves badly cooking the coke over a flame. The inexperienced or the impatient lit up before the ether had entirely evaporated, and the mixture would blow up in his or her face.

Then people discovered that baking soda worked as well as ammonia or ether. The coke–baking soda mixture could be cooked safely in a microwave, in a double boiler, even in a coffee maker. The cooked form of this concoction was a fractured, crystal-like grayish blob that vaguely resembled rock candy. And thus was born rock cocaine, or crack.

In short order, the drug created its own market of hard-core abusers. Twenty dollars could buy a couple of hours of pleasure—but after people smoked up what they had, they immediately craved more. The euphoric high the drug produced was an intense, false nirvana gloriously devoid of worry and bad feelings. Even many drug treatment counselors accustomed to the grip of heroin said they had never seen a drug that took so strong a hold in so short a period of time.

Prior to crack, street dealers overtly selling their product were unique to the city's large housing projects. Heroin, cocaine, marijuana—all were sold primarily through an underground economy. But crack created its own network of street vendors, just as cheap VCRs gave meteoric rise to video rental stores in strip malls across the country. The simple economics of the drug made it the perfect commodity for the enterprising street dealer, unconcerned with its long-term effects on customers: what else created its own supply of customers anxious—indeed, desperate—to purchase your product as many as five or ten times a day? Your inventory could be carried around in your pocket or secreted in your mouth in a pinch.

Within a year's time, crack was brazenly sold on street corners throughout the flatlands of Oakland. "[It's] like one day they just popped up through the cement," says Sgt. Mike Beal of the street dealers he battles as head of the police department's special drug task force, charged with busting this new breed of drug dealer.

The crack trade never became centralized, as heroin had under Felix Mitchell. No longer did the likes of Mitchell shoot it out with two or three major rivals. Fighting sophisticated drug lords like Mitchell was never easy for law enforcement, but busting these small drug "crews" was more difficult still. The cops would close down one corner and another would open nearby. Their busts tended to be small time only, teens caught selling twenty, forty, sixty dollars' worth of rock. Beal's special unit has managed to jam the courts, and especially the juvenile system, but they've done little to slow the spread of crack. In fact, Beal confesses that the problem has only gotten worse since the mid-1980s, as these bands of small-time drug crews have grown increasingly sophisticated in avoiding arrest.

Crack could not have emerged as the scourge of East Oakland if not for the conditions that allowed it to take hold in the first place. Elmhurst, the East Oakland neighborhood that the Reeds bought into, had suffered many a blow before the advent of this potent new drug, not the least of which was the flight of tens of thousands of blue-collar jobs that had sustained the area through much of the century.

General Motors, Ford, Caterpillar, Mack, International Harvester — all shut down huge plants that had been operating in and around East Oakland for decades. The General Motors plant, in Oakland since 1916, laid off nearly 3,000 workers when it closed its plant at Seventy-third and MacArthur Boulevard in the early 1960s; a second GM plant, in nearby Fremont, laid off another 5,900 workers in 1981 and 1982. The Ford factory building still stands at the edge of East Oakland, but now it is home to a bingo parlor and an indoor flea market. In its heyday Ford employed around 5,000 workers.

International Harvester laid off more than 1,000 employees in 1976. Caterpillar laid off 1,900 between 1979 and 1985. In 1981, 1,400 workers at Mack truck received pink slips. Peterbilt Motors laid off 900 in 1981 and 1982. Transamerica-Delaval Corporation, which manufactured diesel engines in its Oakland factory, laid off more than 2,000 employees as it closed its sixty-acre site in the late 1980s.

Del Monte, Hunt and Wesson, Carnation, Continental Can, and American Can—these and other canneries fled East Oakland. The tens of thousands of seasonal jobs the canneries created are gone, but the lead that had been a staple of the canning industry still lingers: a 1988 state study found an alarmingly high concentration of lead in one of every ten East Oakland kids. (Lead in the blood is thought to retard the healthy development of a child and might be the basis of learning disabilities.) Gerber shut its twenty-acre Oakland site in 1985, the same year Montgomery Ward and Company closed its eight-story west coast catalog center in East Oakland. According to one study, Oakland and the rest of Alameda County lost more than 16,000 blue-collar jobs in the first half of the 1980s.

There's often not much a city can do to prevent a major corporation from fleeing once the decision has been made. Yet long after most other cities had marshaled whatever resources they had to prevent plant closures, Oakland still had no such program in place. It was as if the city wasn't even trying. Government's big push in East Oakland was the turnkeys that some blamed for accelerating the area's decline.

For generations the city was run by a succession of white Republican mayors preoccupied with the development of the city's downtown. Yet no matter how much time passed, Oakland seemed forever five or ten years from its lofty dreams of a thickly forested skyline of office buildings and high-priced condos. Logic demanded that businesses be drawn to downtown Oakland when the price of San Francisco real estate was so high, even if reality didn't. In 1977 the city elected its first black mayor; unfortunately, government seemed no more interested in the woes of East Oakland than it had under past administrations. The new mayor was a conservative black judge who dreamed the same downtown dreams of his predecessors. Nowhere was this preoccupation clearer than in the city's decision through the 1980s to spend most of its annual share of federal antipoverty monies downtown rather than in the city's poor communities.

A city banking its future on its downtown is not unusual. Many a mayor across the country has argued that a burgeoning downtown will create additional revenues that "trickle down" into other parts of the budget. Usually the money never quite reaches the neighborhoods, despite the promises, but in Oakland that was surely not going to happen. The city designated its downtown a redevelopment site, meaning that any supplemental tax dollars raised due to development had to be spent exclusively downtown. East Oakland was going down the tubes, but if city hall noticed, that was news to those unsuccessfully requesting meetings with officials who were always too busy to take their calls.

Their early years at Auseon and Dowling were as the Reeds had imagined when they bought into Elmhurst. Theirs was a sweet little street of modest but well-maintained homes. They weren't particularly close with their neighbors, but there weren't any problems, either. People seemed generally friendly and everyone minded his or her own business. Castlemont High's ball fields were practically in their front yard. When they lived in the projects, Annette felt compelled to keep her kids housebound more than she would have liked. In Elmhurst she let them play outside without much worry. It seemed to be the sort of neighborhood where you could rear your kids to be good, well-rounded Christians, as Annette intended.

There were problems, to be sure. Money was always tight, their home life cramped. Their sixth child, Shannon, was born in 1976. Kevin, their seventh, was born the next year. At first all of the kids slept in the second bedroom, several to a bed. Then the reverend told them about a home loan program aimed at helping Oakland's low-income families. The Reeds qualified for a cash grant, allowing them to build an additional room. At least the two girls would have a room of their own.

Times could be tough, but Annette figured that growing up poor and black had steeled her against the worst life could offer. Growing up black, she liked to say, made her appreciate what she had rather than dwelling on that which she lacked in her life. Her kids were healthy and her marriage was going well. Donald was clean and they were finally off welfare altogether. They had enough money to put food on the table and even to take the kids out for an occasional splurge. Annette cared for her family and wiled away any free time she had tending to her vegetable garden. She read her Bible and faithfully integrated the family into her father-in-law's church. Their future looked bright.

For Annette, the first sign that something was amiss in East Oakland was in the late 1970s, when the media started reporting on Felix Mitchell's heroin operation. That was the sort of thing that might take hold in West Oakland, but not East. Worse still were the news accounts of deadly shooting wars played out against the backdrop of seemingly quiet and peaceful East Oakland neighborhoods. One day the television cameras were only a few blocks away, where two of Mitchell's lieutenants had just been murdered by a rival. A gangland slaying in her neighborhood? She had to pinch herself as she watched the news, that's how improbable it seemed.

Nothing prepared her for the legions of crack street dealers suddenly everywhere throughout the neighborhood. "Like I went to bed one night and there they were when I woke up the next morning," Annette said— and once they appeared, they never left. In 1985, the closest drug hot spot was a good half dozen blocks away. Not long after, a crew started selling at Eighty-fourth and Dowling, only three blocks away. Everyone in the family avoided that corner as best they could, but eventually a crew set up shop at Eighty-sixth and Dowling, just around the corner from their home. Some days it was like living around the corner from a McDonald's drive-through, except of course these young men were selling a highly addictive product and were known to pack high-caliber handguns and semiautomatic carbines.

With the crack crews came a new term working its way into the vocabulary of urban dwellers around the country: the drive-by shooting. As new crews formed, they invariably intruded on someone else's territory. Funks—wars over turf—broke out throughout the area. The favored means for exacting revenge was the drive-by—a particularly inefficient and sloppy method for attempting murder, but it was safer than approaching a rival on foot. Not coincidentally, the year crack took hold in urban areas across the country—1985—is also the year cited by researchers tracing back the gun violence epidemic plaguing inner-city teens.

The Reeds watched helplessly as their neighborhood grew visibly shabbier. According to one police study, Elmhurst accounted for more than one in three drug hot spots throughout the city in 1988, although it was only one of the city's nine community districts. People fled even when they couldn't find buyers for their homes. Better to rent out our home and become renters ourselves, some families reasoned, than to live where we no longer feel safe. Naturally, the renters didn't maintain their property as well as the owners had, just as owners, given the general disrepair of the neighborhood, no longer had the same incentive to keep things up.

People installed bars on their windows and replaced wooden doors with heavy metal mesh contraptions that appeared to be designed for a fortress. Some critical threshold, it seemed, had been crossed. Like a crack smoker who had passed from a weekend user to a daily addict, Elmhurst's spiraling collapse seemed inevitable once people agreed they were no longer a community in transition but one in precipitous decline.

By the late 1980s, the signs of decline were everywhere and unmistakable in postcrack Elmhurst. The Safeway supermarket a half dozen blocks away from the Reed home closed its MacArthur Boulevard store for good, leaving a vast swatch of East Oakland without a decent local grocery store. Wells Fargo closed its branch office on East Fourteenth Street at Ninety-sixth Avenue; the Bank of America closed *its* East Fourteenth branch, at Ninety-eighth Avenue, not long afterward. In 1982, eleven banks were located in East Oakland south of Seventy-third Avenue; by 1990 only two were left. During that same period, the number of check-cashing shops—which charge between 2 and 5 percent to cash a check—had swollen from two to eight. One bank had been housed in a dignified brick building at the corner of MacArthur and Seventy-third Avenue; Marge and Jerry's pawn shop now occupies that same space. Eventually even J. C. Penney and Mervyn's, the twin anchors of the shopping mall across the road from Marge and Jerry's, fled Elmhurst.

There was also a steady erosion of once-sound smaller businesses along MacArthur Boulevard, no longer the jewel of Elmhurst. MacArthur had never been a high-class street, but it had always bustled with life. The boulevard was lined with hardware stores, jewelry shops, five-and-dimes, motels, and restaurants. The completion of Interstate 580 in the early 1960s killed MacArthur's bustling motel and restaurant business; the steady decline of the surrounding community of Elmhurst killed most everything else. That meant the loss of even more jobs. The owner of the fruit and vegetable market, the butcher down the street, the florist on the corner—all closed their doors, whether out of fear or because they could no longer make a go of it. Doctors fled, as did the dentists and most other professionals with offices located on MacArthur. By the late 1980s, little else remained but the beauty parlors, wig shops, storefront churches, fast-food joints, and liquor stores.

Elmhurst didn't suddenly become a fearsome place, like something out of a *Road Warrior* film. The Reeds' neighbors continued to be decent people who went to work in the morning and could be found out in their yards on the weekend. The people walking the street were by and large polite, at worst indifferent. Kids walked around carrying basketballs, footballs, or baseball mitts, depending on the season. The drug dealers generally left you alone if you left them alone.

The difference, however, was that in East Oakland things occasionally occurred that were unthinkable elsewhere. In the flatlands, a drunk, or a crazy, or someone strung out on drugs—who knew?—would be walking down the block muttering loudly to himself, brandishing a baseball bat; in Elmhurst, the sounds of gunfire became commonplace, so much so that most people didn't bother calling the police when they heard shots unless they were certain someone had been injured. In contrast, a single shot fired in the hills would light up the 911 switchboard. Once one of Annette's kids ran home from school with the news that two kids he knew had just been shot while hanging out in front of the car wash. Every kid seemed to know at least one or two peers who had been killed.

The schools were something else that set Elmhurst apart. When Annette was a girl, Castlemont High was thought of citywide as a good school, though one in a tough, working-class community. Now her children came home with stories of classrooms so out of control and nerve-jangling that it would be something of a miracle if even the most studious child could learn as much as his or her counterpart in the suburbs. Her kids told Annette of constant fighting; a few confessed that they were frightened about going to school altogether. Standardized test scores ranked Castlemont among the worst high schools in the state; there was also an alarmingly high pregnancy rate and a dropout rate that hovered around 50 percent—this once-proud school was now no better than some of the country's worst inner-city schools. Annette wished she could send her kids to a private school, but that was financially impossible.

In 1984 approximately eight hundred Castlemont students signed petitions saying they were fed up with the gang fights and guns that had become part of their school life. The petition drive became page-one news throughout the Bay Area when the school board complied with the students' number-one demand—the dismissal of the principal, whom they characterized as scared and out of touch. "Dealers come on campus all the time, every single day," one senior had told the school board. "Outsiders almost control this school if you ask me."

Castlemont fell into police beat number thirty-four, which by the end of the decade would rank as the most murderous among the city's thirty-five beats. In whichever direction you walked home from Castlemont, you passed a corner where crack was being sold. No matter how assiduously you tried avoiding trouble, you never knew if suddenly you'd be confronted by a challenge because you happened to glance at someone the wrong way. That was life growing up in Elmhurst: you could be a good kid who one day turned down the wrong street at the wrong time and suddenly struck a land mine.

Annette and Donald spoke about moving, but where would they go? They could have searched for a better neighborhood, but the truth was they wouldn't get much for the Auseon house, if they could sell it at all. Even if they could move, the only neighborhoods they could afford weren't any safer. So they did as they had always done—they made do with what they had and prayed their kids would make it to adulthood in one piece.

Annette Reed was inclined to see culprits everywhere. She blamed urban renewal, she pointed an accusing finger at the Housing Authority for swamping East Oakland with these unsightly turnkeys. Though she was a West Oakland expatriate herself, she grumbled about these crude West Oaklanders living among them. She was a strict mother who at least attempted to keep a tight watch over her kids and had no tolerance for those who didn't even try to raise their children in the same manner.

She blamed a government that sat on its hands as corporations large and small gave up on East Oakland in the wake of white flight. Places like Elmhurst, Annette would tell her kids, don't just happen, they're *allowed* to happen—through ignorance, neglect, misguided policies, and prejudice. The shame was that the decline was as predictable as it was tragic. The federal government during the Reagan years drastically slashed funds to state and local governments, which in turn were forced to cut funding to a range of social service agencies, both public and private, attempting to do something to reach this generation of kids without hope. Instead government countered the problem by relying more heavily on the police and the prison system, because building more prisons was simpler and seemed more cost-effective than actually trying to do something about the problem. Her children would tease her about her minipolitical lessons—"Aw, Mama, don't be getting deep on us"—but they'd listen to her just the same.

To Annette, the people who ran the city were no better than those who sat in Washington, D.C., or Sacramento. To her, the city used the police mainly to keep the drugs and violence corralled within the flatlands. If a dozen teenagers started selling on a corner up in the hills, she was sure that the cops would have them all in jail before the night was over. She firmly believed that if hers had been a white, middle-class neighborhood suffering this same decline, somebody—the feds, the state, the city—would call out the troops.

She was furious with the street dealers who had invaded her community, yet she sympathized with them just the same. It took a special kid with unusual perseverance to see past Elmhurst. These kids, whom people tended to see as ignorant, were smart enough to understand that there was reason to be cynical. With the lousy schools and a pervading culture of violence, the easy availability of guns, the drunks they saw everywhere around them, and the drug abusers and the despair, it was a small miracle that so many kids endured. Twenty years earlier, a teenager just getting by in school could have found work at one of the hundreds of factories in East Oakland. By the mid-1980s, East Oakland's sole growth industry seemed to be drug dealing. Even a job as a bag boy was out of the question because the nearest supermarket was now miles away.

Annette blamed the cops, too, especially those who were part of the drug task force assembled to rid the flatlands of these ubiquitous young dealers. The task force cops were typically young, white, and brash. They patrolled the streets dressed in jogging shoes, jeans, baseball hats, and blue windbreakers with POLICE stitched across the front and back so that when they chased a suspect, no one could claim he'd shot this white guy running through his yard because he had no idea the guy was a cop.

The task force cops tended to swarm a corner in much the same manner as a gang would rob a bank. They waved their guns and barked out commands. They were quick to shove people and throw them to the ground if they didn't respond fast enough. They'd push people up against a wall or a car and cuff them without telling them what they may have done wrong. If a kid allowed it, they searched his pockets; sometimes they'd do it anyway, even though it might constitute an illegal search. Then they'd park their suspect in the backseat of a squad car and run his name through the computer for outstanding warrants and the like.

The problem with this protocol was that a young man standing on the corner could be a drug dealer, but he could also be an innocent kid just laughing with his friends. Often the cops busted people who were carrying drugs or were wanted on an outstanding felony warrant. Yet they also hassled plenty of uncorrupted teens. A kid on the corner swimming in gold chains could be a crack dealer, but he could also be a kid earning $4.25 an hour at McDonald's who chose to spend every last dime on jewelry. The beeper he carries might indicate he's peddling drugs, or it might mean he's just trying to look cool. Or maybe his mother worries so much about him morning, noon, and night that she insists he wear it.

Annette was as frightened as the next person to contemplate a world without the police. Yet to her it was like they didn't comprehend that the flatlands included not only the bad guys but a majority of the victims as well. Even her son Dermmell, the one her other boys teased for being so quiet and straight, was jacked—roughed up—several times by the cops.

One time he was on his way to the store when the task force, guns drawn, pushed him against a wall, cuffed him, and kept him in the back of a squad car for ten or fifteen minutes. They ran his name for outstanding warrants, found he had none, then let him go without so much as a word of apology.

It's no wonder kids harbor hostile feelings toward cops nowadays, Annette thought. With guns and nightsticks dangling from their belts, cops swagger and act tough around the young men in our neighborhood. They treat our kids as if they're no better than common thieves, and then are surprised that children return their hostility with disrespect. She may have made people flinch when she said that that's why cops occasionally get blown away.

Donald Jr., Annette and Donald's oldest son, was quiet and moody. He steered clear of trouble but by the time he reached Castlemont he seemed to have lost his way. His mother's mantra was, "Watch your company," but Donald got caught up in the wrong crowd and dropped out of high school anyway. He wasn't headed anywhere, and eventually he got into the street life. Later he would have to attend adult school to earn his high school diploma.

Annette finagled it so that Curtis, her second son, attended Redwood Heights Elementary, a predominantly white school in the hills. Annette blamed the neighborhood schools at least in part for Donald's downward slide, so she saw to it that Curtis transferred to Redwood Heights when he was around eleven. Curtis had always been an outgoing, boisterous kid, but at this new school he suddenly didn't know how to handle himself. He had never before been around so many white people. He didn't know what to say or how to act around his classmates, so he kept to himself, trying to make himself invisible. He had gotten good grades at his neighborhood school, but at Redwood Heights he was having a hard time in his classes. It wasn't long after he enrolled there that he started getting into trouble.

Like most kids, he wiled away his time watching the television shows of his generation—*Silver Spoons, Diff'rent Strokes*, reruns of *The Brady Bunch*. He was a poor kid who shared a room with four brothers, all dreaming of a life like those of the television characters: they never got whupped and they never wanted for anything. And of course, Curtis noticed, they were white—unless they were two black kids from the ghetto taken in by a wealthy white man, as on *Diff'rent Strokes*. More familiar were the struggles and pains of the black family on *Good Times*. It got so that he believed that he could attain the finer things in life only if he could magically make himself white.

Curtis was fourteen when he first started selling crack. To avoid the watchful eye of his mother (his father was working so hard in those days, he wasn't around to see much of anything), he hooked up with a crew that sold on Ninety-second Avenue and D Street, more than a dozen blocks from his house. At first he was nickeling and diming, but eventually he got much deeper into the life. He entertained his friends with talk of fancy cars and the mansion he'd own worthy of a spot on *Lifestyles of the Rich and Famous*.

"Man, Curt, you ain't nothing but a dreamer," they'd tease him, but he'd shine them on. He was fueled by a mix of drive and rage that had him believing he could be the next Felix Mitchell, only bigger. "Living in the ghetto, man," he'd tell his partners, "it's all 'bout greed. Greed pure and simple 'cause you never know when it's all gonna end." Curtis was fifteen when he was picked up on a petty theft charge, and sixteen when he was given probation for carrying a firearm. That would be only the start of his troubles.

Dermmell, Annette and Donald's middle son, was no one's idea of a bad kid. He was shy and sweet, well-mannered and courteous. He had a gift for athletics, or at least football. Dermmell was the kind who hung back from everyone else, keeping mainly to himself. He had his best friend, David, but that was about it. When he wasn't playing football, he could usually be found at home, watching television or playing video games.

Trouble began when he was in the sixth grade. One kid, whatever the reason, decided he didn't like Dermmell. The kid made constant fun of him—for being so shy, for being so straight, for not responding to his insults. This kid was picking on Dermmell all the time, every day. One day the kid pushed Dermmell, and Dermmell cracked. He could withstand the taunts, but not someone laying his hand on him. He beat the kid up, but from then on had to contend with his new reputation as someone who thought he was tough.

Demmell was like a reluctant gunslinger from the Wild West who suffered his reputation as a fast draw. Every kid in school, it seemed, wanted to have a piece of him to see how tough he really was. It was like, "Oh, you think you's bad? Let's see how bad you are."

Eventually, Demmell got himself into fights that were avoidable. A kid would accidentally bump into him in school and he'd take it as a challenge. His thinking then was that he didn't want that kid thinking he could jostle him anytime he wanted and get away with it. Demmell would say something to the kid and his adversary would say something right back, and like that they'd be duking it out. He developed a code. You could say whatever you wanted to him, but if you so much as touched him you were taking away his right to be left alone.

In elementary school he got As and Bs, but his grades started slipping when he hit Elmhurst Middle School. He blamed this on his own attitude, not on the teachers at Elmhurst. He was too busy thinking about fighting to pay any attention to his work. He did well enough each year to continue on to the next grade, but just barely. At Castlemont he ran track and was a star on the football team. He was a starting defensive back and, during his junior year, Castlemont's quarterback. That became his sole motivation for maintaining a passing average: to continue playing football and running track.

Organized athletics also served as Demmell's inspiration for avoiding the lures of the street that seduced so many of his peers and even a few of his friends. He was not without temptation, however: he lost a girlfriend he really cared for to a drug dealer with a car and the other "props." Curtis was always on Demmell to stay clear of the life he was living—he even bought him a car to reduce some of the temptation—but Demmell's friends who had taken up the trade would cajole him to hook up with them. And why not? His buddies were fourteen- and fifteen-year-old kids having a hard time in school who had discovered a quick route to Easy Street. They didn't seem to be working, not really—they hung out each night, joking with friends and making an occasional sale—and they never seemed to get caught.

Demmell recognized that there were downsides to dealing. There were the cops and rival dealers with guns; he always hated guns. There was also his mother's wrath to consider should she catch him. But the truth was that the only thing really standing in his way was sports. He wondered about kids who weren't the athletes he was. Demmell had football, and there was no way he could play well if he was up half the night selling dope.

Shannon, the son born after Demmell, was much like Curtis, which both delighted and frightened Annette. He was bright and funny, but it seemed like the better a personality a boy had growing up in Elmhurst, the more likely he was to meet trouble. Shannon, like Demmell, was a fighter. He always seemed to have something to prove. He was an average student through elementary school, but that changed when he hit middle school. Every year he would need to attend summer school to avoid being left back a grade.

Kevin, the baby of the family, wasn't as quiet as Donald and Demmell, nor was he outgoing like Curtis and Shannon. He was a sweet kid who could seem reserved when he was around his more garrulous brothers, but out in the world he was chatty and lively. He was also an affectionate boy who, while still in elementary school, picked flowers from empty lots to give to his mother. "After you, Mrs. Reed," he'd say, holding the door open for Annette. He was funny that way, always doing things that kids don't normally do. He would even tell his mother not to go overboard at Christmas because all he really needed was a single toy.

To Annette, her baby's most extraordinary attribute was that he alone among her boys liked school. He loved doing well, loved the social nature of learning with other kids. He'd parade around like a peacock when he brought home an award and he'd chide himself when he thought he hadn't performed up to his potential. Annette never had to get after him about anything, never had to yell at him like she did the other boys.

Occasionally he'd stay out past his curfew or wander off when he was supposed to be home, but even that was an endearing trait. He'd strike up a conversation with anyone, no matter what the person's age, and lose track of the time. Like a miniature adult, people said. He was smart and friendly, with big dreams for his life. He was the baby of the family and also a kid who seemed to be headed places. If anything, his only problem was the weight of burdens that had been placed on his shoulders. He had become, it seemed, everyone's best hope.

6

BAD INFLUENCES

Tony was thirteen, not six months out of the San Antonio Villa, when the woman next door approached him and a friend about selling crack. She'd give them the rock on consignment, they'd pay her back after they'd sold it. "It ain't nothing you two boys can't handle," she told them. "It's easy money." The pair eagerly agreed to give it a try.

Tony sold for a few weeks, but standing outside waiting for customers was as boring as school, although selling dope didn't make him feel stupid. Besides, it wasn't long before Paula figured out what he was up to. She got so angry at her neighbor she practically got herself arrested on an assault charge.

Tony might not have been heading down the wrong path to street selling, but he wasn't heading anywhere positive, either. He didn't dream the dreams that were automatic to kids living in other neighborhoods. It was never "I want to be a fireman" or "I want to be a veterinarian." If he thought about the future at all, it was about tomorrow, not adulthood. He was spared the expectations parents often impose on their children yet denied an innate belief that life offered a world of possibilities from which to choose. He wasn't a suburban kid who worried about his "permanent record" or about the grades a college admissions officer would see, but he also didn't fantasize about being a grown-up father who put food on the table. About the only thing that lit up his dreams was money.

In that way he was like every other kid who imagines himself driving a souped-up sports car or living in a fancy house with a swimming pool—except that there was more to dream for, since he had so little.

Surrounding Tony were people getting by on government assistance or folks just barely surviving. There were more negative influences as well. His uncles O.D. and Larry—more like brothers, really, given their ages and the fact that they shared a room with Tony—were both pioneers in Oakland's burgeoning crack trade. Larry was twenty-one years old when Tony was twelve. He sold over on Sunnyside, not far from their Ninety-second Avenue turnkey. O.D., only six years older than Tony, sold down the block from where they lived, by a bank of thirteen spindly palm trees that towered so high above Ninety-second Avenue they could be seen for blocks.

O.D. was always Tony's favorite uncle. He idolized O.D., looking up to him in the adoring way a boy might look up to his father. Tony spent countless hours watching O.D. and his friends work. He'd sit off to the side, not saying a word, yet he seemed to absorb every word and every gesture.

O.D. tried discouraging Tony from following in his footsteps. Sometimes he'd shoo him away, but mainly he bought him things—the latest basketball shoes, a Raiders football jacket, a soda and a burrito from the minimart—to strip Tony of a motivation to sell. But the fact that O.D. could peel off a few twenties to give to Vera or Paula served only to impress Tony rather than stifle his motivation.

Paula might have insisted that O.D. at least sell somewhere far from the building, but she was in no position to get on her high horse. Paula, too, sold drugs out by the palm trees, though briefly. She was drawn by the potential for earning fast money, but she gave it up because she was petrified standing there exposed to every hard-up crackhead and would-be rival.

No one worried that Larry might be a bad influence on Tony and his siblings, because he was leading a life that no one could envy. He violated the cardinal rule of selling that dictates you never use your product. Larry's fall was precipitous, like that of nearly every crack addict. He smoked "gremmies"—joints dusted with crack, named (in a perverse display of affection) in honor of Everett Gremminger, the local police department's top narcotics investigator.

Larry stole to support his habit. Several times he came home looking like a beat-up alley dog, bandages and bruises everywhere. The story was the same every time: he had gotten caught trying to rip somebody off. When Tony was fourteen, Larry was found guilty of robbing seventy dollars from a woman. He caught a break, getting three years' probation, but was arrested again the following year, again for robbing a woman. The story that she told the cops was this: A man said he was lost and needed directions. Then, holding a tire iron, he told her, "Give me everything you got or I'll kill you." He took a few hundred dollars' worth of jewelry and maybe one hundred dollars in cash. Larry pled guilty and was sentenced to two years in the state penitentiary.

Less than a month after his release, he was picked up on another robbery charge. The victim was again a woman, his ruse again to ask for directions. This time he was sentenced to eight years in the penitentiary—three years for the robbery and an additional five years because of a prior conviction for the same felony charge.

O.D.'s drug-dealing days came to an end at around the same time as Larry's third robbery charge. O.D. was arrested for helping a friend exact his revenge against a woman who had supposedly ripped off some of his friend's coke. The woman was beaten, shot in each wrist, strafed by a shotgun blast aimed at her scalp, and then left tied up and bloody in the Elmhurst Middle School playground. When O.D.'s friend was later picked up by the cops, he said O.D. and a third man with them were guilty of nothing but helping him push the woman into a car so he could take her someplace out of the way. The victim, however, told the cops that the other men cheered on their friend and urinated on her as she was writhing on the ground.

O.D. pled guilty to one charge of kidnapping. "I just wasn't thinking," he told a probation officer. "I did it because my homeboys asked me to do it." He was sentenced to seven years in prison.

Tony was fourteen when O.D. went away, and he brooded over O.D.'s incarceration for a long time. He recalls being angry at O.D., like somehow O.D. had betrayed Tony instead of having betrayed himself.

■ ■ ■

One day, before either of his uncles was in prison, Tony was by the palm trees with his friend Patrick. He was in a terrible mood. The previous night Larry had returned home beaten and covered with bandages. He had been beaten up so severely that his leg was in a cast.

The incident hit Tony hard, perhaps because of the parallels to his mother's battle with drugs. He felt sympathetic toward Larry, yet he simultaneously felt scorn for the pathetic state into which his life had deteriorated. "He's like a thief, man," Tony told Patrick. "He always be coming home all fucked up." Tony crossed his heart and swore to the heavens that he would never become a dealer like his uncles. He told Patrick: "I ain't never going to smoke no dope, man. I ain't never gonna be selling." He made this promise as the two sat watching O.D. and his partners go about their business.

7

JUNEBUG

Life in the housing project on Ninety-second Avenue was even worse than Ann Benjamin had imagined. Chunks of plaster occasionally dropped from the ceiling; the floors wouldn't come clean no matter how hard or how often she scrubbed them. When the building's sewer system backed up, the toilet in her apartment was the one that would overflow with sewage. Housing would dispatch a crew to blow out the sewer lines and everything would be fine—except that her apartment reeked for weeks, and the same calamity repeated itself just about every year she lived there.

The garbage was another problem. The Housing Authority provided a pair of standard-size garbage cans to handle the weekly trash of a five-unit building. The residents complained that the cans were always overflowing, but for years Housing did nothing. People put out their garbage anyway, even if both cans were full, so by week's end, garbage was strewn everywhere. No doubt there were people on the block wondering about the slobbish habits of these people who lived in public housing. For Ann, perception was the least of her worries. Her bedroom window faced the garbage cans; in the summer the stench was overpowering.

The neighbors were another source of irritation, if not outright fear. Shortly after Ann moved to Ninety-second Avenue, one of her kids got into an argument with a boy next door. The year was 1980, when John was still living there. (Ann's relationship with the father of her kids didn't last twelve months into her move to Ninety-second Avenue.) John and the woman next door traded accusations about whose kid was at fault. Then Ann heard a gunshot. The woman, who everyone knew was messing around with a hotshot in the Felix Mitchell gang (the copper-colored Mercedes often parked out front was all the confirmation people needed), had taken a shot at John. The cops came but made no arrests. For days Ann braced herself for the retaliation that, thankfully, never came.

The Clays—Vera and her brood—were another problem. There were the small things, like the items they were borrowing—a mop, a broom—without returning, but that wasn't the half of it. To Ann's mind, Vera was a sweet enough woman, but her kids were another story altogether. One son sold dope a few blocks away, another just down the street. Vera's eldest daughter was apparently a junkie, and her youngest daughter, Paula, got under Ann's skin worse than the rest. She was still a teenager when Ann moved in, but she was always giving Ann lip for supposedly looking down on the others who lived in her building. Ann's crime, apparently, was that she alone among the residents of the building worked a full-time job. Ann didn't know if she should laugh or cry over this foulmouthed teenager telling her how to live her life.

The couple living in the unit between Ann's place and Vera's were no more neighborly. He was a heroin addict, she an alcoholic, and they were always fighting. Ann and her kids could hear the screaming and the threats through walls that seemed as thin as rice paper. On bad nights there were also the sounds of broken dishes. One time a knot appeared on their side of the wall after they heard a body thud against the wall. After that, every time the couple next door started fighting, Ann half expected one or both of them to come tumbling into her kitchen through shattered plaster.

Ann had long dreamed of becoming a nurse, so before moving to Ninety-second Avenue she enrolled at a local college to start the prerequisites. But her bills began to mount, and she was forced to quit school to find a job. She found work providing private duty care to well-off elderly people who were homebound. She liked the job, but the pay was lousy and the demands upon her great. Her goal was to save enough money to move, but in truth she was barely getting by.

"If I was in section eight housing, I could've looked around for another place," Ann said later. "But it was Housing [Authority housing], and once you're in Housing, you're just stuck at that particular place until you leave."

Near the end of her first year on Ninety-second Avenue, Ann returned home after an outing with the kids to find John with another woman. Ann grabbed the gun she knew John kept stashed away and started waving it around, demanding that he start packing his things immediately. John barricaded himself inside their bedroom and called the cops. "I would've shot him if it was loaded," she told the police when they arrived. Whether true or not, she was rid of John for good.

Psychologically, the ensuing months were tough. She had put up with her ex all those years because she had allowed him to convince her that she was the weak one. She looked at herself as a hayseed too naive to survive the city on her own. Yet working a job and providing for her kids showed her that she was the strong one.

She was in her early twenties during a time in which many of her peers spoke about "finding" themselves. That was a luxury Ann couldn't afford. She had recently given birth to her and John's third child, Hakeem, born shortly after she moved to Ninety-second Avenue. One might say that she was coming into her own, except that she was a single mom raising three kids stuck in a community that would challenge the abilities of even the most devout and attentive set of parents. And in 1984 she had another child, a son she named Demonte, meaning that at the age of twenty-seven she was the mother of four.

The first time Ann was burglarized, she didn't think to connect it to the drug dealing going on down the street. She felt violated and angry and frustrated at how hard she had worked for what the crooks had stolen: a small stereo, an iron, various hair products. After the second break-in, a neighbor told her that the culprits were the guys hanging out by the palm trees. That second time they took a replacement stereo, a clock radio, a jar filled with pennies, and a sweater a girlfriend had knitted for Ann for her birthday. The third time they didn't take much because there wasn't much else to take. But they left the place a mess of overturned mattresses and dumped drawers. Because Ann was working, her kids were the ones to find the apartment this way after school.

The culprits stopped breaking into Ann's place—what was there to take?—and started stealing from the woman who lived in the apartment right above Ann's. That was bad news for the woman upstairs but good news for Ann. She now had someone she could call whenever something crazy happened in the building.

Ann's oldest, Junebug, was a sensitive kid, fragile and easily nicked. More than anything else he wanted to be accepted by his peers. That was a normal part of adolescence, of course, but frightening for Ann to contemplate given all that awaited him outside their front door. He was always a good student, which made Ann believe he was headed for a better life than her own. Yet his emotional makeup made her fear he was destined for a fate far worse.

He had the look of someone who could be on the verge of laughing or crying: both emotions were at home on his face. At times he could seem like the most carefree of children, flashing a toothy grin that prompted everyone to note the resemblance between mother and son. The "Benjamin look," everybody said—and Ann would beam.

But there was that other face, a brooding look that made Junebug appear older than his years. It was more like an adult's face, preoccupied and set with worry. Even when he grew older and learned to better mask his deepest feelings, his emotions were protected by a thin membrane that was easily penetrated. Occasionally he would explode with anger, but mainly he pouted, quietly tending to the emotions bubbling up inside of him. The slightest tease, the most minor of slights, the natural frustrations attendant to childhood—every psychological nick or cut would send him deep inside himself.

Junebug was reading by age four, earlier than most kids. As far back as anyone could remember, he had his head buried in one book or another. He skipped from the first grade to the third. He was placed in the fast track with other promising kids.

The realm of facts and figures seemed his forte. He was like a calculator, his mother would boast, adding and multiplying numbers in his head just for the fun of it. He'd sit on the couch, looking up census figures and then writing them down in a notebook, as if preparing for some kind of test. He'd tick off odd tidbits, such as the population of China, never failing to tickle the funny bones of the adults for whom he seemed to be performing.

He was in the sixth grade when he and the rest of his classmates studied the stock market. Stocks became another of his passions. Every night he came home and pored over the financial pages of the newspaper, carefully charting the various stocks that had caught his interest. He continued tending to his paper portfolio long after the assignment was over. The movie *Trading Places* was a big hit then, and secretly he dreamed that someday someone would pluck him from East Oakland, much like fate had given Eddie Murphy's character his chance. Ann swelled with pride when, later that year, Junebug was called to the podium at his elementary school graduation to receive an "outstanding student" award.

Yet there was another side to Junebug's academic career. In the fourth grade he started to become what the authorities might have labeled a "problem child." Ann started getting phone calls from school. He was disrupting the class, talking out of turn, demanding his teacher's attention. He had been caught stealing another student's pencil but refused to admit to taking it. He yanked on a little girl's pigtails and made her cry.

It was always little stuff like that, and not just at school. He would fight with his sister, it seemed, just to upset Ann. He was often doing that, acting out for no apparent reason except that misbehavior was the surest way to get his mother's attention.

Junebug had been particularly close with his father when he was younger. He had always gravitated toward his dad when they lived together as a family. Yet now that they had split up, their dad hardly ever came around to see the kids anymore, even though he lived just twenty blocks away. There were no Sunday afternoon excursions with Dad, no weekend sleep-over dates. Every year Junebug's father would forget his birthday; there were no presents, no visits, not even a phone call. The same with Christmas.

Even a grade school teacher was able to pinpoint the transformation. By coincidence, Junebug had the same teacher two years running when he was in the third and fourth grades. The first year Junebug struck her as a sweet little boy with an open face and an engaging smile. But the next year it was as if a different child had enrolled in her class, one who was ill-adjusted and moody. She was kind when she phoned Ann. "Is there something wrong at home, Ms. Benjamin?" she gently prodded. The phone rang every year with another teacher voicing his or her concern. It was always the same: "Your son has so much promise, Ms. Benjamin. Is there a problem at home?"

As the oldest child and with no father around, Junebug looked on himself as the little man of the house, assuming a burden well beyond his years. To his child's mind, even the string of burglaries his family had suffered were somehow a sign of disrespect for him, as if by breaking into his apartment they had cast him as weak. When he was twelve he decided he should be contributing more to the household, so he took a job selling newspaper subscriptions door-to-door.

Ann tried to be attentive. She'd try drawing him out, she'd try reasoning with him. "I'm working hard and doing the best I can," she would tell him. But nothing she said seemed to work. Her probing would typically prompt either silent tears or a moody "I dunno." All she knew for certain was that whatever it was that was eating at him at any given moment it was something deep and tender because of the currents of emotion on his face.

On those rare occasions when he would unleash his feelings, they were directed at his mother and not his father. "I hate you," he would yell at her with such vehemence that it was as if the hatred were an entity in the room with them.

In private moments, Junebug recognized that his mother was working hard and doing her best. He would then turn that same anger on himself. He was, he told himself, the most unappreciative of sons. Only later could he tell Ann that what he wanted from her was her encouragement as he pursued his interests. "It's like there's no time for that," he half-cried when revealing himself to her.

Ann, too, tended to blame herself for her son's moods. Maybe it was the hours she was working; maybe she should quit her job and live on aid, she told herself. That way she wouldn't be walking through life half exhausted, trying to be both mother and father to her kids and at the same time their sole provider. Then she'd be able to give Junebug and the rest of her kids the attention they deserved. The rub, however, was that then she'd never get them off Ninety-second Avenue. Then they'd be stuck in public housing forever.

When Junebug would recall the day his family moved to Ninety-second Avenue, he'd remember their dinner by candlelight and the family sleeping on a mess of blankets and pillows sprawled across the floor. He'd also remember this chubby kid a couple of years older than he was hanging around while they moved in. That was the first time he met Tony.

Junebug was six and Tony eight, but they became quick friends. They were constantly together in those first years after the move to Ninety-second Avenue. They watched cartoons and played made-up games; they threw around a ball and wasted too much time playing video games.

Yet from almost the moment they met, there was a tension that was as much a part of their friendship as any bond they shared. For Tony it was a jealousy that Junebug had his mother and even his father when he first moved in.

For Junebug it was an uneasy sense whenever he was over at Tony's apartment. It wasn't fear so much as his presence in an alien world in which he didn't feel comfortable. He didn't know what to make of Tony's family, it was so different than his own. Ann set rules and curfews for Junebug. He had to be home by a certain time, he needed to ask permission before heading off to the arcade or to the store. Tony never seemed to have a bedtime or a time he had to be back inside the apartment. Never once could Junebug recall Vera calling Tony inside. It was as if she stayed in her room, unaware or unconcerned.

"Miss Clay, she means well, but it's like she don't care," Junebug would tell his mother. "It was like she was oblivious to their goings-on."

Ann never liked Junebug's spending so much time with Tony and his family, and she made no effort to hide her feelings from her son. Tony was two years older than her son, no small difference at that age. His family reminded Ann of her in-laws and the way they spoke to one another. Tony struck Ann as this sweet sad sack of a kid, yet the truth was that he seemed headed nowhere good in his life. By the time Junebug was eleven, two of Tony's uncles were in prison on felony convictions. His father wasn't in the picture and his mother was constantly in and out of jail. Ann didn't know what impact a mother like Tony's would have on a kid, but she was certain he wasn't a boy her son should be with.

"Mark my words," Ann told her son, "he's going to be the downfall of you one day if you don't watch yourself."

For Junebug, his relationship with Tony was always complicated. He recognized unpleasant traits in Tony's family that he came to see in Tony. He'd vow to stop being his friend, but then he'd get to feeling lonely. His resolve would weaken, either out of sympathy or out of need. There were practical considerations as well. Junebug was a skinny whip of a kid who had no father or older brother to stick up for him. There are advantages, especially in a place like East Oakland, to having the biggest kid out there as your friend.

8

KING OF
THE CORNER

Tony was fifteen when an older kid named Bootsie and his mother moved into the apartment above Vera's. Almost immediately Bootsie started selling crack out in front. Uncle O.D. had sold just down the street, but Bootsie was the first to open a concession right in front of the building.

Bootsie was only a couple of years older than Tony, but he struck Tony as much wiser and more mature. He seemed to know everything about setting up his own business. Unlike most small-time dealers, Bootsie cooked the cocaine himself rather than buying it in its crack form. That alone impressed Tony.

Bootsie shooed away the other kids from the block, but he allowed Tony, bigger than the rest of his peers, to hang around with him. He would invite Tony inside to watch him cook the coke to make crack. Bootsie had a killer stereo, a terrific television, and all sorts of other cool stuff. He also owned a safe in which he banked his profits.

Tony liked hanging around with Boots because it made him feel more grown up. He also liked the things that Bootsie bought him. Boots would invite Tony along on a shopping expedition and then buy him something that he knew would light up any fifteen-year-old's eyes. "This here's for being my lookout," Boots would say with a big smile. One time he bought him a leather jacket, another time a pair of designer jeans.

Tony loved these trips to the mall, but he considered how much better it would be to buy himself whatever he wanted. For the third time in his young life he found himself contemplating dealing.

Tony was thinking about broaching the subject with his new friend when Boots brought it up himself. They were hanging out in front of their building at the start of a new month. Boots was telling Tony how he'd be out through the night because on the first of the month the General Assistance (welfare for those without children) and disability checks arrive in the mail. (AFDC—Aid to Families with Dependent Children—arrives in the middle of the month.) There'd be so many customers wanting crack he'd have a hard time keeping up. He brought Tony inside to show him the stash he had cooked to prepare for the night. From his safe he pulled a bag of rock that made Tony's eyes bulge.

"How much you buy that for?" Tony asked him.

"Two thousand."

"How much you gonna take in?"

"Almost seven thousand. Sixty-five hundred."

"That right?"

"Yah." While the safe was open, Tony caught a glimpse of the bills stacked neatly inside. Bootsie noticed him staring. With a smile, he told Tony he had more than ten thousand dollars stashed away.

"So what you want to do? Wanna hook up with me?"

"Yah, I'll hook up wit'choo."

That night, true to Bootsie's claims, there were so many customers that at times they had as many as a half dozen people awaiting their turn. Tony didn't get to bed until after daylight. Bootsie took a healthy cut of his profits, but that still left Tony with nearly one thousand dollars cash—not bad for a single night's work.

The transition to street dealing was easy for Tony. He had observed O.D. and his friends and then Bootsie. There was, too, the street smarts assimilated by virtue of growing up in East Oakland. All of the kids he knew used the lingo the street dealers had invented—a *dove* for twenty dollars' worth of crack, *Five-O* (the cops), *hubba* (crack), *slangin' rock*. So natural was this patter to Tony by the time he hooked up with Bootsie that later he couldn't remember a thing about his first sale.

Tony was making between two and three hundred dollars a day in those first months; more around the first and the fifteenth of the month. School stunted his profits, so he stopped going except for occasional appearances. He avoided selling when either Vera or Paula was around, though Paula grew wise to Tony soon enough. Even Vera eventually figured out what was going on. "You ain't hanging out in front no more, are you boy?" his grandmother would ask him. Tony would tell her no because, to him, lying wasn't as bad as disappointing her with news she didn't want to hear.

For a time Paula put up a fight, but by now she had given birth to a baby of her own. She no longer had the time to look after Tony like she once had, nor could she afford to buy him things to counterbalance his desire to deal drugs. He was fifteen years old with a teen's desires — a car, a stereo, and the like. She lectured him about ending up in jail like O.D. and Larry. She even broached the forbidden topic of his own mother's drug problem. Tony would vow to stop, but then he'd start selling anyway. Eventually Paula gave up.

"You getting too old for me to be telling you what to do," she said to him. "You just gonna do it behind my back anyways, so at least be careful." Paula still lectured Tony every once in a while, but only when Vera was after her about her suspicions that Tony might still be dealing drugs outside.

The partnership between Tony and Bootsie lasted only six months. It was a stormy breakup that began when Boots was busted. Earlier in the day, Tony had given him around a thousand dollars for some crack. Normally Boots would give Tony his crack right there, but his stash was low, so he told him he needed to cook some up. Boots was busted before he had time to consummate the deal.

Tony asked Boots's girlfriend, who was going to visit Boots at the county jail, to see about getting his money back. She passed along a message when she returned: "He says he'll be out soon. He says just to wait."

Apparently this was Boots's first bust, because he was out in a week. He pled guilty to simple possession, got his lecture from a judge, and was released. But Tony didn't greet his friend with a "How ya doing, what's up?" He didn't express concern about his friend's brief incarceration. It was just, "Where's my money, man?"

"You don't trust me no more?"

By then Tony had grown accustomed to the money he was making. He had been walking around broke, tending to his anger. He spent most of the seven days his friend was locked up thinking about all of the money he would be making if he had some rock to sell.

"You holding me up, man," Tony said. "I want my money now." Bootsie told him to go fuck himself and Tony started hitting him. By chance, a pair of Housing cops happened by and broke up the fight. "You ain't getting nothing now," Boots told Tony.

An hour later Tony came back to the turnkey with a cousin and a friend from up the street. Boots wasn't around, so Tony kicked in his door. The three of them grabbed the safe and lugged it across the street to Tony's friend's apartment. They beat on it for a while, with no success. They were carrying it back outside to take it to a guy they knew with a torch when a rod fell out. The safe popped open.

Inside were four rocks that collectively weighed about a quarter of a pound—worth around two thousand dollars altogether. There was also nine thousand dollars in cash. Tony took half of the money and kept two rocks for himself. His coconspirators split the remaining rocks and cash.

When Bootsie discovered what had happened, Tony didn't bother lying to him. Boots told Tony he could keep his thousand but he wanted the rest back, no hard feelings. Tony told him to fuck off; he wasn't giving him anything. And that was the last Tony saw of him. Bootsie moved off Ninety-second Avenue without so much as making an empty threat.

Tony couldn't believe Boots hadn't put up more of a fight. He was braced for the possibility that Bootsie might come at him with a gun, but that was before he started asking around about him. He learned that Boots had been ripped off before by a doper who took him for a few hundred dollars. Boots had done nothing to get his money then, a violation of one of the cardinal rules of dealing: never let a crack addict take you. Tony also learned that Bootsie had been telling people that Tony was his bodyguard. The leather jacket and the jeans hadn't been gifts at all but cheap payments for his services.

He was not yet sixteen, but Tony had a corner all to himself. He had enough cash and crack to start his own small crew. He felt no remorse that his success had come by virtue of ripping off a friend and business partner, but instead was incredulous that he could have been so naive. That was the only thing suppressing the exhilaration he was otherwise feeling. He couldn't believe that he had ever looked up to a chump like Bootsie.

9

A SENSE
OF BELONGING

The drug dealers out front were bad news for everyone living in the turnkey on Ninety-second Avenue, but it was worse for Ann Benjamin and her young family. They lived in the ground-floor apartment facing the street, adjacent to the small parking lot where Tony and his crew liked to hang out. Ann lived with the fear that they were directly in harm's way should a rival fire upon Tony, and with the constant intrusions of an all-night drug operation right outside her bedroom window.

When Tony and his gang became bored, they'd light a few joints and blast their music. Their foulmouthed bantering, the booming bass, and the comings and goings of customers made it next to impossible for Ann to fall asleep. The young men did stupid things like bang on the garbage cans. Or at two in the morning there might be an argument with a crackhead complaining that he got less than he'd paid for. Every few weeks Ann would be out with Pine Sol, a bucket, and a scrub brush. Her window was by the corner the crew apparently used as its after-hours urinal.

Ann occasionally called the police, but then she would wonder why she bothered. The dispatcher would promise to send a squad car right away, although everyone—Ann, the cops, and the dealers themselves—understood there wasn't much the law could do short of catching a kid in the middle of a transaction. Half the time the cops didn't bother showing up at all. Ann was always careful to call from a pay phone because she knew that the 911 system automatically registered the number of the phone being used, even if you requested anonymity. The last thing she wanted was to give the dealers cause for devising even worse tortures to bedevil her and her family.

The urination and the noise were minor concerns stacked up against Ann's fear that Tony would drag Junebug into his dirty business. Tony and Junebug no longer hung around with each other now that Tony was big man on the corner. Tony's friends teased Junebug, who was much smaller and a couple of years younger than they were. They called him a nerd and a punk—someone who couldn't handle himself. Tony stood among his friend's tormentors without saying a word in Junebug's defense. Junebug vowed to have nothing more to do with Tony, which might have been music to Ann's ears except that she had heard it all before. Junebug would be through with Tony forever—until the next time they were inseparable friends.

At first Ann tried encouraging Junebug to stay inside more, but that meant his sitting in front of the television all day. Besides, it was an order she couldn't enforce. By the time Junebug had entered junior high, Ann found a better-paying job working for the post office. She worked maintenance on the second shift, which meant that she didn't get home until after eleven in the evening. So desperate was she for child care that Ann turned to her mother for help. Medication was helping her with her schizophrenia, but she was partially deaf and seemed oblivious to her grandkids' presence. It was "hi, Grandma, bye, Grandma" whenever it suited Junebug. Practically speaking, he was on his own.

Ann did what she could to keep Junebug off Ninety-second Avenue. On the weekends she started bringing him and his siblings to Union City to be with their cousins. They'd have little outings that put distance between Junebug and Tony. But mainly she just prayed that her son was smart enough to see that he had too bright a future to flush it away dealing drugs.

In the late 1980s, author (and former teacher) Jonathan Kozol traveled the country comparing schools in wealthier, predominantly white communities and those of poor, predominantly minority city neighborhoods.

In the book that grew out of that effort, *Savage Inequalities*, Kozol provides grim portraits of a half dozen inner-city school systems ("by and large, extraordinarily unhappy places") that crush the spirits and hopes of all but the inner city's most fiercely determined students. The book's main theme might have been encapsulated by a Missouri school superintendent who told Kozol, "Gifted children are everywhere in East St. Louis, but their gifts are lost to poverty and turmoil and the damage done by knowing they are written off by their society."

One does not need to travel far from Oakland to find the kind of savage inequalities that Kozol documented so convincingly. Piedmont is a geographic anomaly, a separate township entirely within Oakland's borders. The Piedmont school district spent forty-nine hundred dollars per student in 1990, compared to thirty-one hundred dollars per student in Oakland. That additional money bought Piedmont an extra school period each day, smaller class sizes, reading specialists, librarians, and an array of extracurricular activities that the Oakland public schools no longer offered. Where in Piedmont the district searches out the most highly qualified teachers available, Oakland seeks teachers with fewer than three years' experience because they are cheaper. Due to the district's budget woes, the Oakland school board in recent years has cut back or eliminated entirely its music programs, elementary school science classes, high school business courses, vocational training, and supervised after-school programs.

Ninety-five percent of the graduating seniors in Piedmont go on to college. In Oakland, as revealed in a 1990 study, nearly half of the high school students—47 percent—were carrying a D or F grade average. In Oakland basic supplies like chalk, pencils, and paper are hard to come by, and textbooks are often in such short supply that students must share. By 1990 the Oakland schools were the stuff of national headlines when a state auditor concluded, "We found problems and deficiencies just about everywhere we looked." Mismanagement, corruption, widespread patronage, pending bankruptcy—these were the scourges of the Oakland schools through the 1980s. Typical was a $2.5 million scholarship fund the district created in the mid-1980s to help underprivileged kids with college tuition. Two years later the fund was in the headlines because the district had failed to set aside any money to pay for the program and the $130,000 raised privately sat in a bank, unused. Piedmont, in contrast, was featured in slick city magazines that sang the praises of its superior schools.

Deep inequities exist not only between Oakland and nearby suburban schools but also within the district. The economic disparities between the hills and the flatlands are deepened by the quality of the schools serving those areas. In 1993 a reporter for the Oakland *Tribune* dropped in on middle school classrooms around the district. In the flatland schools she witnessed students sitting idle and apparently bored, no pen or pencil in hand. In virtually every classroom she visited, she saw students with their heads resting on crossed arms, yet rarely would a teacher roust them.

By contrast, the kids in a typical hills classroom were alert. Supplies were bountiful. The teachers, she found, were more demanding of their students. The kids in the hills went home each afternoon loaded down with assignments. Kids in the flats, she found, had little if any homework assigned. The difference seemed one of expectations.

Not surprisingly, the standardized test scores of the flatland schools are abysmal compared to those of schools in the hills. The district and its teachers aren't entirely to blame, of course—even the best academic program won't work unless something is done about the environment in which many of these kids are growing up, and there are the inequities born of the generations of parents who were deprived of a decent education by the Jim Crow practices of the South—but from the perspective of the parents, the flatlands' inferior schools are yet another encumbrance born of their modest means.

Junebug was supposed to attend Elmhurst Middle School, six blocks from his home. Even among the city's flatland schools, Elmhurst stood out then as a notoriously bad junior high. One street north of the school, the most brutal crack crew in all of Oakland lorded over a three-block stretch of Ninety-sixth Avenue. This crew been blamed for burning a man's home because he was organizing to get them off the street and for beating a man who moved into a home that the crew had come to consider their turf because it had been temporarily unoccupied. Elmhurst's eighth graders consistently rank in the bottom 5 percent in statewide assessment exams, while students at the Montera Junior High in the hills rank in the top 10 percent. An Elmhurst teacher quoted in one newspaper said she had only eight social studies textbooks, five math texts, and no English books for a class of twenty-five.

Ann was intent on distancing Junebug from their life on Ninety-second Avenue, so she finagled an admission to Bret Harte Junior High, a racially mixed school that included kids from both the hills and the flats. She used the mailing address of a cousin who lived in a better part of Oakland, and no one was the wiser.

Compared to Elmhurst, Bret Harte was peaceful, almost serene. At Elmhurst, Junebug's friends told him, there was constant fighting. Occasionally a kid would flash a gun—more to show off than to use it, but it was dangerous nonetheless; Junebug couldn't imagine a kid pulling a gun at Bret Harte. As Ann saw it, the main advantage to Bret Harte was that Junebug wouldn't be in constant contact with the kids from their block. Also, Bret Harte's students went on to Skyline, regarded to be the city's best high school, rather than Castlemont, one of the city's two worst.

Junebug was placed in classes with the advanced kids at Bret Harte. His counselor got him into a special writing program at the University of California at Berkeley for promising minority students. Junebug was suddenly dreaming of life as a writer. He was also among fifty Bret Harte students who piled onto a bus one Saturday morning to take the SATs with the eleventh and twelfth graders. Their test scores wouldn't count, of course, but the exercise was devised to get disadvantaged kids excited about the prospects of attending college. Junebug also took part in a peer-tutoring program at Bret Harte. It's hard to say who got more out of the program, the kids receiving the extra instruction or the tutors themselves, enthralled both by the hourly wage they were paid and their newfound worth.

Junebug thrived on the academic challenges thrown his way. He seemed happiest and most at ease when preparing for a precollege test designed for older kids or working on an assignment for his summer writing course. Yet concurrently there raged convulsive currents just beneath the surface that portended disaster. Several times Ann caught Junebug stealing money from her purse. He got into a couple of fights at school, apparently (so he told his mother) because he needed to prove he was no punk. He began ditching classes starting in the eighth grade—and then boasted to his friends back on Ninety-second Avenue, "Just taking me a vacation in the middle of the day." At first it was a class here and there, but then it was an afternoon or a morning and eventually the entire day.

Where in the seventh grade his acceptance into Bret Harte's advanced classes was a source of pride, by the end of the eighth grade Junebug was telling his mother he wanted out. He invented all sorts of high-minded reasons, but the truth was that he was fed up with the neighborhood kids making him out to be a nerd, taunting him about his fancy school in the hills and his good grades. "You think you better than us," they'd say with obvious hostility.

Ultimately Junebug's participation in any advanced program became a moot point. The A's of his earlier report cards were replaced by B's and C's, even an occasional D. "I just want to be like other kids," he'd complain to his mother. Ann just shook her head. Who would *want* to end up like the dead-end kids hanging out in front of their building?

Junebug's ultimate act of defiance occurred when he revealed his true address to the school authorities, confessing that he should be going to Castlemont next year, not Skyline. Ann felt like screaming, but what was there to say once the damage was done? Skyline was the kind of school that could have helped him get into college, Junebug knew, and Castlemont was the kind of school where college was possible, of course, but the obstacles were far greater. He wanted to make something of his life, sure, but mainly he just wanted to fit in.

Even before Keisha was born, Ann knew the kind of relationship she wanted should she ever have a girl. She dreamed of an intimate mother-daughter bond, the kind she had never had with her own mother. She was always on firm ground when thinking through her approach to raising Keisha, if for no other reason than she was certain she wanted to do things differently than her own mother had done.

When contemplating her rearing of Junebug, however, Ann was wracked by doubts. Maybe she was mothering him too much, she told herself. Maybe that's why he was acting out in school. Should she allow distance to form between them? Could she be both a mother and father to Junebug? Should she even try?

Junebug was always invoking his father during a fight. "My father wouldn't talk to me like that," he'd yell at her when he was angry or hurt. "My father wouldn't do that." In truth, Junebug didn't like his father very much, and Ann knew that, but that made his verbal assaults no less painful. It seemed Junebug was ending every one of their arguments the same way: "I'll go live with my daddy then."

Junebug talked about his father so often that Ann began thinking it might not be a bad idea. Both she and John had grown up in broken homes, but only her ex had the experience of a boy being raised by his mother. So, despite serious reservations, Ann packed up Junebug's things when he was thirteen and prayed for the best. Any hopes she might have had were dashed when she heard from one of John's sisters that John had applied for AFDC right after Junebug moved in, but had been turned down. She knew then that it was just a matter of time before her son was back home.

Junebug lasted three months at his father's place. He said his dad would often take off in the morning, leaving him to fend for himself. A cousin sold dope from out of the house. If he went to school, he got there on his own; there was no one offering a ride or, for that matter, making sure he went at all. Some days he sat on the couch watching TV, bored, thinking how much better it had been at his mother's house but too proud to ask about moving back.

He often went hungry because no one paid attention to his meals. Everyone was family inside the apartment, but people locked their bedroom doors just the same, which meant that Junebug often didn't have access to a bathroom. He urinated in the backyard when he couldn't hold it any longer, and hoped he didn't have to do anything more involved once people had left or locked themselves in their rooms. When he would get tired of his own smell, he'd walk the twenty blocks to his mother's house to take a shower.

Junebug's friend Aaron would stop by occasionally to pick him up. Aaron also lived on Ninety-second Avenue, so he had come across his share of frightening characters. When he visited Junebug at his father's place, however, he felt fear. Some of the people entering and leaving the house appeared to him like they must be wanted for crimes you wouldn't even want to know about. "They'd be looking at me like, 'Who is you and what you doing here?' " Aaron said.

Aaron was no more impressed with Junebug's father. "He was like, 'I'm living,' " Aaron recalled. "That's about it. That was about all he was doing—just living, just surviving." He wasn't surprised when Junebug sometimes came straight to his house after school to spend the night. Who would want to stay over there?

Before moving in with his dad, Junebug had one truly terrific father-son memory of a fishing trip when he had been around six years old. Initially he had brought up his father only to get under his mother's skin, but after a time he truly believed it might be the best solution. It was as if he had embroidered an elaborate dream around that one remembrance, when the truth was that he was resentful of his father and embarrassed about the way he looked and dressed.

For Junebug, the last straw came on his fourteenth birthday. At his mother's place everyone would have been fussing over him. He didn't expect that kind of commotion at his dad's, but he expected *something*. Instead there was no mention of the day. He told his father he was going over to his mother's because it was his birthday.

"Oh, OK, tell them I said hi," his father said. There was no "happy birthday," no apology for having forgotten, nothing. And with that his experiment with living with his father was over.

Junebug recognized that he was too thin-skinned for his own good. He tried to take in stride the ribbing that was an everyday part of adolescent life. He tried putting up walls to shield his innermost feelings. Yet the smallest psychological pinprick could stir within him immense emotions. He didn't dwell on his feelings like some—he wasn't the type to play his resentments over and over in his head like a repeating loop of tape—but instead would feel them in the extreme. His mood swings came over him like sudden changes in the weather, a squall of fury replacing sunny blue skies. He'd be feeling great, believing himself to be smart and confident, but later that same day a tidal wave of feelings could come crashing down on him, washing away everything but anger, self-blame, and confusion. In these moments, the intensity of the feelings he felt coursing through his body frightened him.

Junebug longed to fit in, but he knew in his heart that he was different from most of the people around him. He had dreams of flight. He fantasized about fleeing Oakland and creating a new life for himself, somewhere where no one knew who he was. It was as if only then could he become the person he wanted to be.

Honesty, loyalty, and openness were virtues to his mind, yet on his block they were the characteristics of chumps and fools. It was as if people around them were operating on street speed but he and his family were still in Pine Grove, Louisiana. We don't belong here, Junebug would tell himself. These people aren't doing anything with their lives. Morals-wise, we're above all them.

And yet he was drawn to their life despite himself—to a life that promised excitement and money and, first and foremost, acceptance. He felt disengaged from his family, so he would try conforming to the streets, even though he was no more in synch with the people he knew there than he was with his family.

With time Junebug learned how to handle himself so that he was no one's easy prey. People would have to think twice before taking advantage of him or disrespecting him. In this he would take great pride. But learning to handle oneself physically was one thing; psychologically he seemed far too fragile to survive Ninety-second Avenue.

10

KICKIN' IT
ON THE CORNER

There's nothing glamorous about street dealing. The slang the dealers themselves use—"grinding," "clocking," "slangin'"—connotes images of the daily grind of a job, of punching the clock, of slinging hash. In East Oakland, in the early 1990s at least, the preferred term was "grinding." "Slangin' rock" would do, but "clocking" was strictly East Coast.

They had no grand name for themselves, these young men who sold dope on Ninety-second Avenue a block from a main artery, East Fourteenth Street. They were just "Ninety-second" or "Ninety-second and Holly," or, if looking to give themselves a more gangsterish sound, "nine-deuce."

The pipeheads in the area knew Ninety-second to be a corner that was almost always open for business. Ninety-second was like an all-night convenience store for crack, except that it was staffed not by an immigrant family but by young men just as hungry for a piece of the American dream, even if tainted by their dirty money.

The nine-deuce crew was sure to keep "turf guns" stashed within reach—in the bushes, stuffed into a discarded easy chair Housing never came to pick up, even in a garbage can. Among themselves they agreed that they would be willing to use the guns if necessary, while privately at least a few wondered if they really had it in them to pull the trigger.

They stomped customers who violated their unwritten codes. Sometimes they'd slap someone around just because one of them was in the mood. On Tuesday they'd laugh at the pathetic coke whore, skinny as a pipe because eating meant less money for crack. She'd beg them for a dove's worth, claiming to be six dollars short because her man had stolen her stash, but then she would produce the entire twenty bucks when they held out. But when someone else would try this same sort of gambit on Thursday they'd be on him like he was a thief. They were kids, ranging in age from fourteen to eighteen, each with his own threshold.

They had their morals, or at least their superstitions. They worked every day except Sunday because, they told themselves, God has no mercy on those who grind on his day of rest. Directly next door was the parking lot for the Amos Temple Church, an imposing and handsome white church with stately Corinthian columns. Some were true believers in the ban, because they were religious or because it seemed that the few times any of them had gotten busted it had happened on a Sunday. For others their vow was born of something between guilt and avoidance. Closing down on Sunday meant the well-dressed parishioners wouldn't stare them down when retrieving their cars after church.

Junebug took his first timid steps into street dealing in 1988, not long after his brief stay with his father. He had recently turned fourteen; his birthday money, in fact, was his seed money for buying his first few chunks of crack.

In anticipation of turning fourteen, he had asked his mother for a quilted black-and-gray Raiders football jacket. Ann told him the jacket was too expensive. He said there was nothing else he wanted, so she gave him cash. Including his mother's gift, he had about one hundred dollars saved up, which still wasn't enough for the jacket.

His friend Tony—now "Fat 'Tone" to friend and foe alike—proposed a solution. Give me the hundred in exchange for some rock. You'll double your money within a few hours. And like that, Junebug Jones, all skin and bones, his clothes hanging from his lanky frame, a baby-faced kid with high cheekbones and delicate features, did his best to look confident and tough and cool while awaiting his turn selling to his next customer.

'Tone helped Junebug in those first few hours and over the coming weeks. Whenever it was Junebug's turn, 'Tone would nod if a person was a regular. That first night Junebug was a bundle of nerves, but he also felt something resembling exhilaration. He was suddenly part of a whole new world, forbidden and alluring.

'Tone enjoyed teaching Junebug the ropes. He showed him how to use a razor to cut the rocks into twenty-dollar chunks. They walked together to the drugstore around the corner, where they bought the plastic sandwich bags and the blades that are immensely popular with teenagers in that part of town.

'Tone was never school smart, but he was wise in the ways of the street. He was always offering aphorisms of the trade. "Never carry the shit on you," he'd say, stash it somewhere nearby. That way if the cops come around, they can't bust you with a bag full of rocks in your pocket. Sell to people we see everyday 'cause you never know who might be an undercover. Don't sell to someone while they're still in their car because otherwise they can shoot and be gone before you know it. Never do your product. Smoke pot, drink, but never touch crack. "That shit'll make you crazy," counseled 'Tone, whose mother was all the proof either of them needed.

Not all of the crew was ready to embrace Junebug, but 'Tone told everyone that if they had a problem with Junebug, they had a problem with him. 'Tone felt pangs of guilt, teaching his bright but impressionable friend the ins and outs of dealing, but who was he to tell a friend he has no right to earn a living? Besides, countering the guilt were feelings of pride. Because of him, no one looked at Junebug as a nerd anymore.

"My little cousin," 'Tone said when referring to Junebug—the ultimate term of affection in East Oakland, short of referring to someone not related to you as "my brother."

It wouldn't be quite right to say that Fat 'Tone was the jefe lording over a crew of about a dozen or so young men. Theirs wasn't a gang in the traditional sense. There were no initiation rights, no colors, no elaborate handshakes. No leader gave orders or drew up a schedule. Still, 'Tone had been out there longer than anyone else and he was everybody's supplier. He was also the oldest. If nothing else he was the de facto leader by virtue of his experience, his connections, and his considerable heft.

He was the biggest kid on the block and also the toughest. He was deceptively strong beneath his baby fat. He claimed never to have lost a fight, a boast that friends and partners backed up. His most worthy adversary proved to be a guy named Rick, whom 'Tone mixed it up with after an argument over money and drugs. Rick had a year and several inches on him but the two fought to a draw. More typical was the time he drove over to Castlemont to confront a guy who, after losing everything he had playing dice, stole it all back from a member of 'Tone's crew. 'Tone hit the kid so hard he lay there flat on his back. "You don't be ripping off my pahtnah," he told the kid.

'Tone didn't dream of becoming East Oakland's next Felix Mitchell. He didn't think in terms of moving in on other crews. He wanted to make his bones by piling up so much money working their corner that he would demand attention, not by murdering his way to the top.

'Tone's supplier—a guy he knew from the street, a few years older than he was—sold him crack at five hundred dollars an ounce. 'Tone bought it already cooked because doing it himself wasn't possible at his grandmother's apartment. All he needed to do was carve large chunks into twenty-dollar lots, around the size of a molar. An ounce worth of crack sold on the streets for about thirteen hundred dollars. That meant approximately eight hundred dollars pure profit for every ounce he sold.

A good day meant maybe one thousand dollars in sales, or profits exceeding five hundred dollars; an average day netted two to three hundred dollars. Around the first and fifteenth of the month, when people received their government checks, they could make as much as two thousand dollars each.

'Tone blew a ton of money on drugs and food, but he managed to save a modest amount in a safe he kept in his room. He figured he had around ten thousand dollars in cash and drugs in his safe when it was stolen. He immediately suspected his mother, but he chased that thought from his mind. It had to have been someone in his family, though, because there was no sign of a forced entry and nothing else in the apartment had been disturbed.

'Tone's mother used to hit him up for drugs and money. She had been strictly a heroin user but with the arrival of crack she was happy to have either drug in her hands. 'Tone never gave her any drugs but he was always good for a twenty, if not more. He'd lean on her about her drug dependency and she'd always tell him the same thing. "I'm trying, baby, I'm trying." She had been through several programs, with no long-term success.

'Tone's father also came around after learning that his son had his own little crew. He asked him to hook him up with some rock. It took 'Tone a few moments to place the face. When he realized who it was, 'Tone threatened to beat up his father if he ever came around again looking for a handout. That was the last time 'Tone would ever see his dad.

Partaking in the world of the dealers just outside his door opened Junebug's eyes to dazzling possibilities. A virtual smorgasbord of material rewards rolled by. Beepers, silk shirts, designer jeans, VCRs, televisions, porterhouse steaks—if it fit into a trunk, someone cruised by to see if these young men with pockets stuffed with cash were interested. You could buy a gold chain or a ring for your honey from these inner-city traveling salesmen—unless you wanted to drive her downtown so the two of you could lean over the glass cases in a jewelry store to pick out an expensive bauble that was hers for the asking because she had chosen to be with you.

Guns, too, were sold in this same fashion. Men of all races came around with trunks crammed with an assortment of weapons that made an adolescent's eyes dance. A .22 for easy hiding; a .45 with ample pop; a 9 mm assault pistol like the Intratec Tec-9; the automatics that turned dealers into modern-day mobsters armed with sleek new tommy guns—any of these could be yours without stepping foot outside the neighborhood and without filling out any bothersome paperwork. The weapons still in boxes were sold at a premium, well above the store price, but you could get a used handgun for as little as twenty-five to fifty dollars.

Their main turf gun was a .38 that 'Tone had bought from a pipehead for a couple of doves. The gun might have been dirty, but that wasn't something 'Tone even stopped to think about. Even if it had been used in a homicide, he wouldn't have cared. Back then he didn't think the cops would ever catch him.

After some trouble with a rival crew, Tony bought a Tec-9 from out of someone's trunk for seven hundred dollars. The pistol was a bulky and inaccurate weapon favored by drug gangs in the United States and by Third-World militias; for several years running, the Tec-9 was confiscated during law enforcement busts at a higher rate than any other weapon. The "nine," as it was sold over the counter before California banned its sale in 1989, was a semiautomatic, but it had already been converted (illegally) to an automatic when 'Tone bought it. As modified, the gun could spit out a clip of thirty-two bullets in fewer than ten seconds.

Anything could be yours when you were holding crack. For a mere twenty bucks' worth, you could rent a dope fiend's car for the night. A hubba rental wasn't usually necessary, though, because several members of the nine-deuce crew owned their own cars, even though they were well below the legal driving age.

Tony drove an "old school"—a 1972 Chevy Impala. Their "turf" car was a Dodge Dart that was beat up and bruised but drove just fine and didn't draw attention. They weren't like the drug gangsters in movies who bought themselves BMWs with smoked-out windows and loaded with chrome. On Ninety-second Avenue, common sense dictated that you buy yourself a modest ride so as not to beg Five-O to pull you over. Grinding was about business, they'd tell themselves, not about buying yourself ostentatious toys.

Junebug wasn't all that serious about his selling in those first months. He hung out with Tony and the crew after school and in the evenings, careful to quit before his mother came home from work. He'd dash into the apartment, rip off his clothes, and feign sleep. He sold for spending money—and of course for the acceptance it gained him.

The more he stood outside selling, though, the more grown up he felt. He could walk into the minimart and, like any adult, buy whatever he desired: onion ring chips, a can of Tahitian Treat, frozen pizza for dinner. He worked more hours when he wanted an expensive toy like the hand-held video game he kept hidden away in his room. He told himself that he was helping out his mother the same way a towheaded boy of yesteryear worked as a box boy after school and on Saturdays to help take the financial strain off his ma and pa.

Yet privately Junebug was always wrestling with giving it up entirely. For a time he considered working at someplace like McDonald's, but the more he thought about it, the more he realized that the humiliation of flipping burgers for minimum wage would have been too great. He considered those times he had joined other members of his crew for a trip to the McDonald's on Ninety-eighth. They'd plead with some kid they knew from school to hook them up with a freebie. Then they'd eat their meal while laughing at this same kid. He was nothing but a chump slaving away for maybe a hundred and fifty dollars in take-home pay every other week. They were clearing fifteen hundred dollars easy in those same two weeks, hanging out in the street with friends.

There were dangers, of course, not part of the work shift at Mickie-D's. There were rival dealers and the cops; their customers were addicts known for rash and desperate acts. Yet Junebug had that teenager's ability to blot those thoughts from his mind. He saw himself as impervious to harm. Small-time street dealers are murdered, and they go to jail for murder all the time, but that's on TV, not on Ninety-second Avenue.

Ann phoned her ex the first few times she caught Junebug outside with Tony's crew. "Let me come back home and this wouldn't happen," he'd invariably tell her, so it wasn't long before she stopped calling him about Junebug altogether. She'd have to handle him on her own.

She lectured Junebug. She appealed to reason. She tried exploiting whatever fears he might be feeling deep inside. "I know you're out there," she would say, "I know what you're up to, and all I got to say is you're going to learn one day the hard way." It was never "I order you to stay in the house," and she never hit him for defying her wishes. Instead she let him know at every opportunity that she strongly disapproved of what he was doing.

It seemed that Ann was always up on a soapbox about something — the earring Junebug had started wearing, his sudden fondness for the slang he once considered "ignorant," the tattoo he got from a guy up the street. The tattoo made Ann's blood boil. Junebug had inked "92," for Ninety-second Avenue, on his bicep: BUG 92 (actually, he had wanted JUNEBUG 92, but at the last minute he got scared it would hurt, so he shortened his nickname to save himself four letters of potential pain).

"It's bad enough we got to live here, but why you have to go puttin' it on your arm forever?" she demanded. "You think that's something to be proud of, you hanging out with them fools out front?" She raised her voice, but of course it was too late. The mark was indelibly tattooed to his arm. No amount of yelling would rub it off.

Junebug always hoped that his mother would be more like the parents of other kids he knew, resigned to whatever their sons was up to if not eager for the extra cash they brought into the household. Junebug would always hear his mother out, never confessing that her voice was in his head, eating away at his conscience despite his best efforts to beat it back.

For a time Junebug carefully hid the things he had bought with his drug money, but eventually that seemed silly, so instead he showed his mother her proper respect, to his mind at least, by never consummating a deal in her presence. By the age of fifteen he stopped bugging her about money altogether. He was grown up now, he told himself; he'd pull his own weight. He wished she'd accept some money, but he knew without having to ask her that she would never accept a dime earned selling drugs.

Junebug recognized the delicacy of his living at home. He feared that his mother would kick him out of the house, if for no other reason than his influence on his siblings. What he didn't know is that kicking him out might be the last thing she would ever do, given her own past. Eventually Junebug started dreaming of moving into his own place with a friend. That way he could minimize both his exposure to his mother's lectures and also his guilt.

Junebug hated it that his little brothers were exposed to the life he had taken on. "See what I'm doing," he would tell them. "Don't ever turn out like the way I'm turning out." But he figured that they might look at him in much the same way that he had looked at adults when he was their age: hypocrites who said one thing but did another. He told himself he'd be on them never to start, but if they got into it anyway, he would teach them like 'Tone had taught him, so they didn't end up in jail or dead.

Keisha, too, became Junebug's concern, even when his ministering was not welcome. When he caught her drinking with her friends when she was fourteen, he was on her like a strict father. "You ain't my daddy," she yelled at him.

Still, his message was a powerful one. He knew the kind of girls she was starting to hang around with. They drank and cursed and ended up pregnant in the tenth grade. She'd point out that he had no right to talk to her like that, given his own life, but that was exactly the point. "You start hanging around with them girls," he'd tell her, "and you'll end up no better than me."

11

NO WAY OUT

By the spring of 1990, the Oakland police unit responsible for ridding East Oakland of small-time drug dealers had received so many complaints about Ninety-second Avenue that busting Fat 'Tone and his crew was made a top priority. The unit's commander, Sgt. Mike Beal, does not want to admit that he decides strategy based on the frequency of calls to his office. But back then, in 1990, Beal and the ten men under his command were responsible for a twenty-five-square-mile area home to between 125 and 150 drug hot spots. Then, as now, the squeaky wheel tended to get the grease.

Beal's unit was created after pressure was put on city hall to do something about the drug crews that had taken hold in the flatland neighborhoods. The dealers refer to them as the "task force," but officially the unit responsible for all of East Oakland was known as Special Duty Unit No. 2. Beal had been on the force six years when he took command over SDU-2 in 1988.

Beal works out of a windowless office in the basement of police headquarters downtown, miles from the vast majority of drug hot spots his unit was created to shut down. The tiled ceiling sags and industrial-grade filing cabinets groan and squeak under the weight of the thousands of arrest reports his unit fills out each year. Based on arrest figures, the bureaucracy touts SDU-2 as one of its great successes, yet to Beal the reality is a lot more complicated than bottom-line numbers. He figures that most of the names he has in his files are still dealing, unless they're dead or serving time for a more serious offense.

Even if they make a good bust, the measly rock or two they'll find in a kid's pocket invariably means that the DA will accept a simple possession plea rather than the more serious intent-to-sell charge. The task force switched its focus to undercover and surveillance work, but both demand an enormous number of man-hours. Besides, with prosecutors overwhelmed by murders, rapes, and other serious assaults, there's little time for these kids busted for selling twenty, forty, or a hundred dollars' worth of crack.

"The way things stand now, we're not going to cure things out there," Beal says, "but if I can give the citizenry relief for just one night . . ."

Yet for all Beal's claims of his modest goals, there are plenty of people who believe the men under his charge are too aggressive. That includes some of Beal's fellow officers, including an East Oakland cop named Marv Jackson.

Jackson was born and raised back East, in the rough and tumble of Brooklyn's Bedford-Stuyvesant. He was thirteen and seemed headed nowhere in particular when his mother earned a degree and was able to move the family to a nicer neighborhood. Suddenly he was hanging around with kids who talked of college and beyond instead of kids who stared in wonder at dope dealers awash in money and respect. To Jackson, that's the main difference between him and the young men he's been policing since 1980: he got out in time.

Like Beal, Jackson feels the frustration of combating the drug crews that plague East Oakland. "All day long I'd hear the same dozen addresses over the radio," Jackson says. "Ninety-six hundred Walnut. Ninety-second and Holly. It'd be the same twelve or fifteen guys hanging out in the same spot all day. They got sick of seeing us and we got sick of seeing them."

Yet where the task force cops envision that they're ridding East Oakland of this vermin among them, Jackson believes he's dealing with young men who've taken a series of wrong turns in their lives. As he views it, his job is to know who is who so that he'll have the requisite intelligence when the real trouble begins.

"We're not the judge and jury out here," Jackson says. "We can drive by [in a patrol car] and make their job harder. You harass them when you can. But there's the Constitution and the department's rules, so basically you do the best you can within those limits."

Like other black cops on the force, Jackson grumbles that the task force is too white. But mainly he complains that as a beat cop he would be called on by Beal's squad or other special duty units to cuff and interrogate someone without being told what a suspect was being accused of. More times than he cared to count, he's fought someone into handcuffs and pressed him to confess, only to learn ten minutes later that they've sent him after the wrong guy. Sometimes the suspect would be hauled downtown anyway, booked for resisting arrest even though there's no other charge against him.

And of course it was up to Jackson and the other beat cops to deal with any lingering resentment among those who had been mistreated. After the task force jacked up a corner, the kids there acted crazy over the next few days, as if there were a full moon.

In the flesh, Mike Beal is not nearly the macho cowboy that his detractors portray him to be. He confesses that it's scary working the streets of East Oakland. You run down dark alleys not knowing what awaits you around the next corner. You jump over a fence knowing there's a chance someone's stopped to train a gun on you. If on occasion a member or two of his unit is overly aggressive, Beal says, then maybe it's a matter of self-preservation.

Beal doesn't doubt that there are those like Annette Reed who resent his tactics, but there are also countless East Oakland residents who think he isn't nearly tough enough. He tells of one typical caller, an older woman who used to have her family over for Sunday night dinner. They are no longer able to do so because she doesn't feel they're safe coming to her block. The answer, she told Beal, was military personnel carrying rifles.

Beal's reputation is that of a straight-arrow, by-the-book kind of cop, despite the notoriety of the unit under his charge. Despite himself, he's come to respect some of the young men he busts. They're "these little assholes I'd like to beat into the ground" one moment, but the next minute he can extol their intelligence and their wasted potential. "Their problem is a lack of conflict resolution skills," he says, sounding very much like an at-risk youth counselor.

Over the years he's come to know any number of the dealers by their first names. He even confessed to liking a few of them. Later, he couldn't recall the name Tony Davis, but "Fat 'Tone" rang a bell, and he remembered that closing down that corner proved futile, an impossible task given the lack of officers under his charge, a toothless criminal justice system, and the straitjacket imposed by the Fourth Amendment's search and seizure protections.

In the spring of 1990, Fat 'Tone was eighteen years old and weighed more than 250 pounds. He had full, round cheeks, a thick double chin, and hair piled in a scruffy high top. He typically wore a white T-shirt, loose-fitting jeans that tended to slip down his ass, and whatever athletic shoes were stylish at the moment.

When there was any bit of a chill outside or if there was trouble in the air, 'Tone wore the Derby jacket that was the rage in East Oakland then. The Derby had an inside pocket ideal for hiding a gun. Even teens who wouldn't consider owning a piece pestered their folks for a Derby because of its status and because it never hurt to have someone wondering whether you might be packing.

'Tone stood five feet ten inches tall, but people seemed to think of him as even bigger than he was, presumably because he was so imposing a young man. The few times he was arrested, the cops tended to make him six feet or taller. Those same reports identified him as "unemployed," but that was true only in the narrowest sense of the word. In fact, he was making money at a faster clip than any of the cops charged with busting him.

'Tone took great pride that not once had an undercover cop fooled him into thinking he was a genuine customer. "It's in the way they carry themselves," he counseled Junebug. "They can say everything right, but they've got this pushiness that a dope fiend don't have. A dope fiend knows there's always 'nother corner, but the cops, they's always like desperate to do a deal."

Still, 'Tone looked at the task force with something between fear and respect. They were easy to spot because every task force cop drove the same no-frills black Dodge Diplomat, but that made them no less worthy an adversary. In contrast, he saw the cops working for the Oakland Housing Authority as fools. Housing had created its own unit to fight drug dealing on its property, but it tended to hire less experienced cops or those who couldn't get a job with a city police force.

The Housing cops used the same approach every time they came after 'Tone and his crew, driving down Holly three or four Chevy Caprice Classics deep. At night the Housing cops used the same strategy but turned off their headlights. They weren't fooling anyone. The crew typically had someone sitting on the fence separating their turnkey from the church parking lot. From there one could see a couple of blocks up Holly. A lookout yelled when he spotted the approaching caravan of darkened cars and they'd scatter, foiling yet another supposedly clandestine mission.

Junebug was still fourteen the first time he was arrested. He was standing outside in front of the building one Sunday evening, talking with some other kids, when the drug task force rolled up on them. He wasn't selling at the moment, so he didn't run like everyone else. Only after it was too late did he remember that a friend had asked him to hold a Baggie with two twenty-dollar rocks in it. He tossed it over his shoulder, but the cop saw him dump his dope.

Ironically, Ann had just finished delivering one of her many lectures about the wrongs of drug dealing. At that point she wasn't entirely sure whether he was dealing or just kicking it with his friends outside, as he was still maintaining back then. There in the kitchen she tried impressing upon him that if he was selling, he didn't need to; she was making enough money without his help. And if he wasn't grinding, then at least he ought to be smart enough to stay away from these guys when they're out there selling. "The cops are getting wise to what's going on," she told him, "so even hanging around outside can get you arrested."

Not thirty minutes later, a neighbor knocked anxiously at Ann's door. "They arresting Junebug," she yelled. Ann rushed outside in time to see a cop leading her son away in handcuffs. She asked Junebug if it was true that he had been holding drugs. He answered yes. He didn't want his mother working herself up into a state of righteous indignation when he had been caught dead to rights. He also didn't want to get his friend in trouble with the cops. If he claimed that the dope wasn't his, he knew the cop would only ask him whose it was, and then he'd be in a worse bind.

Junebug didn't allow himself to show any emotion as he was being led away. It seemed like every guy working that corner had been busted at least once, so what counted most at that moment was the pose. The cop who arrested him, Junebug later claimed, called him "stupid" and told him that if it was up to him, he'd force him to stand naked in the street with a sign around his neck saying he was nothing but a lowlife dope dealer. He wouldn't give the cop the satisfaction of a response.

The police report listed Junebug as five feet nine inches tall and a mere 115 pounds. He was one month shy of his fifteenth birthday. He was charged with simple possession and released the next day. Because it was his first offense, he was sentenced to six months' probation.

Ann was hoping a night in juvenile lockup would teach Junebug a lesson. Yet to Junebug's mind, the thing to learn was that he had to be more careful now that he had a conviction on his record. The courts would no doubt treat him tougher the next time around.

With time he would get much more serious about dope dealing and the task force would target his corner, yet his arrest on a simple possession in 1989 was the one and only time in his life he'd be busted, at least on a drug-related charge.

By the spring of 1990, Tony was getting high every day, all day. He never touched the crack he sold, but he'd smoke pot around the clock, sometimes burning as many as a dozen joints in a day. He also consumed a staggering amount of alcohol. He'd go through as many as four forty-ounce bottles of Old English malt liquor in a day. He guzzled Hennessy, gin, whatever someone was offering. He was partial, too, to Cisco, a potent concoction favored by teenagers and winos—five ounces of alcohol dressed up in twelve ounces of fruity flavors.

He was always clowning, trying to make people laugh, but when he was wasted he would be paranoid and moody. He did crazy things after smoking and drinking all day. Late one night 'Tone was hanging out in the church parking lot with his friend Billy and a guy named John Banks. John did something to anger him, so he pulled out his Tec-9 and let it rip. He didn't hurt anybody—he had just wanted to see them jump—but that made it no less potentially fatal a prank, and foolhardy as well from a business standpoint. Shooting an automatic only made their corner that much hotter.

'Tone had gotten into so many fights at Castlemont High School that the administration sent him to the East Side Center for Redirection, across the street from the Lockwood Gardens housing project—like exiling a kid to Mars, according to one school official. East Side is an alternative school for troublemakers, pregnant teens, and others the district doesn't want in one of the city's five regular high schools. A teacher there took a special interest in Tony and tried delving into whatever it was that was preventing him from trying at school. The way 'Tone saw it, however, she was too late. He appreciated the effort, but by the time she entered his life, he cared little about school.

That winter he had moved out of Vera's apartment to give his grandmother some peace of mind. He knew that another bit of her heart broke every time she caught him hanging out front. There was also her security to consider. Under Housing's new rules, his grandmother could be booted from the building if he was caught dealing. Paula had moved into an apartment with extra room a few months earlier; when she invited 'Tone to live with her, he jumped at his good luck.

Paula moved into a place on Ninetieth Avenue, ideally situated between two main streets, MacArthur and Bancroft. That was another advantage in moving. Whenever Ninety-second got too hot, 'Tone and his friends would start selling in front of Paula's place.

Paula was hip to what was going on. She knew, too, that 'Tone stored some kind of nasty gun under his bed. They were close and there were few secrets between them, but she felt it was no longer her place to tell him how to live his life. So instead she prayed that he didn't lose his head out there and end up in jail for something stupid, like her brother O.D., or dead.

Junebug, meanwhile, was getting more into dealing with each passing month. By the first half of 1990, he was as hungry for profits as anyone out there. Like an ambitious entrepreneur, he set daily and weekly goals for himself. He motivated himself by calculating, recalculating, and then calculating again his potential profits if he kept selling at his current pace.

Goals were easy to hit in the days after people received their government checks, but Junebug's ambitions ranked him among the corner's stalwarts. He clocked his hours even during the slowest days of the month. He even began selling on credit to those he knew worked a steady job. Others called him foolish, but he racked up more customers—and more sales—that way.

Junebug preferred working the late shift. By himself he had nothing to prove to anybody. Sometimes he sold with his friend Aaron Estill. Aaron was a year younger and less experienced than Junebug. It was Junebug, in fact, who got Aaron into dealing, much like Fat 'Tone had gotten him into the life.

Aaron lived down the street with his mother and his two older brothers. His middle brother, Anthony, had been a partner of 'Tone's right after Tony started on his own. "Skinny 'Tone," everyone called him. Skinny 'Tone gave up dealing in 1989 after being busted and sent to the California Youth Authority. There he worked on a fire crew stationed in the California mountains. After battling blazes for about seven months, he returned to Oakland saying that he wanted to train as a mechanic and eventually build high-performance cars. He'd still be talking—but only talking—about that same plan five years later.

Aaron's father was in the navy and his mother worked in a bank when Aaron was born. Their marriage broke apart when Aaron was around five years old, after a friend of his father's showed up AWOL. His friend needed money to disappear, but Aaron's father was the one holding the gun when the pair of them were caught trying to rob two white men. His father was sentenced to ten years in jail.

"What kind of fool holds the gun?" Doreatha Estill asked herself that question so many times it made her head ache. "Maybe you drive the car for a friend. I'm not saying that's right, but you don't hold the gun." It became a bitter mantra of hers even long after she had gone about rebuilding her life.

They had been living in Virginia, where her husband was stationed. Doreatha moved back home to East Oakland and worked at the Carnation plant until it closed in 1983. She worked hard at being a good mother. She was always piling the boys into the car to take them on a picnic, to a carnival, or to the fair. When she was a girl, her mother was a single parent who always claimed she was too busy working to take her and her siblings on little outings. Doreatha was determined to raise her kids differently.

Aaron was twelve or thirteen the first time he saw a dead person lying in the street. He was leaving Booker's, a store on Ninetieth Avenue, with a bag of chips and a soda when he saw a car peel away from the gas station across the street. Someone had just taken out a middle-tier drug dealer with a shotgun blast to the brain. Aaron was among the first few witnesses on the scene, arriving before the cops or the paramedics. Staring at the man's shattered skull and the gore leaking out left him queasy inside, but he stood there in shocked disbelief. He would beat the cops to the scene of a couple more shootings, but it would never be as unnerving—or as oddly exhilarating—as that first time.

In the spring of 1990, Aaron was a smallish young man of fifteen who once was outgoing and carefree but now was passive and aloof, because indifference is a wiser strategy for surviving the streets. To his mother's mind, his curiosity and spirit were casualties of the everyday violence around him. Where once she used to find him chattering with strangers of all ages, he was now quiet and cautious. Later people would recall him as a kid hanging around the fringes of the nine-deuce crew, never really a part of their gang.

Aaron was kicked out of Elmhurst Middle School while he was still in the eighth grade. He had asked his teacher for permission to go to the bathroom, but the teacher told him that it was near the end of the day, so he'd have to wait for the bell. He claimed he needed to go really bad, she still said no, so he simply walked out of class. The vice principal was waiting for him when he exited the bathroom. She ordered him into her office, but by then the bell had rung, so he said he was going home. She grabbed him by the shoulder; he pushed her arm away to break free. She threatened to bring him up on an assault charge and Aaron told her he didn't care. She never pressed charges.

Like 'Tone, Aaron was sent to East Side, even though it was a high school for grades nine through twelve. For a time Aaron stuck with the program at East Side, but eventually his interest dwindled. "They got me in this school like I'm stupid or something like that," he complained to his mother. "The teachers, they ain't trying to teach us nothing. People, they laughing and cracking jokes. People'd be in the back of the room smoking weed and the teachers ain't saying nothing but, 'Okay, settle down y'all.'" Despite his mother's protests, he stopped attending classes altogether.

His brother Anthony's life had taken pretty much the same trajectory. Anthony did OK at Elmhurst—mainly B's and C's, he said—but he felt Castlemont was a joke, so he stopped going to classes. "You get tired of hanging around up there so you start hanging around the house," he said. "You get tired of hanging around the house so you start hanging around outside. Then you just pick it up—the grinding."

For Aaron, the decision to start dealing wasn't any more complicated. He wasn't up to much else, so why not? His inauguration into dealing went this way: Junebug asked him, "Wanna start grindin'?" and Aaron told him "Awright." He spent his profits on junk food and clothes and dreamed of the day he could buy himself a car.

Through the night, Junebug and Aaron sat in the disabled Cadillac Junebug's uncle—Ann's brother Ben—kept parked across the street. Sometimes they'd be out there past sunrise. They'd do anything to keep themselves awake. Junebug made up raps, including one paying homage to their little crew, but mainly they messed around or reminisced and, on occasion, got deep. They shared dreams of striking it rich in the music business. Aaron never touched drugs, but occasionally Junebug got really stoned, blasting the heat while smoking a joint. "Going back to the land," they called it on Ninety-second.

A set of headlights would pass and they'd slump down low in the car seat so they wouldn't be seen. The regulars knew to park their cars and walk toward the turnkey. Only then would Junebug and Aaron get out of the car. "Let them stand out there exposing themselves instead a' us," they told each other.

Junebug went through one of several regular routines created both to elude arrest and to protect his stash. His favorite was to hide his crack inside empty cans stowed in the garbage can. A customer would hand over the money—nothing illegal about that—and he'd send him or her around to the side of the building. Out of sight, Junebug would retrieve the appropriate amount of rock from the garbage. Then, when the customer was in view again, he'd reach into some obvious place like the bushes, pretending to grab something. And of course the addict was watching his every move when Junebug was within his sights.

No matter how careful they might be, however, the experience was nerve-racking. The passing lights might be someone shopping for a dealer at three in the morning, but they also might be an addict with a .38 in his lap, desperate for another hit. A "drug 211-187" the cops call it: a drug robbery that ends in a 187, a murder. For all the homicide rate climbed in Oakland in the late 1980s and early 1990s, no category swelled as quickly as this one. A "victimless" crime, the more hard-boiled officers in blue would joke.

In Junebug's first year at Castlemont, he was placed in the advanced track classes with the smarter kids. He barely maintained a C average. By the eleventh grade he was failing every subject. When he bothered to go to school at all, it was only as a place to see and be seen. There were countless times he hung out at Castlemont without bothering to attend a single class. Instead he and his friends hung outside, making fun of the chumps trying to learn inside.

He dressed in the stylish clothes he was able to buy with his illegal profits. He wore pricey dress shirts and designer jeans and the jewelry he fancied, until a Muslim street preacher convinced him that gold and diamonds represented the oppression of the black man. For a time he even wore a beeper on his belt, though they weren't big enough players to need beepers.

At Castlemont, Junebug believed he had finally come into his own. There were plenty of students who couldn't stand these brash, self-adoring dealers who were turning Elmhurst into a veritable war zone, but they were easy enough to ignore when there were so many others who were impressed. Girls vied for his attention. Other kids looked up to him.

Yet inside he was all balled up. Every semester started with the same debate raging inside his head. He'd buckle down. He wouldn't waste his life, he'd make his mother proud. But then he'd quickly grow bored with his classes. The hard work and struggle often required to master a new subject seemed a waste of time. Again he'd be cutting a class to smoke a joint with a friend. And of course any homework assignments got in the way of what he called his "business." Grinding always seemed to win out over homework.

Junebug recognized that he was mortgaging his future for the immediate gratification offered by drug dealing. But he also knew the odds were stacked heavily against his making it. In 1990, one in three black men in their twenties in California were in jail, on parole, or on probation—four times the rate of African-American males enrolled in a four-year college program. He rationalized his life choice this way: I'm a smart kid from the inner city who's been cut off from all forms of American privilege. My prospects for anything resembling the middle-class dream are bleak. Why bother with school when I'm making good money?

His logic was no different than a kid growing up in Detroit twenty years ago who figured he didn't need to care about his grades because he'd only be getting a job on the assembly line once done with school. Working at a General Motors plant isn't illegal, of course, but GM—or Ford or Chrysler—hasn't hired many people from Oakland in years. The truth was that the crack trade offered ambitious young men work in a part of town in which a job even a cut or two above McDonald's was hard to come by.

In the first half of 1990, Ann Benjamin suffered insomnia for the first time in her life. Some nights Ann lay awake in bed, never even bothering to close her eyes. She'd fret and plot her escape and question the

God who was putting her through such hell. Other times she'd sit at the kitchen table and stare with such intensity it was as if she were looking through the walls clear across the continent to Louisiana, desperately trying to figure out what she had left behind in Pine Grove. She dreamed of the simplicity of her life there. She pictured her kids as she remembered herself, a carefree girl running down dusty roads scattered with children and chickens. She had known pain back then, but it was nothing like the confusion confronting teenagers nowadays.

A young man barely older than Junebug had burst into her apartment with a gun shortly before her bout with insomnia. It turned out he had the wrong apartment, but staring down the barrel of a gun had frightened her speechless. She stood there with her mouth agape, unable to answer him. He slapped her face with the back of his other hand. Ann's brother, who was watching TV in the other room, rushed toward the door. The kid fired an errant shot and ran.

Ann hated doctors, but after three or four months of walking around exhausted from lack of sleep, she finally broke down and made an appointment. She told the doctor she was a single mom raising four kids and hated where she lived, but she didn't mention anything about the violence that seemed a natural part of her life or her eldest son's drug dealing.

The doctor prescribed what he described as "sleeping pills." They left her feeling drugged and heavy lidded, so she read about them in a medical dictionary. She gasped. The doctor had prescribed a strong antidepressive. I'm not crazy! she told herself. Does this man think I'm *crazy?* She stopped taking the pills, but then she found herself chain-smoking Salems.

Ann didn't really confide in many people back then. She had a few friends, but they lived in a world far apart from public housing. Besides, what was there to say? What was there to do but complain? Mainly she kept whatever she was feeling to herself because it seemed pointless to share her misery with anyone else.

She was angry at Junebug for a great many things, but foremost among them was the role he played in putting his family in harm's way. "How could you sell right out front?" she yelled at him. "If anyone wants to get you, they know where you live. And that means they're shooting at where me, your sister, and your brothers live." Fat 'Tone had already moved to Paula's house; Junebug alone among those dealing outside lived in their building.

'Tone was the intended target when a couple of guys shot up the corner with a twelve gauge in the first half of 1990. 'Tone glimpsed the shotgun just before they fired and got out of the way just in time. But buckshot ended up in Ann's dresser and in a wall in her daughter Keisha's room next door. Fortunately, no one was home that evening, but for a time the family took to sleeping on the floor. Ann's two youngest, Hakeem and Demonte, cried inconsolably whenever they heard gunshots. If the shooting out front made it harder for her two youngest to sleep, who knew what it did to their ability to learn in school, or to have anything that resembled a happy, normal childhood?

Yet the low point for Ann those first few months of 1990 had nothing to do with Junebug's dealing. It occurred instead when Junebug got into the kind of stupid fight that's strictly the province of teenage boys. He was sitting talking with a friend in his friend's car when an older kid came along. The driver invited the older boy to join them for a ride. The older kid ordered Junebug out of the front seat, but Junebug wouldn't budge. The older kid was much bigger, but Junebug drew a line in the sand. "I ain't getting out of no front seat for you," he told him.

One thing led to another, and the older kid threw a busted car tape deck at him. "Better not throw it back at me," the boy warned. Of course that's exactly what Junebug did; the tape deck hit the kid in the back of the head.

Junebug ran into his apartment, into his room for the .22 he kept stashed between his mattress and boxspring. He told himself he didn't intend to actually use the gun. He'd wave the piece around to scare the kid off. That the other guy might pull a gun of his own and force the issue was something that Junebug never stopped to consider.

Ann was home when her son started rummaging through his bed in search of the .22. "I know whatchoo looking for," she said, anger in her voice. One of her other kids had discovered the gun and she had already removed it. "Guns don't solve your problems," she lectured him, "guns just end you up dead or in jail."

Junebug tried acting cool around guns, as if one hooked into his waistband was no big thing, yet the truth was that guns petrified him. He wasn't like other guys, who occasionally would pull one out and fire it in the air a few times, making it easier to shoot in that split second you have to decide whether or not to shoot at another human being. Junebug couldn't even bring himself to squeeze off a few rounds on New Year's Eve, when it seemed that half of East Oakland ushered in the new year with gunfire. Once he had gone off on his own in the middle of the day to a desolate stretch of East Oakland among the train tracks and abandoned buildings to see what it felt like to pull the trigger. It was only one round, yet he thought half the cops in Oakland would be all over him as the noise of the gun reverberated in his ears. He couldn't imagine anyone getting away with murder, given the booming sound a gun made.

Junebug didn't admit any of this to his mother but instead returned her stare with a scowl. For all her problems following her separation from Junebug's father, Ann never felt so defeated as she did that day. She vowed to work even harder. She took on work as a private duty nurse whenever she could find it, even though that meant working days and then going to the post office to work the second shift. I'll get us out of here as fast as I can, she told herself. What else can I do?

PART TWO
THE MURDER

12

BAD BLOOD

The driver was an older man named Burley whose friends called him Phil. The way Fat 'Tone and his crew would tell it, his companion was some mouthy dope fiend who brought on all that befell the two of them her own fool self. Kept after them about buying dope on a night Five-O were on them like theirs was the only hot spot in all of Oakland. Feeling woozy in the hospital later that night, Phil of course gave their intentions on that Tuesday in April of 1990 purely innocent airs: Just minding our business, me and my lady friend, when these four boys surrounded us near the corner of Ninety-second and Holly. They're demanding my keys, they force me out of the car, and the next thing I know's I'm lying in the street bleeding from the mouth and from the back of my head.

Years later the young men working Ninety-second Avenue would remember that night as much for the hours preceding Phil and his friend's arrival as for all that happened afterward. For hours they seemed trapped in a game of cops and robbers that wouldn't end. Typically the cops would swoop down on them once in a day, or maybe twice over a twenty-four-hour period when they had something special going. But on this night the task force came by once, twice, and again a third time in less than a few hours. Fat 'Tone, Junebug, and everyone else out there that night scattered down alleys and over fences, eluding capture each time, but they called it quits after the task force's third go at them. They stashed their dope and wrote the night off as a loss, like businessmen closing early because of foul weather.

Not five minutes later, this old guy and his lady rolled up on them. "You all got sumpin'?" the woman asked them. "Y'all gotta dove?"

They probably would've suspected their own people of being an undercover on this particular night, let alone some pipehead they didn't recognize driving through with a guy forty years her senior. But they realized that of course Five-O wasn't about to employ some guy in his sixties to nail them on a twenty-dollar buy. They sized her up to be some pain-in-the-ass coke whore who might prove fun for a few minutes.

"Whatchoo talkin' 'bout, lady? We ain't no dope dealers."

"Ain't no one out here doin' sumpin'?"

"We're good boys over here," they teased her. "We don't sell no dope."

"Baby, I ain't the poe-lease. Can't y'all tell me where I can get me some?"

"How we s'posta know somepin' like that?" another kid asked. It was Junebug. For good measure, he added, "You ought to stop smokin' that shit your own self. That shit'll kill ya." And of course they all broke up laughing over that one.

"Ain't no reason for you boys to be like that. I ain't given you no cause." And again she was on them about selling her some rock.

No one can recall who actually made the first move—the whole thing was so stupid that later no one would admit to starting it—but once one of them was involved, they were all involved. Smiles melted into stony-faced visages, as if the cops were on them for a fourth time. Someone said, "Get your ugly ass outta here, lady, 'fore we kick it for ya." But by then escaping was too late. They surrounded Phil and his car so fast it was as if stealing his rickety old 1981 Escort had been their intention all along.

Phil later said in court that he was at a friend's house when his buddy's daughter hit him up for a ride to the store. She needed Pampers for her baby, she had said. On their way over, she asked him to stop on Ninety-second Avenue. "I'm looking for somebody," she told him vaguely.

Safely inside a courtroom, Phil placed himself valiantly outside his car, defending his friend's daughter. But the way Fat 'Tone, Junebug, Aaron, and others in their crew remembered it, the man had sat stoically without saying a word while his companion pleaded for some rock. They had even felt momentary sympathy for the man, whom they imagined so hard up for some sugar that he needed to endure scenes like these. But he was there and their mood was what it was. They began rocking his car back and forth. Someone got in his face: "Get your black ass out of the muthafuckin' car, else we yank you out." Once Phil was out of the car, 'Tone smacked him square in the face with a forearm. Phil hit the ground like a fallen tree. The woman ran.

Junebug slipped into the driver's seat. "Where the motherfuckin' keys at?" he asked no one in particular. Someone handed Junebug a set, but he still couldn't start the car. "How you start this thing?" A hand reached in and pointed out a button you had to depress before the ignition would engage. The engine turned over, Aaron jumped into the passenger seat, and the two of them took a short joy ride around the neighborhood.

About all Phil remembered afterward was someone grabbing his keys and his trying to explain about the ignition system. His next recollection had him lying in the street, surrounded by cops and paramedics. His car and the young men were gone. Gone, too, were his keys, his wallet, and his friend's daughter. He told the cops that as best he could tell, the perps were between the ages of twelve and seventeen.

Six days later, a pair of cops were driving down a side street in East Oakland when a black kid twenty years old drove past them in a car heading the other way. "I know from prior arrests for stolen vehicles that stolen vehicles are often recovered in high narcotic areas," a cop named Owens wrote in his arrest report, "so I then looked at my stolen vehicle hot sheet." Which of course was nothing but an official way of saying he spotted a black guy driving a car in East Oakland, figured he might be guilty of something, ran the plates, and got lucky. They arrested a twenty-one-year-old who gave his name as Monroe Brooks and charged him with car theft.

Brooks told the cops that he had borrowed the car from a guy he knew named Trevor. Didn't know a last name, not sure where he lived, had no idea where Trevor might have gotten the car. The only thing he could say for certain was that he knew nothing about a carjacking.

One can imagine the cops shaking their heads wearily. "See, I got me this cousin," some young perp will tell them, and then they waste half a day looking for a kid who is no blood relative at all, only a friend. "Oh, I just call him my cousin," the perp will say matter-of-factly—just like the girl he describes as his "little sister" who isn't his sister but the sibling of his best friend.

It turned out that there was no Trevor, and Brooks's real name wasn't Monroe but Shondell. Shondell broke down and told the cops that his friend's real name was Rick. Shondell gave the cops an address, but neither the manager nor a guy in the apartment next door knew of any Rick. They confronted Shondell and he gave them the correct address, even told him Rick's full name: Ulric Bradley. But then Rick told the cops that he had gotten the car from Shondell, not vice versa. Shondell, Rick said, had claimed to have gotten the car from some hard-up dope fiend.

The cops brought Shondell downtown to stand in a lineup. Phil identified him as the young man who had sat in the driver's seat demanding his keys. He could be certain, Phil told the cops, because while he was lying on the ground, he had gotten a really good look at him as he handed up his keys.

Phil's lady friend refused to view the lineup. She told the cops she hadn't seen much, so what's the use? As she told it, they had just been sitting in the car when these boys came after Phil and she ran. She said some large, fat kid had tried grabbing her, but he had missed and fallen. She said she had asked around the next day and heard that a fat kid was always hanging out on that corner—went by the nickname Fat Tony or something dopey like that.

Police in another of the Oakland Police Department's special duty units—SDU-1, akin to a roving posse crisscrossing Oakland looking for fugitives and others wanted on felony warrants—caught up with 'Tone around the same time Shondell was picked up driving the stolen Escort.

Paula was at her mother's place visiting when a pair of task force cops showed up at Vera's door. "What you want to talk to Fat 'Tone for?" Paula asked the cops. "We just need to talk to him about someone he might know," one of the cops lied. "Well he ain't here," Paula said. She told the cops she had no idea where he was, even though Tony was now living with her.

The two cops were still standing there when Paula told her mother, "Don't tell the police nothing." The way Paula figured it, the cops were always claiming they didn't want to do so-and-so any harm, but then nine times out of ten they slapped the cuffs on your loved one just the same.

The cops arrested 'Tone the next day hanging out on Ninety-second Avenue. Later, in court, he claimed that he hadn't told the police a thing, but in a windowless interrogation room in police headquarters he gave up several friends. Shondell landed the first blow, he told the cops. Rick Bradley was involved. And a kid named John Jones, whom everybody knew as Junebug, was the one who clocked the old man in the face.

'Tone admitted that he had also been there that night, but he put himself innocently on the fence while his foolish friends went about stealing the car. The extent of his involvement, he claimed, was to chase the woman after she made a dash for it. He tried grabbing her, but he missed and fell. That apparently made quite a scene, this 250 pounder, his size forties slipping down his behind and his belly extending out from underneath his T-shirt, flopping on the ground in pursuit of a skinny pipehead. His friends laughed at him, 'Tone told the cops, so he refused to go when they beckoned him inside the car.

The cops picked up Junebug later that same night. "The only question I have," one of the cops asked him, "is why'd you punch the old man in the face?"

"Whatchoo talking about?" Junebug was aiming for a scowl, but the look on his face more closely resembled hurt. "I didn't hit that old man."

The cop didn't argue. Instead he hit the play button on the recorder sitting on the table between them. "Junebug, he hit that old man." It was unmistakably 'Tone's voice. His oversize friend who had sworn he would always be there watching his back, his street guide who had taught him that rule number one above all others was that you don't rat on a friend, had given him up to get himself off the hook.

Junebug would be locked away in juvenile hall for a month. He watched a lot of TV, messed around with friends, and spent the rest of his time seething over Fat 'Tone's betrayal.

13

THE KILLING ZONE

The part of East Oakland that in 1990 was home to Junebug, Fat 'Tone, and their families is officially known to the cops as police beat number thirty-four. Bounded by East Fourteenth Street to the west and MacArthur Boulevard to the east, and between Eighty-second and Ninety-eighth Avenues, beat thirty-four doesn't rank among the city's worst in terms of armed robberies, car thefts, or any of a long list of crimes. Its distinction among the city's thirty-five police beats is murder. Rare is the resident who knows beat thirty-four by its official police demarcation, but even more rare still is that flatlander who has never heard the area referred to by its unofficial name: the killing zone.

The killing zone may not be identified with teen violence in the national mind like South Central Los Angeles, the South Bronx, or the south side of Chicago are, but that has more to do with perception than reality. The homicide rate in Oakland is significantly higher than that of Los Angeles, New York, Chicago, or all but a dozen or so other cities with a population of at least 100,000 people. And it's beat thirty-four where Oakland's murder epidemic takes its greatest toll.

For five straight years, starting in 1988, beat thirty-four ranked first or second in murder among all Oakland beats, but it was in 1990 that beat thirty-four earned its memorable appellation. That year no fewer than 18 of the city's 161 murders—1 of every 9 murders that year, though home to fewer than one in every thirty Oakland residents—took place in beat thirty-four. "The most murderous square mile in Oakland," wrote a San Francisco *Examiner* reporter. Even the city's mayor has spoken of the "killing zone" without irony. Oakland doesn't have a murder problem, Mayor Elihu Harris was quoted as saying, so long as you avoid East Oakland's killing zone.

In 1990 beat thirty-four was home to the city's third, eighth, and eleventh murders that year, all within the first fifteen days of January. The victims were a nineteen-year-old drug dealer, a twenty-three-year-old woman found dead in her home, and a thirty-year-old man out for a walk at six in the evening.

The beat's fourth murder victim was a thirty-year-old gunned down in an early evening Uzi attack. Eleven days later, a twenty-one-year-old was discovered dead on a sidewalk at Ninety-fifth and Birch. The next murder victim was a forty-seven-year-old man stabbed to death by his forty-six-year-old common-law wife. A couple of weeks later, a thirty-six-year-old man would be picked up for stabbing his thirty-year-old girlfriend to death. Another case of a woman stabbing her husband followed two months later. Before the year was half over, a seventeen-year-old woman would be arrested for beating to death her nine-month-old son and a twenty-four-year-old would be found lying dead on a sidewalk just one block from where the body of a twenty-one-year-old had been discovered just two months earlier.

By the halfway point of 1990, beat thirty-four was home to no fewer than a dozen murders. Then in July the killing zone would register another two murders, including perhaps the most tragic and senseless of them all.

The Reed family, too, lived in the killing zone, although their small community behind Castlemont High was not quite as dangerous as Ninety-second Avenue just off East Fourteenth Street. While the cops were called to the fourteen hundred and fifteen hundred blocks of Ninety-second Avenue a combined eighty-six times in 1989 and 1990, they were summoned to the twenty-two hundred and twenty-three hundred blocks of Auseon Avenue only thirteen times over that same two-year period.

There were seven reported shootings on that two-block strip of Ninety-second Avenue, none on Auseon. On Ninety-second Avenue there were six cars reported stolen during that time and no fewer than twenty reported robberies and burglaries. Nine batteries were also reported. Auseon Avenue, by comparison, was relatively quiet, but it was still the scene of five batteries, a burglary, and a rape. Moreover, three of the murders in beat thirty-four during the first half of 1990 occurred within a few blocks of the Reed home.

Yet as violent and frightening as the world around them had become, it was the upheaval within the Reed home that preoccupied its residents. In February, Donald and Annette's second son, Curtis, was questioned in connection with the murder of a dealer the cops described as a kilo man. The dealer's body was discovered in his BMW. He had been wearing a bulletproof vest but died from a single bullet wound to the head. Curtis swore his innocence—the young man was in fact a friend of the family's—but the homicide cop assigned to the case was convinced Curtis knew a lot more than he was letting on. He dragged Curtis downtown right after the murder and then again several weeks later. But with Curtis it was just name, rank, and serial number. He was nineteen at the time, bright and personable but a high school dropout who was still grinding.

Dermmell, the middle son, wasn't in trouble with the law, but he was the source of news no less distressing. That spring Dermmell had been caught forging his teacher's signature on a grade change slip. He was an excellent runner—ran an impressive 38.3 in his best event, the three-hundred-meter intermediate hurdles, placing him among the high school elite in that event—but in 1989 he had been disqualified from participating in track because of his poor grades. He had submitted the forged slip hoping that it would allow him to run track in the spring; instead he was immediately suspended from school.

Yet the most traumatic change inside the Reed household had to do with the parents themselves. The extended period of goodwill that had prevailed in the Reed home for something like fifteen years, dating back to just before they purchased their house, had deteriorated into constant warring between husband and wife. The entire mood of the household had changed. The Reeds fell away from the church, which had for so long played a positive role in their lives. For Annette the decision to cut herself off from the Glory Temple was a difficult one but also obvious. Her father-in-law was the church pastor. Where once the church had been a source of serenity and solace, it was now sticky with family dynamics.

If anything, Rev. Curtis Reed was angrier with his son than with his daughter-in-law. As far as he could tell, after so many years of doing the right thing by his family, Donald had again messed up. "That boy don't want to work," the reverend would tell anyone who asked. "He just won't ever learn to accept responsibility."

The marital problems between Annette and Donald affected all of their children, but none more than the two youngest, Shannon and Kevin. Kevin, the baby of the family, had matriculated to King Estates Junior High in the fall of 1989. The annual test administered to eighth graders around the state showed King's students ranking among the lowest 5 percent in reading, writing, and mathematics. For the first time in his life, Kevin was bringing home less than stellar report cards. King rivaled Elmhurst and Frick for the mantle of the roughest middle school in East Oakland, and the transition to junior high can be a tough one, but Annette knew that her marital woes were the true source of Kevin's troubles.

All through that year, Kevin tried comforting Annette whenever she was obviously upset, as if he were an adult friend instead of her thirteen-year-old son. "Just checking to see how you're doing, Mama," he'd say if she was lying quietly in bed by herself. He always seemed to take his mother's side. Our father's doing this, he'd complain to Dermmell, Daddy's doing that. When Kevin started coming home with B's, C's, and even a couple of D's, Annette sent him and his brother Shannon to stay with a friend. Better he should be shielded from her woes, she reasoned, than to have him getting so involved in their conflicts.

Shannon was acting out, too, over his parents' pending breakup. With him, though, the warning signs had nothing to do with his mediocre grades—unlike Kevin, he had never been much of a student—but with his constant fighting. At the start of the summer of 1990, Shannon was a skinny little fourteen-year-old kid who nonetheless seemed incapable of backing down from a fight. He even challenged Dermmell, even though his brother had three years and considerable bulk on him.

If an older kid told Shannon not to walk down a particular street, he wanted to walk down no other block but that one. When his mother confronted him about his fighting, he told her that the other kids picked on him because he was so small, that he had to fight because otherwise he'd be labeled a punk unable or unwilling to stand up for himself. "I don't know, Mama, these boys just don't like me," he confessed to her.

Annette tried talking sense to him. "You have a right to go where you want," she'd tell him softly, "but if you know there's going to be trouble, why don't you walk around it instead? You don't want to challenge every person nowadays, because that challenge could be your last."

Dermmell, too, tried reasoning with Shannon. He saw some of himself in Shannon, but the world had changed even in the few years since he had been in junior high. He was seventeen, but he had vowed never to mess with a younger kid because they have too much to prove. You could win a fight but then lose when one of them came after you with a gun. Fighting with people isn't going to lead anywhere good, Dermmell would say, but Shannon dismissed his brother as a hypocrite. Dermmell, after all, had been in his share of fights.

In 1990 Shannon started hanging around with a kid around the corner named London Willard. They weren't tight for very long, but when they were, they were the closest of friends. It would be inaccurate to say that London was a bad influence on Shannon or vice versa, but there was something about the two of them together that brought out the worst in both. Shannon was around five feet four inches tall and weighed barely a hundred pounds. London was hardly any bigger. Apart they were anyone's fair game, but together it was like they weighed two hundred pounds and stood ten feet tall.

"I don't know why they be fighting," their friend Alfred Burleigh would write in a statement to the police that summer. "I guess it's because people pick on them 'cause they so small, so the two of them gang up and beat people up." The problem, of course, was that a fight could turn into something far worse if London and Shannon chose a kid with friends equally willing to rumble.

14

NO MERCY
ON A SUNDAY

Junebug was released from juvenile hall in mid-May 1990. The twenty-eight days he spent locked up weren't nearly as bad as he had feared, more resembling summer camp than punishment. He had just turned sixteen, but the authorities placed him with the smaller kids, two to a room. The youngest among them ran around like kids with the house to themselves, kicking in doors, making noise to make noise. It seemed he knew half of the kids in his unit.

His mother visited him only once, not because she was indifferent or supposedly too busy but because she figured the isolation would force him to think about the missteps that had landed him in juvie. But Junebug blamed only Tony, not himself, for his predicament. Not long after Ann's visit, Keisha turned fifteen. Junebug's absence weighed heavily on Ann's heart, spoiling what would have otherwise been a merry day. The truth was that she seemed to be suffering more through his incarceration than he was.

While he was still locked away, Junebug received a letter from 'Tone. "I know you mad at me, Junebug, But honest I never tole the police nothin," he wrote in a crude, childlike hand. But of course his friend's letter only made Junebug angrier.

The crew on Ninety-second Avenue braced for a confrontation the day Junebug was released from juvie. But 'Tone outweighed Junebug by more than a hundred pounds. Short of using a gun, he was no match for his oversize friend.

Junebug played it cool. He saw 'Tone the day he was released, but he said nothing. Instead he looked past him, putting on his face a blank and indifferent mask. Later he stopped in to see his friend Aaron. "I'm done with him," Junebug said when Aaron asked him about Tony. "That fool's bad for my health."

Yet like past vows to rid himself of 'Tone for good, Junebug's seemingly firm resolve lost out to other considerations. Junebug treated 'Tone like he didn't exist for the better part of the month, but the longer the silent treatment lasted, the more absurd it came to seem. They hung around in the same crowd. They were business partners. He still needed 'Tone's connections. Their first few conversations were innocuous, like "Where's so and so at?" or "You need anything?" After a week or two of clipped dialogue, they were were back to being buddies again, though to Junebug's mind their friendship was never the same, despite outward appearances.

Later, after it was too late to undo all that was about to happen in those fateful days in the early summer of 1990, 'Tone admitted that he had done his friend wrong. But back then, 'Tone never apologized, never said a word to Junebug about what he had done except for the letter he'd written while Junebug was in juvenile hall. But to himself he swore he'd make it up to his friend. If Junebug gave him a second chance, he'd prove he was down for his friend.

Junebug spent the early part of Sunday, July 8, hanging around with Aaron. They played Nintendo for a while and then drove over to the mall on Seventy-third Avenue to scope out girls. Junebug met someone nice who lived down the street from where 'Tone stayed with his aunt Paula. She gave him her number and invited him to visit next time he was in the area. It was shaping up to be a great day.

After the mall, Junebug asked Aaron to drop him off at Paula's place. It was Sunday, so no one would be grinding on Ninety-second Avenue, but he figured that Tony or someone might be hanging around on Ninetieth. Maybe he'd sell or maybe he'd just hang out for a few hours.

'Tone was inside with his girlfriend Tonette. A couple of guys were outside, but they weren't selling so much as kicking it—hanging around. They'd sell if anyone came looking for something, but they'd also go somewhere if the mood struck them. The three of them smoked a joint. After a while, the other two guys left. Junebug felt a sudden urge for a cherry ball candy. He was stoned and he had the munchies.

"You or Tonette want something from the store?" Junebug asked 'Tone.

"I'm cool. We's cool."

A kid was sitting on a bicycle out front. He was one of those wide-eyed waifs around eleven or twelve years old who would hang around drug hot spots hoping one of the older kids would notice them. Lend me your bike, Junebug told him, and I'll buy you whatever you want from the store. The store was only a couple of blocks away, but no one who was part of the nine-deuce crew walked if they could ride. The kid jumped at the deal.

The Rowaid Market was like minimarts all around East Oakland. A Palestinian-owned shop in the first floor of a two-story walk-up, it sold a little bit of everything, from candy bars to milk to the plastic bags the kids used to sell their rock. Its staple item, though, was alcohol. A row of refrigerated cases filled with beer and malt liquor lined the back wall. The shelves running the length of another wall were heavy with bottles of cheap wines, mostly the fortified, twist-off-cap variety. Steel grates protected the plate glass windows on either side of a front door that was itself made of crisscrossed mesh wire.

Junebug arrived at the store sometime between seven and nine that night. He placed the black-and-blue Sonic Six bike he had borrowed against the store's outside wall. Several kids were hanging around in the abandoned lot next door. Junebug noticed them, but he wasn't worried that they would rip off the bike; his ego wouldn't allow him to entertain such a possibility. They were a few years younger than he, and he was slangin' rock down the street. Wearing a pair of black shorts and a black tank top that revealed his thin frame, he walked inside the store feeling imperious and immune from harm.

Two of the kids followed him into the store. He caught one of them staring at him out of the corner of his eye. He felt a fleeting sense of worry like he sometimes got outside selling in the street, but he chased it away. He locked eyes with one of them, doing his best to stare him down, but they followed him out of the store. That's when he knew something was up beyond the usual posturing part of everyday life in East Oakland. It was as if they recognized him.

The pair of them stood in Junebug's way as he grabbed the bike to pedal away. That was the first good look he got at the second kid. He couldn't place either of them. They were both skinny kids no older than thirteen or fourteen. They stood there with their jaws set, trying to look tough. Junebug might have laughed had he not been surrounded by six kids all together. If anything, the others were even younger and smaller than the two who had followed him into the store.

"You got a sister Tameka?" one of the kids who'd been inside the store asked him.

"Nope," Junebug said.

"Why you tellin' everyone you gonna beat up a coupl'a dudes named Kevin and Shannon?" It was the same boy who had asked him the first question.

Junebug's mind raced. Maybe they want to steal the bike, he thought. Maybe all this stuff about Tameka and Kevin and Shannon is just a ruse. Or maybe their aim was stealing all of the gold he was wearing—two chains, a ring, a watch. Junebug didn't answer them. He just kept walking, making the circle of kids move with him.

"You was so anxious to fight the other day, so let's fight."

Junebug had no time to react. The kid asking him the questions punched him in the face before the words *let's fight* could even register. Then he noticed that the other kid from inside the store had a length of metal pipe in his hand. Maybe he had been holding it in plain view the entire time, maybe he had been hiding it behind his back. The kid swung the pipe at Junebug's head and Junebug instinctively threw up an arm. The pipe struck him on the forearm with a crack.

"Y'all don't know who you fuckin' with," Junebug yelled. His voice cracked. He retreated as fast as he could. He was angry and scared and feeling trapped. "Y'all have the wrong dude," he said with a whine. The kid who'd thrown the first punch was removing his shirt and hat, presumably readying himself for a second round. Junebug bolted. A few of the smaller kids gave chase, but he proved too fast for them. He headed for Paula's place to get 'Tone and anyone else who might be around.

'Tone was standing outside talking to a guy who had come around looking for some dope to sell. Junebug ran up to them. "These fools tried to jump me," he told them between breaths. They asked him who. "I don't know, just some fools up at the store," he said. Only when he noticed the little kid standing there did he remember the bike.

Junebug, 'Tone, and the third guy ran over to the store. By then everyone was gone. So, too, was the bike. The three of them walked back to Paula's. Pretty soon three more guys who were part of their crew—Patrick, a fourteen-year-old called Fig, and John Banks—came around. The newcomers could tell something was going on because everyone was so pumped up. Junebug filled them in on what had happened and the six of them walked back to the store. Again no one was there.

At that point nobody said let's go get 'em, since no one had any clue who they were or where they lived. That seemed to be the end of it. Patrick went home and 'Tone went back in the house to hang with Tonette. 'Tone didn't give the incident another thought until Junebug came to get him the next night.

The rule in the Reed household was that if you failed a course during the regular school year, you made it up during the summer. That summer Shannon was taking a couple of courses at Elmhurst. That's where the trouble started.

Trouble was a girl named Tameka. Tameka was five feet seven inches tall and tipped the scales at around 165 pounds. It's anyone's best guess who started what with whom. Supposedly she called Shannon a name and he called her a fat bitch. She towered over him, but the way Shannon's friend Kevin related it later, she enlisted her brother to threaten both him and Shannon. "You and your friend better leave my sister alone," he warned Kevin, "or I'll kick the shit outta the both of you."

Tameka's brother Damon was, like Junebug, sixteen years old in July of 1990. Damon was an inch or two shorter than Junebug but just as skinny. They both had faces that were long rather than round, and each sported a Louisville cut (hair shorn close to the scalp). They had the same mouth and similar eyes, wide and friendly but somehow sad just the same. They only vaguely resembled each other, but Shannon had never met Tameka's brother. The only time he had actually laid eyes on him was when Kevin pointed him out to him.

That Sunday, Shannon was with his family at a picnic. Afterward he hooked up with his friend London. Nothing was going on, so they walked over to the store, where they met a few kids from London's block. They were just kicking it in the lot next to Rowaid's when Shannon saw Junebug pedal up. He told London he thought that might be the kid who had threatened him and Kevin, so they followed Junebug into the store to give Shannon a better look. "That's him," Shannon said with certainty. Right there they agreed they'd teach him a lesson about making threats.

Shannon punched the kid in the face. He was about to punch him again, but he backed off when London came forward with the pipe. London was aiming for Junebug's head.

As far as Shannon and London were concerned, their confrontation at the store was the end of it. The lesson had been administered and they had even gotten a bike out of it. All of them—Shannon, London, and their entourage of smaller kids—walked to Eighty-seventh Avenue, where all but Shannon lived.

Junebug's forearm throbbed where the pipe had struck him, but what really ached was his pride. He was a street dealer, yet he had been forced to run from a bunch of smaller kids. He had let another kid's bike be stolen. And worst of all, now it was everyone's business.

Junebug felt relieved when 'Tone and Patrick left—especially Patrick. When Patrick was around, Junebug acted different, despite himself. Patrick always seemed to be messing with his head. Patrick never kept it a secret that he only tolerated Junebug. The funny thing was,

Junebug cared even though he shouldn't have, because he thought even less of Patrick than Patrick thought of him. Patrick was bad news. He was always doing crazy things, like the time he tried to carjack a red 'vette only because a couple of guys had dared him to do it. He blew out the car's back window with a shotgun after the driver peeled away without handing over the keys.

With Patrick gone, Junebug wanted to smoke another joint and forget the whole thing. He was angry, but he was also feeling resigned. He knew nothing about these kids, not their names or where they hung out.

In his head, he was already entertaining a solution. As he had done several times before, he had vowed that he'd finally buckle down and show his teachers what he was capable of doing when he put his mind to it. But his resolve was already weakening just a few days into the summer school session. This clinched it. He'd work that next day and use the profits to buy the kid a new bike. He was ready to chalk the whole thing up to some bad luck, but this one guy, John Banks, just wouldn't let it go.

Banks had been tight with their crew for only a short time. Junebug never thought much about Banks one way or another, but for a while 'Tone liked having him around. Eventually 'Tone concluded that Banks was more interested in smoking their weed and drinking their alcohol than slanging their rock, and he landed some hard blows one night when he suspected Banks of stealing some dope. But back then Banks was a part of their group, and by extension he was Junebug's partner whether he liked it or not.

The three of them—Junebug, Banks, and Fig—stood in front of Paula's building, passing a joint. Banks kept pushing Junebug to talk about what had happened. Neither of them had ever taken much interest in each other's life, yet now Banks kept asking, "Tell me again what happened," like somehow he could fix it for him. "Describe 'em," Banks asked, and Junebug shook his head.

"I told you, man, I don't know who they are, just a bunch of little kids."

"Try, man. You ain't even trying, like you don't even care."

Junebug's instincts told him to ignore Banks's goading. People got shot in Oakland for less than a stolen bike. He suspected the worst of Banks, but he attributed his paranoia to the pot.

"I don't know," Junebug said. "Six of them between the ages of ten and fourteen. The two bigger kids were around thirteen or fourteen, real skinny-like and short."

"I think I know the boys you're talking about," Banks said. He told him he thought their names might be Shannon and London.

That comment hit Junebug like a shotgun blast to the chest. How could he know them from so generic a description? The strangest part was that Banks didn't live anywhere near Rowaid's. He stayed on Ninety-sixth Avenue, by East Fourteenth Street. How would he know kids hung around a minimart a dozen blocks from his house?

Banks offered an address. "Let's get on over there and have a look," he said. And like that, Junebug recognized how difficult a jam this was going to be to finesse.

"Man, fuck it," Junebug said. "Ain't no big deal."

"Fool, you was the one who got jumped, not me. You a punk or sumpin'?"

"I ain't no punk," Junebug shot back. The comment may have come out sounding pouty, though he meant to sound tough. He felt trapped. So the three of them—Junebug, Banks, and Fig—walked to an apartment on Eighty-seventh Avenue just behind Castlemont High to see about retrieving the stolen bike and maybe even some of Junebug's wounded pride.

Junebug had barely turned onto Eighty-seventh Avenue when he saw one of the kids who had jumped him. But Banks beat him to the punch. "That's one of them boys I was telling you about," Banks said. "Name's Shannon Reed."

Shannon was with a couple of other kids, but Junebug couldn't be sure if the other two had been at Rowaid's or not. The three of them spotted Junebug and took off. Junebug, Banks, and Fig chased them into a nearby apartment building.

Terry Walton was at his girlfriend's place watching television when one of her kids and two of his friends ran inside the house. It was around eleven o'clock in the evening. Not a minute later, three bigger boys were pounding on the door. "Where they at? Where's Shannon at? Where

London at?" Walton was twenty-six. He stands six feet, three inches tall. Yet this one kid, skinny as a rail and dressed in black shorts and a black tank top shirt, was demanding answers like he was Five-O.

Walton told the kid he had the wrong house. "I saw 'em run in here," the kid shot back. In a rush of words, he told him about the kids who had jumped him and stolen his bike. He seemed convinced that at least a couple of the kids lived there.

At first only the skinny kid spoke, but then a second kid, a couple of inches shorter than the first and thicker across the chest, chimed in, "Fuck it, man. Let's get the fuck outta here." They left, but not before the second kid left Walton to consider these ominous words: "We'll get them. You'll be reading about it in the newspaper tomorrow." The kid pointed to his jacket pocket as he made the threat. Walton couldn't be sure what was in there that caused his jacket to bulge, but he never doubted that it was a gun.

Walton and his girlfriend hurried to an upstairs apartment to talk with London Willard and his mother Alice. They were both there, as was Shannon Reed. Walton told Alice what the boy had said her son and his friends had done. He also passed on the other boy's threat. "He said somebody's gonna die," Walton said, adding that he thought the kid had had a pistol.

"How you know they gotta gun?" It was Shannon.

"I saw it."

"He showed it to you? No fool's gonna show you his gun if he's about to shoot somebody."

"Well, I could see it in his coat like this." He jammed his fist into his own jacket pocket.

"He ain't got no gun," Shannon said.

"Don't be hanging around with my son no more," Walton's girlfriend warned London. "Seems whenever he's with you, he's getting hisself into trouble." The hour was approaching midnight on a Sunday night and three older boys had just shown up on her doorstep. They were talking about killing people, and hers was the only address they had.

15

DOWN FOR A FRIEND

Later Junebug would claim that he woke up on Monday, July 9, without a thought about the previous day. His sore arm would suggest otherwise, but denial would be a natural reaction to all that might lay ahead. They had turf guns. He knew where this could lead. If he didn't understand it consciously, he felt it deep in his bones just the same: he was suddenly in the middle of something bigger than himself that was taking on a momentum all its own.

He stepped outside in midmorning. The first person he saw was Banks. Fig was there and also a mutual friend. Junebug groaned. "Wh's up? Wh's up?" And immediately Banks started in.

"I was just telling my pahtnah here about what happened last night."

"That's messed up, man," their friend said, attempting to be sympathetic.

Junebug tried shrugging it off. "Phht. It was no big deal. Just some little kids showing off. I ain't tripping over that."

"You know, man, we should go through there, see if they're out there."

"No, man."

"Come on. You can get the car from Aye-ran. Won't take but a minute."

Junebug proposed that instead they borrow Aaron's car so they could drive over to the mall to scout out girls. Fig said that sounded cool to him, and Junebug jumped at his luck. He stopped in to get the keys from Aaron — just had to say the magic words: "I'll put gas in it" — and they were off.

For a couple of hours they spoke about nothing but that girl or this one, but as much as Junebug tried having a good time, it wasn't working. The previous night was a tape looping over and over again through his head. Deep down he knew he was only prolonging the inevitable. They practically had to drive by Eighty-seventh and Dowling to get back to Ninety-second.

As if on cue, Banks said as they were starting home, "Hey, let's drive through there, see if they're out there." It was as if *he* had been the one who got jumped the previous night, he seemed so obsessed.

Junebug considered that maybe Banks was right. Maybe he was acting like a scared punk. Letting it slide meant allowing these kids to get away with stealing his bike. And what was there to be frightened of? They were probably quaking in their high-tops after Banks's threat the previous night. There was no rule book to consult, of course, but getting jumped seemed a violation that demanded revenge. They'd scare them, or mess them up — *something* to even the score. Besides, if he did nothing, that could mean the end of his reputation on Ninety-second Avenue. If he handled it well, though, then everyone would be talking about how Junebug showed these punks not to mess with the likes of the nine-deuce crew.

Junebug responded to Banks with a "sure," all cool like, as if it were nothing at all. Internally he steeled himself against the worst. With Junebug at the wheel, they turned onto Eighty-seventh Avenue. The block was blessedly empty except for an older man working on his lawn. Junebug suddenly felt cocky. He brought the car to a full stop and then peeled away with a loud screech. He laughed for what seemed the first time in twenty-four hours.

"Stop, stop. I think I saw one of them." It was Banks.

"What?"

"Go back, man. I think I saw one of them."

Junebug knew the wise course of action would have been to keep on driving. But he imagined Banks telling everyone what had happened: "And I told him I saw one of them, but the fool keeps goin', like he's scared to even look." He took a deep breath and turned the wheel for another pass down Eighty-seventh.

"See, there, there. Is that one of them there?"

"Where?"

Junebug glimpsed someone walking into a two-story apartment building a couple of doors down from the one they had been at the night before. "Who you talking about? I just see the back of some fool's head."

Banks swung the door open and was out of the car before Junebug knew what was going on. He squeezed off several rounds from a small-caliber gun. Banks jumped back into the car and Junebug mashed the gas. "What ya doing?" he remembered yelling. "You trying to make Aye-ran's car hot?"

Their corner was only twelve blocks away. Junebug felt overwhelmed by a million thoughts and feelings, but he never for a moment considered that Banks might actually have hit anybody. He parked the car and ran in to drop off the keys with Aaron. He went straight to bed after telling himself he was through with John Banks for good. The next thing he knew, he opened his eyes and it was night.

On that same morning, Monday, July 9, Alfred Burleigh—"June"—ran into London and Shannon hanging out in the street. They were all puffed up with their victory of the previous night. They boasted about the tenth grader the pair of them—both in the eighth grade—had beaten up. The kid had come back later that night with a couple of older dudes, they told June, but they weren't scared.

Terry Walton, however, believed otherwise. He noticed that London, Shannon, and their little gang were walking around with baseball bats and sticks that next day. He didn't know what they were thinking, but Walton himself was expecting trouble.

Among those impressed with Shannon's story was his little brother Kevin. Kevin was the spitting image of his brother, only skinnier and sweeter. He even wore his hair the same way, in a high-top fade. Kevin was thirteen, one year younger than Shannon. He was at that age where his brother could do no wrong. "Teach me to box," he pleaded with Shannon. "Take me to the gym so I can learn to protect myself too."

Shannon promised he would, and he, Kevin, London, and June headed for Castlemont to play some basketball.

A few hours later, a man named Harold Mims was doing some yard work when his attention was drawn by the sound of screeching rubber. He remembered the car, if for no other reason than it was so unsightly. It was a Plymouth or Chrysler circa the late 1960s, a boxy four-door green sedan faded by too many years in the sun. June had already gone home but London, Shannon, and Kevin were rounding the corner as this raggedy green whale of a car screeched away. They didn't give it a second thought, though. It seemed like someone was always burning rubber in their neighborhood.

A few minutes later, the three of them were up in London's room, watching cartoons and messing around. They heard—five days after the Fourth of July—what they figured to be firecrackers. Still, they ran outside. The same boys who had been through a few minutes earlier had returned, Mims told them. He pointed to the building where their friend June lived. "One of them jumps out and just starts shooting," Mims told them. The boys in the car couldn't have been older than sixteen or seventeen, but long ago Harold Mims ceased being surprised by what kids did nowadays.

Shooting at a home is a felony in California, but the police have no record of anyone calling in a complaint. Had someone phoned, a cop would have taken a report, but there the matter would have ended. The cops in Oakland say that with the skyrocketing homicide rate and a parallel increase in nonfatal shootings, they barely have enough time keeping up with cases involving a victim. And in this case no one was hurt.

Junebug hooked up with Aaron at around nine o'clock that night. They were in Aaron's car, heading nowhere in particular, when Junebug told him about the previous couple of days. He pretty much told him everything, though he couldn't bring himself to mention the shooting earlier in the day because he felt bad about implicating Aaron's car. Junebug also skirted around the emotional drain of the previous twenty-four hours. Aaron was Junebug's best friend, but even with him he could lower his pose only so much.

"Want to ride through there?" Aaron asked. And like that, Junebug again felt trapped between his instincts and saving face. "If you want to," he said, hoping to sound nonchalant. Then he said, "Yah, sure, let's drive through there, take a look." Aaron was more levelheaded than Banks, but just the same, Junebug prayed that none of the kids would be there.

London Willard and his brother Damon were hanging out in front of their apartment building. London was fourteen and Damon would be turning sixteen the next day. Shannon had gone home already but his brother Kevin had stuck around.

A girl Kevin knew from the neighborhood, Natasha Buckner, happened by with her friend Tamika. Natasha was fourteen; Tamika, who was spending the night at the Buckners', had turned thirteen nine days earlier. Natasha's mother had hesitated before giving them permission to go out, but relented after Natasha pleaded her case. It was after 9:00 P.M., but it was also summer and her daughter would be starting high school that fall. They were going to the store so Natasha could buy a pair of stockings.

Natasha knew Kevin as the baby brother of Shannon Reed, a boy her age whom she had had a crush on several years earlier. The group chatted for a while before the girls headed off to the store. They spoke some more when Natasha and Tamika passed by on their way home. The girls said they needed to get going, and the boys walked with them up Dowling. They stopped when they reached Auseon. Kevin lived one block to the left and Natasha one block to the right. They stood by a pale yellow bungalow whose owner had long ago installed bars on every window. In early July, the air would have been pungent with the sweet-sick smell of the dying rose bushes in the adjacent yard. The homes in the hills twinkled against the night sky.

They continued talking there on the corner of Auseon and Dowling, despite the time. They were having a nice time; they weren't ready for things to end.

"That's them," Junebug said. "Those are the dudes who jumped me yesterday."

"For real?"

"Yah." They had just turned off Eighty-seventh and onto Dowling. On the corner of Auseon and Dowling, Junebug thought he saw Shannon and London. He was having that kind of luck.

"Watchoo wanna do?" Aaron asked.

Five people, two of them girls, were standing outside. Caution would have told Junebug it was no time for a confrontation. But it was as if coming this far demanded action. "Know what," he said. "Let's go holler at them. I'm getting tired of this." Barely twenty-four hours had passed since he had been jumped, but it was as if this incident had been plaguing him forever. He would "holler" at them—talk tough and hopefully end this once and for all.

"I don't know, man," Aaron said. "What if they got something?" Aaron was worried that one of them might have a weapon.

"Go to 'Tone's house real quick," Junebug suggested. What Aaron would remember his friend saying was something like "We may need something, a bat or a gun or something." 'Tone wasn't much for baseball, but Junebug knew he kept a .45 stashed in his room. Aaron said "awright" and drove the few blocks over to 'Tone's place.

That day 'Tone had slept late, gobbled down a bowl of cereal, and then headed to Ninety-second Avenue. He spent most of the day selling dope and partying with whomever was there. They fired up several joints over the afternoon. Someone picked up forties of something strong, probably Old English unless something else was on sale. For less than two dollars, you could usually buy a forty-ounce malt liquor like Old English, a bottle of brew so oversize and hopped up that drinking one carried nearly the same alcohol punch as a six-pack of beer.

'Tone headed over to a party at around six that night. It was his friend Billy's sixteenth birthday, and there was a small get-together planned in the same apartment complex where he and Paula lived. Joints were passed, coke snorted. Hennessy brandy and a bottle of gin stood on a table and the fridge was packed with malt liquor. 'Tone didn't touch the coke, but he seemed game for everything else.

Billy was forever amazed at how much his large friend could consume, and 'Tone didn't disappoint him that evening. He was a part of the passing circle every time a joint was fired up. He also hogged the Hennessy. Fig, also there that night, figured that 'Tone drank nearly a bottle of Hennessy by himself.

For a while 'Tone staggered around acting loud and stupid, but eventually he collapsed into a chair. People couldn't tell if he had passed out or not because he was wearing a pair of dark sunglasses called "murder ones" (named for the California penal code's term for a premeditated murder). Eventually 'Tone staggered home to Paula's, where Junebug caught up with him.

"Hey."

"Hey."

"Yo, 'Tone, let me see your gat real quick."

"What's up? What's up?"

"Nothing."

"Hold on, hold on." 'Tone had padded off to his room wearing only a T-shirt and his underwear, but he came back fully dressed. He wasn't wearing the eyeglasses he needed to see distances but he was wearing his murder ones. He also had on his Derby. 'Tone never actually said he had the gun, but Junebug never doubted that a .45 semiautomatic was hidden in the Derby's inside pocket.

With 'Tone standing there in his jacket, it was plain that he assumed he was invited along. Junebug hesitated, but only for a moment. Worried that this time his adversaries might have a weapon more powerful than a pipe, securing a gun was as far as Junebug had thought things through. He hadn't contemplated the wisdom of bringing 'Tone along, but then he figured he had no choice. Once he had imposed on him for a gun, he'd have to include him in whatever came next. Besides, 'Tone was always the right guy to have watching your back in a fight.

Aaron rolled his eyes as 'Tone opened the door to get into the backseat. Junebug gave him a look like, What else could I do? Only once the three of them were in the car did Junebug remember the trouble his friend had gotten him into just three months earlier.

■ ■ ■

"That's the car," London had whispered to his brother. Damon looked up fast enough to see the squarish rear end of the old green car that had caught London's attention.

"You sure?" Damon asked.

"Same car or one just like it," London said. No one said anything more, but the mood of their innocent gathering changed. It was as if they were no longer harmlessly flirting beneath a streetlight on a warm summer night but instead toying with fate simply by standing on a corner in East Oakland after dark. They were procrastinating their way through their good-byes when a few minutes later the car reappeared.

No one saw the car this second time until it was too late. Someone inside the car started shooting without a word. London and Damon instinctively turned to flee. Damon looked over his shoulder to see who was shooting at them, but all he saw was the muzzle flash. He also noticed that his brother was lying on the ground.

London had already turned his back to the car and was willing his body to take its first stride when he realized he was hit. He didn't actually feel the bullet penetrate his skin, but his legs crumpled beneath him. Suddenly he found himself lying on the sidewalk. Then his left leg felt like it was on fire. Lying there, he heard Kevin's voice, high-pitched and panicky. "I'm hit, I'm hit," Kevin yelled. London told him to hold on, it would be OK.

"We gonna go get your brother," London reassured him. "Just hold on, man, hold on."

Natasha heard the gunfire but there was a lag before her mind caught up with the chaos around her. She didn't run from the corner, just walked away in a daze, mindlessly. The sight of her friend Tamika running ahead of her awakened her senses. Halfway down the block, Natasha put her hand to her cheek. She felt one bullet hole and then another. It was then she realized that the taste in her mouth was blood and chipped teeth. The first thing Natasha did when she got home was head to the bathroom. She wasn't panicky but instead felt strangely calm. She looked in the mirror expecting the worst. She saw instead that her wounds were two perfect holes, one on each cheek. She always figured that if someone was shot in the face they'd have no face left. She felt relieved that she didn't look grotesque.

Shannon was home playing Nintendo with Dermmell. At 10:30 P.M. they heard what they figured were four or five firecrackers. A minute later the door burst open. "Somebody shot me and got your brother," London yelled. Shannon uttered an automatic response: "Kevin got shot?" He was thinking in slow motion until he noticed the blood soaking through his friend's pant leg. Dermmell was out the door like lightning, but Shannon couldn't find a matching pair of shoes. He slipped on whatever was lying around and took off.

Kevin was lying in the street, his head against the curb, his legs beneath an older-model Lincoln Continental parked at the corner. Dermmell kneeled over Kevin, crying. "Don't die, Kevin," he said. "Don't die." When Shannon arrived, he exploded. "I'm gonna kill somebody!" Shannon yelled. "Get me a gun! Get me a gun!" He ran over to his grandparents' house, just a few doors down.

"Help's on its way," Dermmell whispered in Kevin's ear. "Everything's going to be all right. Just hold on." What frightened him wasn't the blood but the dazed, faraway look in his brother's eyes.

16

MURDER VICTIM NO. 84

The phone rang in Brian Thiem's bedroom at 11:16 P.M. that night. It was Officer Dore from the patrol desk. "We got one at Auseon and Dowling," Dore said. "Three people down. One en route to the hospital code blue." Thiem could later be certain that Dore had used pretty much those exact words because with Dore it was the same dry, personalityless conversation every time. Often there's *something* in the voice on the other end—an apologetic tone, playfulness, sarcasm. But with Dore it's always the facts—an address and a body count—and nothing else.

Thiem was asleep when the phone rang. He always goes to bed early on those weeks he works standby. In Oakland, every homicide cop is assigned the day shift except the two-person team on call that week. Ten investigators worked the city's homicide detail in those years, which meant that every fifth week you and your partner were responsible for any homicide that occurred during that seven-day period. When you're on call, you sleep when you can, because you never know when a ringing phone will mean you'll be awake for the next twenty-four hours.

Thiem's wife no doubt rolled over in bed and asked him, half asleep, "What's this one?" because that's what she always asks. "Got one in East Oakland," Thiem would have said. "Three people shot." They had been married only six weeks, and this was his first late-night call since exchanging their vows. So there may even have been more words this first time, when that kind of intrusion was still exciting—or at least a novelty—instead of merely an annoyance.

Homicide cops on TV arrive at the scene with unkempt hair and pajama bottoms peeking out from under their pants. In the real world, Thiem takes a shower first because it's probably his last chance to freshen up through the night and well into the next day. He dresses in a sport jacket and tie because he doesn't want to be thinking about how he looks if he needs to speak with the victim's family. He's not a paramedic; not every second counts. The rule of thumb among Oakland homicide cops is that you're doing OK so long as you arrive within an hour of a call.

Thiem lives in Lafayette, a quiet bedroom community built on the other side of the coastal hills that separate Oakland from the suburban enclaves of Contra Costa County. Every cop working homicide, at least in 1990, lived outside of Oakland, primarily because they could. The department has no rule about living within the city limits, as do some police departments in other cities. Besides, with a base salary starting around fifty-two thousand dollars a year and thirty-eight dollars–plus an hour in overtime, they can afford to buy some peace of mind far away from the muck of their work life.

The drive from Lafayette can take as long as forty-five minutes during the day, depending on traffic. In the middle of the night, however, Thiem can zip there in around twenty minutes. That night he was driving a bronze-colored Dodge Diplomat, a four-door, no-frills, city-issued car with oversize hubcaps that looked like snub-nosed missile heads. The thing reeked of unmarked cop car. Half asleep, he needed to fish from his pocket the slip of paper on which he scrawled the address the patrol desk had given him. Only then could he give his exact destination when he radioed in to say he was on his way.

In Oakland, the cops always beat the paramedics to a shooting. That's a matter of policy. Even if an ambulance crew happens to be close by, they are under orders to idle around the corner until the police have declared the area secure. A paramedic has never been shot in Oakland, but it's happened elsewhere. Every second is precious with the more serious shooting injuries, but so, too, is a paramedic's well-being, according to a spokeswoman with the Regional Ambulance Company.

About a dozen neighbors telephoned 911 to report the shooting. The first cops arrived not more than two minutes after the initial call. Kevin was unconscious and breathing with extreme difficulty. One of the cops got down on his knees to perform CPR. But Kevin's wound, in his groin, was oozing bright red blood, indicating that the bullet had struck an artery. He was losing blood at an alarming rate. The cop was doing the right thing in providing CPR, but what Kevin needed was a trauma surgeon who could close the puncture.

A sizable crowd had formed before the first paramedic team arrived—more than ten minutes after the initial call into 911. A couple of cops marked off the scene with spools of plastic yellow ribbon. Several others canvassed the crowd looking for potential witnesses. Damon Willard filled the cops in about the twenty-four hours leading up to the shooting. (So accustomed are the police to thinking the worst of any black kid in East Oakland that on Damon's statement form he's listed as "unemployed" even though "student" was the appropriate description.) Greg Buckner, Natasha's father, was also milling around the scene. He had run down the street after seeing Natasha's wounds hoping to catch whoever shot her. That's how the police learned that there were three victims, not two. They had called 911, Buckner told the cops, but they couldn't stand around waiting, so his wife and a nephew drove Natasha to the hospital along with Tamika who was unharmed. The cops also spoke to Terry Walton, who told them about the three young men at his door the previous night.

There were about a dozen uniforms in all working the scene. One each traveled to the hospital with Kevin and London. A third was sent to the hospital to take a statement from Natasha, if and when she was able to give one. The rest fanned out to conduct a door-to-door canvass.

The cops knocked on the door of every home within a block of the shooting. That's the drill no matter what the time, even if it's 3:00 A.M. Rarely do they learn anything when they roust people out of bed. They get a lot of doors slammed in their faces, but they figure that some missed sleep isn't too much to ask when a murder has just taken place. The cops also jot down the make, model, and license plate of every car parked along the street.

Most of the people the cops encountered claimed to have heard and seen nothing. Those with something to offer didn't add up. Taken all together, witnesses had heard between two and six shots sometime between 10:20 and 10:30. A guy named Stephen said he had heard what he thought were firecrackers, but then he heard screaming so he ran outside to see if anyone needed help. His wife Antoinette had been sitting by an open window and figured she was listening to gunshots, but she ignored them because someone shooting off a gun was really no big deal. No one but the kids actually standing on the corner saw the car.

Sgt. Brian Thiem, the son of a refrigerator repairman, grew up in a working-class suburb of Pittsburgh. While in the army, Thiem (pronounced "theme") was stationed at Fort Ord, a couple of hours south and west of Oakland. He could have found a cozy post with a smaller town down the peninsula, writing traffic tickets and dealing with the occasional domestic dispute, but he coveted the cops-and-robbers, car-chase excitement of a big-city department like Oakland's. He joined the force in 1980; by the summer of 1990, he had been working homicide for two years.

In his early days on the force, there were always cops telling him everything that was wrong with working the murder beat—the crazy hours, the aggravations, the pressures—but Thiem never paid attention. From the first time he was a uniform assigned to a murder scene, he knew he wanted to work homicide. The homicide sergeant on the scene garnered a respect that transcended rank. Every cop was anxious to have even a moment of his time, whether to impart some small bit of potentially useful information or to share a dumb crack. No one really much cared about an unsolved robbery in Oakland, but an open homicide on the books was something worth everyone's attention. He was attracted to Oakland so he could be, in his words, "a real cop," and then drawn to homicide to take on the ultimate crime.

Thiem's reputation among defense attorneys and prosecutors alike was that of a plugger. He might not have wowed you with his brilliance, but he'd impress you just the same with his diligence and determination. Thiem may not have been the best homicide investigator in town in 1990, but the consensus was that he belonged on anyone's list of the unit's better cops.

His greatest strength might have been his skill as an interrogator. He's an average-size man with soft, Germanic features. He's fair-skinned with freckles around his nose. His hair, thinning on top, is light brown. His easy, agreeable manner belies most stereotypes about cops. He plays the classic good cop role, friendly and concerned and full of pathos. Those who've partnered with him joke that a suspect catches one glimpse of his brown eyes radiating sincerity and sympathy and it's like they can't help but confess their sins.

The first thing Thiem does when he reaches a crime scene is write down the exact time of his arrival — 12:10 A.M. on this night. He prides himself on working a case from start to finish as if a defense attorney were sitting on his shoulder. You look foolish if, when taking the witness stand, you can't say precisely what time you arrived, as if you are inexact and sloppy in a job that requires precision. That night he wrote down several other observations even before exiting his car: seven-eighths-full moon, clear night, visibility good. (*"Since you don't know, then it's possible it was foggy and difficult to see, isn't that right, Sergeant?"*)

Thiem next sought out the patrol sergeant in charge of the scene. That's how he learned that one victim, Kevin Reed, had died at a couple minutes before midnight. "Victim pronounced at 23:58," Thiem wrote in his notes. The other two victims were in stable condition.

Thiem flinched when the patrol sergeant told him that Kevin was only thirteen. The victim in his last case, Raemy Davis, had also been thirteen. Raemy had been killed by a kid whose coconspirator swore they had meant to scare him, not kill anybody.

Thiem drew himself a crude map as he walked the murder scene. He'd use that when interviewing potential witnesses, so they could show him precisely which way the car was heading and where exactly they were standing when the shooting started. While walking a murder scene, Thiem rarely speaks to anyone except his fellow officers. He talks with the police technician whose job it is to snap pictures and scour for evidence. He reads over the statements the uniforms have collected and tells them whom he wants downtown for a formal taped interview.

Thiem's partner, Sgt. John McKenna, arrived at Oak Knoll Naval Hospital at around the same time that Thiem reached Auseon and Dowling. He eyeballed Kevin's body and spoke to the doctor in charge. He mingled among Kevin's grieving family and friends to see who might know something.

On television, when the homicide cop arrives on the scene, the body conveniently lies there like a prop while the police investigator, the medical examiner, and maybe a guy snapping pictures discuss the case. In real life it's rare for a homicide cop to see a dead body outside the hospital or the morgue. The paramedics "scoop and run" with any body that is the least bit warm. The only murder victim a homicide cop tends to see at the scene is one who is already stinking of rotted flesh, like a body in a ditch, or one who is so obviously dead that the sight would turn an amateur's stomach.

In the hour Thiem typically spends at the murder scene, there'll be the usual patter as he goes about his business. "How many is this for the year, Sarge?" "Good luck on this one, 'cause there ain't *nothing* here." Usually he'll tolerate the demented gallows humor that helps cops place distance between them and the gore, but not tonight. It was the age of the victim and also Thiem's mood. This was his second thirteen-year-old in a row and he was feeling more emotionally involved than usual.

From almost the moment he arrived, Thiem had been working himself up into angry indignation. The uniforms had been working the scene for an hour and a half, but Thiem didn't feel they had anything close to ninety minutes' worth of work to show for their efforts. He could sympathize. He had been a uniform assigned the unpleasant task of knocking on doors late at night. He had taken his share of abuse. But from experience he knew that most cops asked their questions in half-assed fashion, almost guaranteeing no response: "There was a shooting—you didn't see nothing, didja? OK, what's your name for my report?"

Several times that night, Thiem snapped while talking to a patrol officer. He really lost it while talking to some fresh-faced cop who said he had a guy who knew a lot but wouldn't answer his questions. "Grab him and bring him downtown," Thiem barked. The patrol sergeant overheard him and barked back: "No officer of mine is grabbing anybody." Thiem was about to get into it with his fellow sergeant, but he decided the hell with it, he'd grab the guy himself.

"I ain't goin' nowhere," Terry Walton told Thiem. Walton might have mentioned something about knowing his rights, but cops automatically run background checks on the people they interview, at least when they're working a case in the flatlands. Walton was on probation after pleading guilty to a drug possession charge. He had no rights in the limbo land of probation, even if he actually did.

"Mr. Walton, you've got no choice," Thiem told him. "I can violate your probation anytime I want." He was bluffing, of course. It's not a violation of probation to refuse to go down to a police station when you've done nothing wrong. But Thiem's threat worked anyway. Walton sat at police headquarters from 1:00 A.M. until he was called in to give a statement at 5:53 A.M. He might have grumbled while sitting on a plastic chair in a dimly lit hallway for half the night, but as Thiem would remember it, Walton ended up the nicest guy once the two of them started talking.

Body dumps and drive-bys—they're the cases homicide cops hate the most because the killers invariably leave fewer clues. Body dumps are the worst—nothing but a body unconnected to any crime scene, offering an investigator little to go on except for the mode of death.

Thiem's first case had been a body dump, a dead prostitute unloaded in a schoolyard. That taught him lesson number one: you can have skill and the determination, but your success ratio working homicide depends largely on the luck of the draw. A "mom and pop" is every homicide cop's favorite because they often solve themselves. Typical is the case of a black woman from West Oakland named Charlotte Dunn, who a few minutes after midnight one New Year's Eve put in a frantic call to 911. When the cops arrived, she was hunched over her boyfriend Terry's lifeless body, pleading with him not to die. Her prints were still on the bloody knife at her side (and her glasses were on the floor where they landed after her ex punched her).

Drive-by shootings offer little more than do body dumps. The shooter leaves no fingerprints, no fibers, no hairs, or any other telltale clues. Rarely can an eyewitness identify a shooter typically obscured inside the car. The best witnesses tend to be uncooperative, because by nature the drive-by is typically a tactic of warring drug gangs. The rules of the street dictate that you can kill a rival for looking at you wrong, but you would never tell something that might get even a rival dealer arrested.

Even the best clue, the car, typically frustrates an investigator. It was a two-door car, it was a four-door car, it was black, it was blue. Or a homicide cop spends the better part of a week tracking down the car, only to find out it's a "turf car" registered in no one's name, or a "hubba rental"—a car loaned out by a crack addict in exchange for some rock.

Still, Thiem was feeling guardedly optimistic when he left the scene to start interviewing people downtown. For once all of the witnesses were describing the car pretty much the same way: a light green, American-made four-door car, a Plymouth or maybe a Chrysler dating back to the late 1960s or early 1970s. Now if only the car ended up registered to an actual person.

The OPD homicide room has the look of an office conceived in the early 1960s and entirely unchanged since. Two locked interrogation rooms just off the main office are equipped with the most modern sound-proofing technology then available—acoustic tiling covered with a thick coat of paint. The desks are enormous metal things painted steel gray or pale green that seem like they would survive anything short of an atomic blast. Their sole attribute seems to be durability. The office's metal swivel chairs creak and groan like someone suffering an advanced arthritic condition. The plastic cushioning was probably never comfortable, even when new. The file cabinets are of the same era and design as the desks and chairs. The cabinet drawers might actually glide in and out had anyone bothered to oil the tracks in the previous twenty-five years.

The room has all the warmth of a state penitentiary. A heavy metal door, scuffed and dented, is the entranceway into the room. The door handle is stainless steel and cold to the touch. The ceiling tiles are yellowed and stained. Fluorescent bulbs flicker and buzz. Plastic floor tiles vaguely resembling brown flecked with white, the wastepaper baskets, the heavy metal coat rack at the back of the room—all are strictly city issued.

Thiem arrived downtown at this monument to durability at around 1:30 A.M. He lit a fat cigar and put up a pot of coffee before sitting at a computer to run a criminal history on everyone he was about to interview. Damon Willard was clean, but his brother London had a juvie record dating back to when he was nine years old, when the court found that he had attempted to start a fire on public land. He was picked up by the police several more times, but none of the charges ever stuck. Shannon Reed was arrested with London on one of those occasions, but his case, too, was thrown out of court.

Thiem spoke with London, Damon, and Shannon, in that order. London said he had heard six shots. He said the shooter had been sitting in the backseat, but he didn't get much of a look at him—if it even was a him. The murder weapon was a revolver, London said, though Thiem already knew it was a semiautomatic pistol. The tech had found five shell casings at the scene. A semiautomatic leaves casings, a revolver does not.

Damon said that as best he could tell, the shooter was a smallish black male around twenty years old. He figured the weapon was a small-caliber handgun, maybe a .22. Ballistics would give him the precise caliber, but Thiem already knew the weapon had been a much bigger gun, closer to a .45 than a .22.

London and Shannon told Thiem about their fight the night before. They gave Thiem a decent description of Junebug, albeit one so generic that it matched half a dozen kids on every block in East Oakland. Shannon said he couldn't be certain, but he thought the kid was a tenth grader at Castlemont. London said he remembered the kid from his last arrest, when he was locked up in a juvenile holding cell a couple of months earlier.

His final interviewee, Terry Walton, figured he'd heard maybe five gunshots. Walton had phoned 911 but didn't give his name. Then he walked down the street and saw London lying there. He immediately thought of the three kids who had been at his girlfriend's door the previous night. "I don't know if I could identify the three even if I saw them again," he told Thiem.

By 9:30 A.M. Thiem had written up a standard two-paragraph press release and fixed himself a cup of coffee. He called the county coroner's office and found out that the autopsy had begun at 8:45 A.M. Some sleep might be tempting, but talking to the pathologist on a fresh homicide always took precedence over sleep. The start of every homicide was invariably like this one. You're bleary-eyed and fogged in, as if you're afflicted by the same drug stupor that infects some of your more promising suspects.

17

"POP THEM FOOLS"

A police car, its siren wailing and emergency lights flashing, sped across Ninetieth Avenue. Junebug and Aaron, but not Fat 'Tone, watched the squad car slow for the turn on Bancroft. The cop passed not twenty feet from them. The car was moving fast, but for Junebug and Aaron, time moved in slow motion. They couldn't get it out of their minds that the cop was using the same route that they had just taken minutes earlier, though in reverse.

"Don't trip on nothing," 'Tone had said as Aaron eased his car to the curb in front of Paula's apartment. Don't trip—don't even think about it—but of course they could think of nothing else. They were both experiencing a blend of feelings that included confusion, doom, and utter disbelief.

The squad car jogged Aaron out of a daze. "Let's walk on over there, see what happened," he suggested. Junebug immediately balked, but Aaron said he was going anyway. Junebug joined him. For once they walked rather than drove.

The corner that had been so tranquil just twenty minutes earlier was now bathed in the eerie glow of strobe lights flashing against the dark sky. Cops and gawkers were everywhere. Junebug stared at the yellow police tape fluttering from a slight breeze off the bay. It confirmed what he already figured but didn't want to believe: the cops were investigating something far more serious than a few kids frightened by errant gunfire. He killed somebody, he said to himself; that fool Fat 'Tone killed somebody.

Aaron spoke first. "Man, somebody must've got hurt real bad." After a long pause, Junebug said, "They shoulda never jumped me."

The two of them stood away from everyone else. Aaron suggested they move closer but Junebug said they were fine where they were. Aaron didn't push it. They stayed maybe ten minutes. It was unreal how quickly everything had changed. One minute they were small-time street dealers, carefree and smug. The next they're scared kids wanted for what very well might be murder.

They walked back to Paula's. They didn't speak, because anything worth saying should have been said thirty minutes earlier. Aaron reassured himself that he wasn't to blame for what had happened, but deep down he knew he wasn't faultless. He played over in his mind what had just happened. Let's go to 'Tone's house, Junebug had said. *Awright.* With Tony in the car, Aaron had asked, "What we figuring on doing?" "Ride on over there," Junebug had said. *Awright.* He had driven past Auseon and Dowling, heading north without stopping. He had pulled the car over a few blocks away. He remembered Junebug saying, "I want to pop them fools," and 'Tone saying, "I ain't fit to kill nobody."

Aaron had known that there was a gun in the car, yet he had turned the car around and driven back south. His heart had beat faster, sensing danger. And then suddenly it was *blam-blam-blam-blam-blam.* Reflexively, he had ducked his head level with the steering wheel, fearing they were being shot at. Dowling jogs slightly past Auseon. Probably no one noticed but him, but he had nearly crashed into a parked car. They drove in silence the few blocks to 'Tone's apartment.

"I want to pop them fools." Those were the words rattling around in Junebug's mind. "I want to pop them fools." He hadn't had the gun in his hand. They were just words, so easy to say. People offhandedly talked about wishing people dead when they meant nothing of the kind. Every kid he knew used the expression. "I want to pop them fools." It was practically a garden-variety expletive, a way of expressing everyday frustrations, like commuters saying they want to kill the strangers driving the car that just cut them off. "I want to pop them fools." But you don't say it when someone's clutching a .45 inside his jacket pocket.

They walked to the car, still parked in front of 'Tone's. Aaron slipped behind the wheel and Junebug got in the passenger's side—exactly as they had been except for 'Tone, now blessedly absent. Fucking Tony, Mr. Big Man who always wants to handle things. They thought about what might have been if it had been just the two of them. Every available cop was at Auseon and Dowling, but Aaron drove the seven blocks back to Ninety-second Avenue as carefully as a man with a gun to his head.

Junebug headed straight home. He lay in bed, his heart jumping out of his chest. Fractured moments from the previous hour played in his mind like an instant replay machine that wouldn't shut off. The muzzle flash, someone falling to the ground, a girl's scream. He shivered in the dark as if he had just awakened from a bad dream, feeling exposed and vulnerable. A palpable fear rippled through his body; at other times he felt only anger. He was angry at himself, at 'Tone, at John Banks, at the two kids who had jumped him the night before. He could hardly believe that someone had probably lost his life—maybe more than one person—and he had played a part. He wasn't a murderer, he wasn't capable of that kind of violence. He owned a gun, but to his mind it was for self-protection, to defend himself against someone else.

Aaron went home too, but Fig came around looking to catch a ride over to a small party the two of them had been invited to. Aaron said no, but Fig kept pushing and Aaron relented, because "yes" was easier than repeating "no."

Aaron waited outside in the car because he couldn't imagine being with people, but then a girl he knew came out and practically dragged him inside. He sat there mute, feeling suffocated by the chitchat. After about forty-five minutes, he abruptly stood up and said he had to go. Let Fig figure out his own way home.

Home wasn't any better. He lay in bed for hours, seeing himself as if in a movie that was playing in his head: the car slowing down, his body flinching when the gun went off, the muzzle flash, a girl screaming. He kept hearing that girl's scream over and over again. He told himself that he might as well stop thinking about what had happened because there was nothing he could do now, but he couldn't chase the shooting from his mind. He got to sleep at around four.

Aaron was the sort of person everyone teased because he could sleep through anything, but that next morning he was up with the birds. Junebug, too. They both woke up craving news of the previous night's shooting. That's how both of them began their new life as wanted felons—with heavy hearts, desperate to learn what havoc they had wreaked the night before.

'Tone would claim only fuzzy bits of memory after the shooting. Later Junebug would swear that Tony was making himself out to be drunker and more stoned than he was, but 'Tone portrayed himself as so wasted that Junebug and Aaron had to help him out of the car. He said he remembered losing his balance when he tried to stand up. He recalled talking with his friend Billy, but for the life of him he couldn't remember what he might have said.

The way Billy would tell it, 'Tone staggered toward him. "I didn't do it," Billy would quote his friend as saying. "They blaming me, but I didn't do it." Billy kept asking, "Do what? Do what?," but 'Tone never answered him. Billy helped his friend to the door.

'Tone remembered his sister Angela coming in with a couple of her friends. They were abuzz with the news of a shooting a few blocks away. Supposedly there were cop cars and ambulances everywhere. 'Tone managed a "For real?" before stumbling to bed.

Dermmell Reed spent the night brooding over the responsibility that had somehow fallen on his shoulders. He was furious with everyone: his parents, who had left them alone; his older brothers, because neither of them had been home; his grandparents, for not having done more.

He knew his anger wasn't rational. His mother was working the second shift at a Safeway store in the suburbs. His brothers had a right to their social life. But blaming others was preferable to torturing himself with questions that had no answers. "What should I have done that I didn't do?" he asked himself. "Who should I have called?" He wished he had a car, but then he had to admit that he didn't know if speeding Kevin to a hospital would have been the right thing to do.

"That night," Dermmell later confessed, "screwed me up for I don't know how long."

Dermmell had cradled Kevin in his arms while Shannon sprinted to his grandparents' house a few doors away. The reverend was wearing his pajamas when Shannon ran inside the house. "Grandpa, grandpa, come out. They shot Kevin." The reverend told him, "Well, then bring him on in the house."

Shannon, all of fourteen, told him that moving his baby brother wasn't a good idea. "Do something!" Shannon had yelled at his grandfather. Instead the reverend admonished his grandson for speaking to an elder in so rude a fashion.

Later the reverend explained what happened this way: "Wisdom told me not to run. You get to be my age, you just don't go running out there when people might be shooting. Instead I called the police. I ain't medically inclined anyway. Besides, where were his parents at? Fact is, a thirteen-year-old shouldn't be out that late."

Dermmell may have spent more time being angry with his grandparents except that his mother fulminated for the both of them: "A man of the cloth . . . supposed to be there for people in need . . . yet his grandson's laying out in the street bleeding to death . . . he won't get off his bottom. . . . You run out to someone in that position, you try to assist them." There wasn't much anyone could have done to save Kevin short of getting him to the hospital faster. But Annette Reed figured that her father-in-law's attitude might well have cost her son his life.

Dermmell tried talking about that night when the family was gathered together a few months later, but he had bottled up his feelings for so long, they came out in a confused rush. He voice cracked and he got tangled up in his words. Everybody stared at him like he had temporarily lost his mind, but he felt relieved that he had gotten it off his chest just the same.

In the middle of the night, a dark blue Ford station wagon picked up Kevin's body and drove to a handsome two-story building one block off the freeway in downtown Oakland. Bolted into the face of the building is a neon sign that glows red through the night. CORONER'S BUREAU the sign reads. The station wagon backed into the loading bay. On the first floor of the coroner's office, Kevin's body was placed on a long stainless steel tray like a filing cabinet drawer, inside a walk-in freezer.

Kevin had been wearing a blue T-shirt, a pair of faded Levi's, Nike shoes, and a black jacket. In his pocket he had scraps of paper with phone numbers scribbled on them and a balled-up bus transfer. Before the autopsy began, an investigator snapped several head shots of Kevin. With his eyes closed and his lips slightly parted, Kevin appeared asleep, although the deep worry lines creasing his forehead suggested it had been a fitful night. He looked much older than thirteen. He weighed ninety-four pounds at the time of his death.

Dr. Sharon Van Meter performed the autopsy. Speaking into a microphone dangling above the cutting table, she described Kevin as a well-developed, well-nourished adolescent. He had brown eyes and a pierced ear. There was a single bullet entrance wound on his upper left thigh, close to the groin.

The careful, tempered language of a pathologist's report suggests and supposes rather than concludes. The large copper-colored bullet Van Meter removed from Kevin's body was flattened on one side, its sides scraped, as if it had struck a rough surface. The entrance wound was oversize and irregular in shape, suggesting that the cause of the bullet's disfigurement wasn't bone but something else. Van Meter figured that the bullet traveled upward at approximately forty degrees. Taken all together, Van Meter wrote in her report, the evidence suggested that the bullet "struck some intermediate target before it entered the body." She didn't spell out what that object might have been, but she allowed that it very well may have been the pavement. In all likelihood, Kevin died because a ricochet off the street had struck him at the worst possible angle.

The bullet had punctured Kevin's left iliac artery and then perforated the small intestine and the colon. The blow to the iliac was deadly. The right and left iliacs are the primary arteries carrying blood to the lower half of the body. The official cause of death was a bullet wound to the thigh, but more specifically Kevin had bled to death.

■ ■ ■

Sgt. Jerry Harris—"Big Red" to his fellow officers and street corner dealers alike—is a former homicide cop responsible for the constellation of police beats that comprise deep East Oakland. Harris is a large man, maybe six feet three inches tall, with blondish red hair, a ruddy complexion, and a belly that would strain even an extra-extra-large shirt. The joke inside the department is that he never exits his patrol car except for lunch and the end of a shift. Even if he and the officers under his charge are in pursuit of a perp on foot, Big Red remains in his car. He narrates the action over the police radio, driving his car to wherever he can gain the best vantage point, barking out commands so their man doesn't get away.

Big Red spends his days running license plates through the computer and looking out the window for possible fugitives. All through the day, the cops under his charge respond to his radio calls. Typically Big Red calls them to a scene without providing a clue of the crime he suspects a person has committed. He communicates to his officers from inside his car using hand signals, like a third base coach. If he crosses his forearms, then that means the cop should cuff someone. Pretending to scribble with a pen indicates that the cop should ask someone for identification and also interrogate them. A suspect usually complies, while at the same time he pleads to know what this is all about. The beat cop doesn't have to pretend ignorance, because the truth is, he usually doesn't have a clue either.

From Thiem's perspective, Big Red could be a godsend, but he could also be a royal pain. He was forever calling from the cellular phone in his patrol car with any bit of news, big or small. The cops under Red's watch hustled because he left them no choice. Red or one of his officers often had something good. Yet he'd call and then immediately put Thiem on hold because Red had something coming over his radio. Typically, Thiem's been up all night. He's sitting on the edge of his patience, yet he's listening to Red tap-tap-tapping on his in-car computer or talking to someone else on the radio. And sometimes it ends up that Thiem's been holding for several minutes only to learn that Red has nothing to report.

Big Red phoned Thiem three times the day after the murder. The first time was to tell Thiem he had a guy, Harold Mims, claiming to have witnessed the shooting near London Willard's home the previous afternoon. The second and third calls ended up bum leads. Red thought he had a bead on the Tameka whose brother had supposedly threatened Shannon, but then he phoned back to report that his Tameka had no brother.

Big Red phoned six more times over the following two days. His biggest news was that he had found another Tameka. This one went to Elmhurst with Shannon *and* had a sixteen-year-old brother. Red took Shannon to stand outside Castlemont High at the close of the school day to see if he could ID the kid he and London had jumped. When Tameka's brother Damon walked by, he and Shannon locked eyes and glared at each other, but Shannon swore that the kid he'd beaten up wasn't anyone he saw in the crowd that day.

Red also called to say that he had spoken with a gardener who had recovered a .45 caliber slug at the murder scene. The evidence tech assigned this case had marked in chalk the location of every spent casing spit out by the semiautomatic handgun. She had walked off measurements to draw a precise schematic of the corner. Among the things she wrote in her report was that the window of the Lincoln parked on the corner had been shattered, but apparently she didn't follow the likely path of a bullet that would have caused the damage—as had Red, working backward from the bullet lying there by a fence post, partially obscured by weeds. Thiem had never respected the work of this particular evidence tech. He cursed her name and then chided himself for having trusted her work when his instincts told him otherwise.

The first thing both Aaron and Junebug did after waking up the day after the murder was throw on some clothes and go buy a newspaper. Each by himself tore through the morning Oakland *Tribune*. There was nothing about any shooting or murder the night before. Each allowed himself a brief ray of hope, but the reality was that a shooting not reported to the police until after 10:00 P.M. was too late to make the morning *Trib*.

Junebug felt disoriented, as if everything in his world had suddenly been turned upside down. When he was outside fetching a newspaper, he wanted the safety of the indoors. But once he was inside, he felt like he needed to be outside. The moment he walked out his door, though, he regretted it. Fat 'Tone was standing there waiting to talk with him.

Tony, too, had been up early the morning after the murder. He immediately headed to Ninety-second Avenue. He was anxious to talk to Junebug, but he would have even settled for Aaron, though he'd never liked him. He needed to square reality with his fuzzy memory.

'Tone might have been the last person in the world Junebug wanted to see, yet there was no one aside from Aaron and 'Tone with whom he wanted to talk. "I did it for you," 'Tone told him. Junebug felt like screaming, but he bit his lip. If anyone deserved a thrashing for being so dumb, Junebug thought it was himself. How could he have been so foolish? He had violated his vow to never again allow himself to be beholden to 'Tone; now he was linked to him around a shooting, if not a murder.

They spoke for ten, maybe fifteen minutes. They barely talked about the previous night except to agree that neither would tell a soul what had happened. Yet for all they saw of each other in the coming days, that was pretty much the only conversation the two of them had except for a couple of practical discussions about Aaron's car. They'd say "wh's up, wh's up, catch you later," as if nothing out of the ordinary had happened, but the murder always lurked just below the surface. Junebug drew an analogy to a man who's caught having an affair with his wife's sister. The husband and wife might not talk about it, yet it's always there between them nonetheless.

"It loomed over every interaction we had after that," Junebug said later. "Believe me, every time we saw each other, the subject was on our minds."

Junebug told himself he wanted to be as far away from 'Tone as possible, but by late afternoon, he found himself at Paula's house in front of the TV. "Watchoo boys watching the news fo'?" Paula asked them. They were anxiously switching channels, so after a while Paula booted them out of the living room. "Y'all are getting on my nerves," she yelled at them.

A little bit later, Paula walked next door to her friend Clover's place. 'Tone, Junebug, and Aaron were there sitting in front of the TV. She never remembered a single one of them ever watching the news, yet now they couldn't get enough of it. When the news reported a murder around the corner the previous night, she asked them straight out what they knew about it. They assured her that they were curious only because it had happened so close to where everyone lived.

That's how the three of them learned that they had killed a thirteen-year-old boy named Kevin Reed. It was the next day that they saw what Kevin looked like and realized that they had taken aim at the wrong kid.

The following day's *Trib* carried a long front-page article reporting on the shooting, including a picture of Kevin. Donald Reed described his son as "an all-around great kid" who enjoyed computer games, rap, fishing, and hanging out with his family. The paper also reported that the family was still grieving the death of Kevin's cousin, who had been killed when the 1989 earthquake knocked down a section of the double-decker freeway that cut through West Oakland.

"We were just getting over that," Donald told the reporter. "Our family will never be the same."

Aaron read the article once and then several times again. Only then could he convince himself that he really had something to do with something this tragic. Junebug had come by proposing that they drive around looking for girls. The next thing he knew he was speeding away from the murder of a thirteen-year-old boy. He was only fifteen himself.

Seeing the news in black and white also hit Junebug hard. When he first saw the article, he felt a sensation close to exhilaration. The kid pictured wasn't the same kid who had jumped him. This was another murder! But then he realized what had happened, that this was Shannon Reed's brother. After that he felt infinitely worse. He had been telling himself that it was really Shannon and London's fault, that they had started it. But it turned out that the kid they killed was completely innocent.

Junebug sat there alone in his room with the paper on his bed. Emotions crashed down on him: sadness, anger, and of course guilt, because he was to blame no matter how much he tried to convince himself otherwise.

■ ■ ■

Tony was so quiet in the days after the *Tribune* story that Paula feared he was seriously ill. Until that week, he could never stand to be stuck inside the house for even an hour, but now he was lying around Paula's all day or moping at Vera's. It was ominous how quiet and moody he had suddenly become. He hung around her and the baby all day, driving Paula crazy.

He felt, he later said, incapable of being by himself because when he was alone, he couldn't stop thinking of Kevin. He couldn't keep food down. He didn't sleep well, either. Paula wasn't sure what to think except to know he was feeling guilty about something. Several times she asked him what he knew about the boy killed around the corner. He denied knowing anything, but Paula kept after him until finally he broke down and told her something resembling the truth. "It was an accident," he repeated over and over.

"You gotta go to the police, baby," she told him. "Give yourself up and they'll go easier on you. It'll help soothe your guilty mind."

'Tone promised her he'd think about it, but then he dismissed the idea out of hand. They'd throw the book at him, he decided, whether he turned himself in or he waited to get caught. He vowed to God that if he somehow got away with what he had done, he'd never do something like this again. He hoped that if he was caught, he'd get off on a technicality, like you see on TV. With time he even half convinced himself that he hadn't shot the gun, that what had happened had to do with people other than himself.

The first time they saw each other after the murder, Junebug and Aaron tried talking about what had happened. Mostly they just shook their heads and struggled for words that didn't come. About the only thing that either would remember of the conversation was a mutual vow to keep what had happened strictly to themselves.

A few days later, however, they were already talking about turning themselves in. If 'Tone goes down, Junebug reasoned, all three of us are going down. Junebug's own fate after the carjacking was all the convincing that Aaron needed. Then and there they revised their vow of silence. If the cops picked either of them up, they'd come clean. Fuck Tony. And why not? It wasn't like either of them had pulled the trigger.

Not long after that, Junebug mentioned to Aaron that he was thinking about turning himself in. Aaron immediately said that he was thinking the same thing. Or maybe it happened the other way around. Aaron and Junebug traveled around this same circle several times. One or the other of them would talk of confessing, the other would say he was thinking the same. Going to the cops was a good idea, they'd agree—and then wouldn't go, instead wishing the whole thing would go away.

Except for these conversations about maybe turning themselves in to the police, the two of them barely spoke about the murder. What was there to say, really?

Dermmell never felt so alone as he did in the days following his little brother's death. The house was packed with people, but the crowds only made him feel even more lonely. The presence of so many relatives who barely had time for them when everyone was alive made him angry. They hugged him with tears in their eyes and all Dermmell could think was, Who are you?

Dermmell kept mainly to his room. If he wasn't sleeping, he was lying in bed thinking about his brother. He thought of Kevin's infectious nature. Why hadn't he invited Kevin to join him and his friends more often? He recalled Kevin's enthusiasm when the two of them were fishing by the estuary, remembered the easy way about him and how good-natured a kid he was.

He thought about the night Kevin was murdered. Normally, when his parents were out, he would be after his two younger brothers about coming home at a decent hour. He remembered thinking it was getting too late for Kevin to be outside, but for once he decided not to make a big deal of it. "That kind of stuff eats you up," he said.

He tried going to summer school, but those first few days were rough. Mainly he wanted only to be with his friend David. Dermmell loved his brothers—he considered theirs a tight family—but there wasn't that same kind of intimacy that he had with David. He could talk with his friend in the days after Kevin's death more easily than he could with his family.

For Annette Reed, the days after her son's death were a blur of family and friends paying their condolences. All she could really remember was her surprise that Kevin had touched so many lives. Several teachers called to say how sorry they were. He seemed to have made an impression on all sorts of neighbors she had never met before. He had been particularly popular with the girls, who far outnumbered the boys his age who paid their respects.

There were distractions and hassles, not the least of which was raising the money to give Kevin a proper burial. The *Tribune* article reporting on Kevin's death ended with a plea from Rev. Curtis Reed for donations. (They received about eight hundred dollars.) In private the reverend was furious that he had been put in a position to "practically get down on my hands and knees and beg for charity." He reminded them that he had been after them about the importance of burial insurance for them and their kids. "Carelessness and negligence, that's all this is," he lectured them. He had learned the importance of burial insurance from his parents. He had tried to pass it along to his kids, but to the reverend's mind, his eldest son and his daughter-in-law never seemed to understand the first thing about the word *responsibility*.

On Friday, July 13, the Reverend Curtis Reed stood among a small group of ministers gathered to meet the press at the corner of Auseon and Dowling. Heading up the press conference was Rev. J. Alfred Smith, the highly regarded pastor at the Allen Temple Baptist Church, on Eighty-fifth Avenue just below East Fourteenth Street. There were those parishioners who wished Smith would move the church to quiet environs, but one essential piece of Allen Temple's magic is the link it creates between black professionals who've left the neighborhood and those who've stayed behind. The church sponsors a scholarship fund, a credit union, a job referral service, and a legal assistance program.

"No one is safe in the city of Oakland," Smith told the few reporters who had gathered. He proposed a gun amnesty program that would allow people to turn in their illegal weapons with no questions asked. He acknowledged the limits of what he was proposing but added, "At least it would be a first step. The worst thing people can do is sit down and do nothing."

Smith challenged the incumbent mayor to embrace his program. The mayor's press secretary told local reporters that the mayor would talk over the idea with his chief of staff. There, apparently, the idea died until a few years later, when gun amnesty programs—offering such inducements as cash, basketball tickets, free passes to an amusement park—would be the rage here and across the country.

Kevin's funeral was held one week to the day after the murder. Smith delivered the eulogy; the area's city councilman, Carter Gilmore, also said a few words. Several of Kevin's classmates made up jackets emblazoned with R.I.P. KEV on the back—a growing custom among teens in East Oakland. A choir performed a rap song that Kevin had written, "The Streets of Oakland," during the service.

At the next day's city council meeting, Carter Gilmore pushed a resolution in Kevin's memory. "The city of Oakland extends its deepest sympathy to you in the loss of your loved one, Kevin Reed," it began. A copy of the proclamation in a dime-store frame was presented to the Reeds a few weeks later.

One of the two candidates in the city's pending mayoral runoff, Elihu Harris, asked for and received Annette's permission to use Kevin's rap song. She agreed, but then his campaign people got the words wrong. To Annette's mind, their snafu distorted the meaning Kevin had invested in his song. "People just want to use things for their own advantage and don't really care how it makes other people feel," she said. "I don't know what he thought he was doing, but it really hurt me and my kids." It was yet one more aggravation in those months when her youngest child's murder was still a raw memory.

Natasha Buckner was a normal teenager who spent too many hours talking on the phone with friends. She was fourteen when she was shot, a pretty girl, sweet and bubbly. She had just recently graduated from a local parochial school, where she had been an honor student and a cheerleader. That fall she would be attending Bishop O'Dowd High School, an East Oakland parochial school that promised a brighter future than Castlemont. Her dream back then was to become an obstetrician.

Sheila Buckner, Natasha's mother, was on vacation from her job as a manager at an Oakland department store. Instead of enjoying her daughter and her free time, she spent her vacation at her daughter's bedside—if not in the bed with Natasha. After a couple of nights, the hospital staff had to tell Mrs. Buckner she could no longer sleep in her daughter's bed. Greg Buckner worked for a local paint company. He, too, took off as much time as he could manage so as to be with his daughter.

The *Tribune* ran a small feature story about Natasha three days after the shooting. Natasha wasn't up to an interview, nor were her parents, so the article was based mostly on an interview with her cousin, James Renfro, who was staying with the Buckners for the summer. Renfro was a college student at Santa Clara University who had grown up in the neighborhood.

"It was like déjà vu for me," he told the reporter. "My brother was shot and I wound up driving him to the hospital then, too."

Twice in the days following the murder, Greg Buckner called to speak to Thiem. The first time was to pass along something he had learned talking with Shannon. Supposedly the kids responsible for the shooting lived in a green apartment building across from Castlemont High, at Eighty-sixth and MacArthur. That was exactly what an anonymous caller had told the police. The second time was to tell Thiem about his conversation with Shannon's brother Curtis. The kids who killed his brother, Curtis had told Buckner, lived in a blue two-story house on Eighty-fifth Avenue near East Fourteenth, more than a dozen blocks from Castlemont. But when Thiem tried talking to Curtis himself, Curtis refused to talk to him. "He's talking to me like he suspects that I had something to do with my brother's murder," Curtis told friends. "You don't talk to people with that kind of disrespect and then expect their help."

Buckner was an ex-marine who struck Thiem as a man struggling to remain patient while the cops did their job. "Let me handle this," he told Thiem. Generally Thiem didn't think much of the sort of people who lived in parts of the city like Elmhurst. "Not like us," he would say.

"Not exactly the kind of place where you're dealing with Joe Average Citizen." His was a disheartening, all-inclusive condemnation of those he had sworn to serve and protect. But despite his biases, Thiem took immediately to Buckner, a real four-square guy who struck him as his kind of man.

When Thiem heard a rumor that the Reed brothers were plotting their revenge, he felt nothing but contempt for these young punks and their street justice. Greg Buckner, however, was a father and a former Marine. Thiem had a stepdaughter only a few years younger than Natasha, and he could easily imagine what he'd be feeling if it were his stepdaughter instead of Natasha. He too would be struggling with the urge to hunt down the young men who had done this to her.

18

THE CHASE

In the days after Kevin Reed's murder, several people phoned homicide to say they knew of an older-model green car driven by the sort of person who might very well commit murder. One anonymous caller was more definitive. The owner of the car used in the murder, the caller said as if it were fact, lives in an apartment building at MacArthur and Eighty-sixth Avenue.

Another caller—again anonymous—told Thiem that he would crack the case if he tracked down a recent juvenile hall escapee named Floyd Lawrence. Lawrence's name came up again that day, when Rev. Curtis Reed mentioned to Thiem that he had heard the same rumor. Thiem ran Lawrence's name through the computer. Twice in the previous eighteen months Lawrence had been sent to a juvenile facility on a drug conviction. The second time he had run from Los Cerros, a youth camp one step short of a commitment to the California Youth Authority.

Still, Thiem figured his best lead was something London had told him the night of the murder. London had seen the kid he and Shannon jumped, at the county's juvenile lockup a few months earlier at Fourth and Broadway. Thiem found out when London was at the detention center and then obtained a printout of all juveniles booked around that same time.

Thiem's next stop was the school district's central office. Shannon had said he thought the kid was a tenth grader at Castlemont. So Thiem spent a few hours checking his juvie printout against a list of Castlemont High students. He found five matches.

That was on Wednesday, two days after the murder. On Thursday morning, at a little before six, Thiem and his partner were awakened after a body was discovered on the hill above the Caldecott Tunnel. The victim, Gregory Gardner, was an eighteen-year-old kid who lived on Dowling, four blocks from the Reed family. Gardner, his family said, was a good kid who harbored dreams of becoming a cop.

Thiem's partner served as the lead investigator on the Gardner killing, but the case still took Thiem's undivided attention over the next couple of days. He felt confident about the Reed case—he already had a likely motive and two solid leads in Floyd Lawrence and Damon—but the Gardner murder would be only the first of nineteen murders, not to mention the demands of previously unsolved homicides still piled on his desk, that would temporarily pull him off the Reed case.

Junebug, Aaron, and maybe a couple of other guys were hanging out on Ninety-second Avenue when John Banks happened along. It had been two or three days since the murder.

"You all is fools," Banks said.

Aaron played dumb. "What you talking 'bout?" he asked. Junebug remained silent.

"Man, you all's just stupid," Banks responded.

Banks's next words weren't addressed to Junebug directly, but it was said for his benefit, that much was clear. "You know that boy in the *Trib* who was murdered?" he asked. "That's my friend's little brother. I've known him since we were little." You could have pushed Junebug over with a finger.

The car and the murder weapon ate away at any remaining bond between Junebug, 'Tone, and Aaron, especially between 'Tone and

Aaron. 'Tone felt like screaming every time he saw the car over on Ninety-second, but Aaron refused to dump it.

Aaron had bought the car only a week or two before the murder. It was homely but it was fast, equipped with one of those enormous engines American car manufacturers were installing before miles per gallon became part of the national lexicon. Aaron had fallen in love with it the first time he noticed it whizzing down Ninety-second Avenue. He was standing there talking with his brother Anthony when he interrupted himself to admire the car. By coincidence, Anthony knew the owner, a friend of his named Lance. Lance was looking to sell the thing for around two hundred dollars, Anthony told him. Aaron said "sold." "My mob car," he called it not because of any fascination with 1930s gangsters but because it could fit so many people. It was a 1967 Chrysler Newport, a big old bucket that allowed six or seven of them to crowd in for a cruise.

Despite the murder, Aaron was still burning rubber in the Newport, acting like a kid with a new toy. One day not long after the murder, he hit a corner too fast and, as he struggled to regain control of the car, he heard a couple of gun blasts. He brought the car to a quick stop. A big-time drug dealer in their neighborhood stood there with a rifle in his hands. "Don't be driving like that when there're kids out here," he yelled at Aaron. The dealer had put two bullet holes in the passenger-side fender.

Aaron exploded in anger, but the dealer just laughed. He held out the rifle to Aaron. "Want to shoot up my car so now we're even?" he asked. Aaron reached for it, but then the guy pulled it back fast. He threw Aaron a few twenties for his troubles and told him to be more careful next time.

'Tone was apoplectic when he heard about Aaron's run-in with the dealer. Was he *trying* to draw the attention of the police? He offered to give Aaron the two hundred dollars he had paid for the car. He said he'd buy him a plane ticket (one way) to anywhere in the country if he got rid of it. But Aaron held firm. It was his first car. Was he supposed to dump it just because Fat 'Tone had acted like an idiot? It was as if he couldn't get rid of it because he could never resolve the unfairness of it all.

'Tone thought about beating Aaron up. In his fantasies, he'd punch him until he relented. But then he realized that a beating might provide Aaron, the least culpable of the three, cause to go to the police. So 'Tone was left staring impotently at the thing, feeling doomed every time he looked at it. "When you gonna get rid of that fuckin' car?" he'd growl. Or he'd say to Aaron, "You's a fool, you know that?" He would say it out of the blue, but he was confident that Aaron knew exactly what he was talking about.

Junebug agreed with 'Tone. He too felt like a sitting duck every time he looked at the car. He put it to Aaron straight: "ditch the thing." He was surprised he even had to mention it. You remove the plates, you leave it somewhere far away, and then you take a bus home. But Aaron would say, "I don't know, man."

'Tone and Junebug spoke about stealing the car. They'd set it aflame somewhere out in the boonies and let Aaron think it had been stolen. It got so that Tony wished Aaron would die, that's how much he hated seeing that car on the street. The crazy part was that Aaron hardly drove it anymore. He just kept it parked out front, unwilling to sell it but afraid to drive a vehicle that had become the bane of his life.

Aaron decided that if the cops came around asking questions, he would claim it had been stolen sometime around the Fourth of July. To the obvious follow-up question—Then how'd you get it back?—he'd say that the thief must have ditched it, because he had just come across it one day while walking down the street. He didn't report the car stolen, he would say, because it wasn't registered and he was under age.

It would have been simpler, of course, to dump a car that sat so long without moving that eventually it would be towed as an abandoned vehicle. But being fifteen and owning a car in East Oakland was a status symbol, even if the big beast of a thing was hot.

'Tone had committed a major blunder of his own. He had failed to dump the gun and now the police had it. It would be some time before Brian Thiem would learn that it had been confiscated, but as far as the three conspirators knew, Five-O had the piece and were now that much closer to busting them.

The morning after the murder, 'Tone had hidden the gun inside the grimy recliner that sat between his grandmother's apartment and Junebug's. Not twenty-four hours later, the chair had been removed. 'Tone had just about had a heart attack when he noticed it was missing. A neighbor told him that a Housing clean-up crew had been around earlier in the day to remove the unsightly easy chair. Supposedly the gun clattered to the ground as they were heaving it onto the truck.

When Junebug heard that the cops had found a gun there between the two apartments, he assumed it was one of their turf guns. East Oakland is bordered by an estuary; San Francisco, thirty minutes away, is surrounded by water on three sides. If a gun's been used in a murder, you drive to a body of water and fling the thing as far as you can. It couldn't have been the murder weapon because 'Tone couldn't be that dumb.

But 'Tone told Junebug the truth, or something resembling it. He admitted that the cops now had the murder weapon, but what he couldn't bring himself to say aloud was that he hadn't rubbed off his fingerprints. It hadn't even dawned on him to do so until after the fact.

'Tone cursed his stupidity, but mainly he blamed the gun fiasco on Aaron. It made no sense, but he told himself that if Aaron hadn't parked his car in front of their building, then Housing wouldn't have known where to look for a gun. Neither Junebug nor 'Tone bothered telling Aaron that the cops now had the gun. Not forty-eight hours had passed since the killing and Five-O had the murder weapon, but it would be months before Aaron would learn this fact.

To Junebug, it was like his friends were asking to get caught. He told himself that he had nothing to worry about because it was 'Tone's gun, and the car tied Aaron to the shooting. He wasn't connected to either. If anyone talks, it'll be their word against mine, Junebug told himself. That notion would soothe his fears for the moment, but there was never any stretch of time after the gun was found that Junebug didn't figure it was only a matter of time before they would all be caught.

That summer, Junebug and his family drove to Louisiana to visit kin. Aaron, too, was on the road to visit family; with his mother and two brothers he traveled to Tennessee to spend time with relatives. For each of them, the vacation from Oakland prompted dreams of flight. After their return, they spoke about running away to Louisiana together. Aaron, too, had people there. But all they ever did was talk about the idea.

'Tone harbored similar fantasies. He dreamed of escaping to Bakersfield, a modest-size city that for most Californians was nothing more than a rest stop along the interstate. Bakersfield was where his girlfriend Tonette had been born. 'Tone couldn't have placed Bakersfield on a map. He had no idea what life might be like there, how hellishly hot the summers were or how different it was from a city like Oakland. Yet he found himself thinking of Bakersfield just the same, as if it were a bit of paradise and a solution all at once. He didn't mention it to Tonette, but he figured that if the cops ever got close, he could convince her to disappear with him into this glorious wonderland he called Bakersfield.

The homicide cops call them the "sweat rooms." There, inside one of two tiny rooms, detectives "sweat" their more promising suspects. The rooms are about the same size as a prison cell, maybe six feet by ten feet. Each is furnished with a bulky table and several chairs, making them more claustrophobic still.

Homicide cops routinely park a suspect or a reluctant witness inside a locked sweat room for hours at a time while they go about their business. They'll make phone calls, they'll run names through the computer, they'll grab a burrito at the Mi Rancho across the street. They'll trade insults and jokes with their fellow investigators, typically about drugs ("You must be smoking that Buddha weed") or sex ("Jocko, do you stare at every investigator's crotch while you're talking to them or just mine?"). All the while their suspect or witness sits there with nothing to do but stare at the walls. Not surprisingly, the acoustic tiling covering the sweat rooms' walls are heavily gouged and scratched with graffiti.

The posse—the OPD special duty unit specializing in the capture of fugitives and violent felons—picked up Floyd Lawrence less than a week after a tipster had told Thiem that Lawrence knew something about the murder. Thiem had the posse place him in a sweat room and he locked the door. Lawrence was lucky. Thiem sweated him for only three hours before walking in to talk.

Lawrence was seventeen at the time. He claimed he knew nothing about the murder except what people on the street were saying. He said that on the evening of July 9 he was probably hanging around at Eighty-second and MacArthur, placing him only six or eight blocks from the murder scene. Big Red had told Thiem that a guy from Lawrence's crew had been busted driving an older-model green sedan. Lawrence claimed he didn't own a car, but Thiem noticed that he kept a Ford key on his key chain. Lawrence said the key was to his cousin's car.

Thiem showed Lawrence photographs of London and Shannon. He claimed he recognized neither of them. He shrugged in ignorance when Thiem showed him mug shots of the five Castlemont students who had been booked at the same time as London. Lawrence seemed to be telling the truth, but Thiem had long ago decided that he possessed no magic power that told him when someone was lying. "His eyes will go a certain way," the experts say. "It's in his body language, it's the way he crosses his legs." To Thiem nothing much counted short of catching someone contradicting an incontrovertible fact.

Thiem didn't push Lawrence very hard, but there was no reason to. He was an escapee from a juvenile facility who was now facing a narcotics charge. He wouldn't be going anywhere for a long time.

That same day, Thiem drove to Terry Walton's apartment to show him a photo lineup that he had assembled. He showed him mug shots of Tameka's brother Damon, Floyd Lawrence, and the Castlemont five. Walton said that suspect number six, John "Junebug" Jones, looked like one of the kids at his front door the night before the murder, but he couldn't be certain. None of the others struck a chord.

Two days after Walton's shaky ID of John Jones, Thiem and his partner John McKenna were in the area, so they decided to drive by Jones's address to have a look. Thiem couldn't believe his luck. Parked in front of Jones's building was an older-model, green four-door Chrysler Newport—a perfect match with their murder vehicle. Jones was standing there in the parking lot, but Thiem resisted his impulse to talk with him.

Thiem and McKenna swung by London's place to show him the same photo lineup they had shown Terry Walton. London didn't hesitate before IDing John Jones as the kid they had jumped at the store the night before the murder.

Back at his office, Thiem ran Jones to check his police record. He had been by himself when he was arrested on a drug sales charge when he was fourteen, but a car theft back in April offered several potential suspects. He focused on the two other young men incarcerated for the crime. Rick Bradley was still in the county jail at the time of the murder, but Shondell Brooks was out on bail between June 5 and July 24. Thiem added another possible suspect to his list.

Thiem ran the license plate number from the Chrysler Newport. The official owner was listed as a sixty-six-year-old man who lived thirty blocks from where the car was parked. Thiem sighed. He couldn't say for certain what it meant, but he was sure it was going to require plenty of leg work.

At first there was so much going on around her that Annette Reed was numb to pain. There were always people at their house or friends to talk with on the phone. But after a few weeks, most everyone returned to their normal routine and there were few people around outside her immediate family. She was now pretty much on her own, with no one to distract her from her grief.

Annette had started working at the Safeway only a couple of months before Kevin's murder. Her manager was at first as supportive as she could have hoped, but she returned not long after the funeral anyway. She was hoping that work would take her mind off Kevin, but that was a mistake. She suffered a breakdown. The second time her employers weren't nearly as understanding.

The union might have been more to blame than the store management. She had received a notice in the mail about some union dues she owed, but it had come right after Kevin was killed and she'd forgotten about it. When she returned to work, she was told to either pay up or be terminated. Annette tried explaining her catch-22—that she couldn't afford the dues unless she started working again—but people kept passing the buck, and eventually she just gave up.

It seemed like everything was falling apart at once. With the stress of the murder, her relationship with Donald quickly deteriorated from bad to worse. They were there for each other in the days right after the shooting, but that was short-lived. Donald too lost his job in the aftermath of the shooting. Not long after Kevin's death, they missed their first mortgage payment. Now they had a mortgage company after them as well.

Annette was also balled up with worry over Shannon. Whoever had killed Kevin had been gunning for Shannon, and he or they were still out there. She figured the cops would never catch the kid or kids who had killed her son, even though a good friend of hers worked for the department. With so many murders, she told herself, what were the odds that they'd put in the time to crack one case that hadn't merited even a word in the media since the first few days after the murder?

Annette sent Shannon to live with a friend to keep him away from Auseon and Dowling. He was supposed to start at Castlemont that fall, but Annette was granted permission to send him to another high school. She had never wanted him to go to Castlemont anyway. Now she had an excuse to get him transferred to Oakland Tech, a better school.

Annette suggested to her family that they go to therapy as a group, but no one else seemed keen on the idea. She knew she should go by herself anyway, but something more immediate always seemed to demand her attention—the hassles around her job, the threats that they might lose their house, Shannon's schooling. And there were the obvious financial considerations as well. Therapy, it seemed, would have to wait.

Kevin's death was affecting his siblings in different ways. According to Annette, Donald, Jr., at twenty-one the oldest of the five boys, seemed to enter a prolonged trance, for which he was ultimately hospitalized. He had never been much of a talker, but it was as if he went mute after his baby brother's death. "He couldn't function," Annette recalled later. "He wasn't responsive at all." Donald, Jr., would go for long walks in the middle of the night. At three or four in the morning, they'd find him standing where Kevin was killed, a picture of his little brother in his hand. That was *his* picture of Kevin, off limits to anyone else. If anyone so much as touched the photo, he would erupt. They had him admitted to the county hospital, but the doctors there didn't know what to say. There was nothing medically wrong with him. "You just have to hope he snaps out of it," one doctor told her.

Curtis avoided his parents' house as much as he could. The few times he spent the night there in the aftermath of Kevin's death he lay in bed unable to sleep, haunted by the thought that Kevin was going to reach down and touch him, as if his baby brother were a palpable spirit there in the room. Whenever he was there during the day, he was obsessed by the clock: this is when Kevin would be arriving home from school, this is when Kevin would be sitting in front of the television watching a favorite show. Out on the streets, he was like every other guy he knew, speaking casually about killing somebody without giving a thought to the impact of that kid's death on his parents, his siblings, and his extended family. He saw the pain his family—his mother especially—was experiencing, and almost immediately he began plotting his revenge. "I'm going to get them," he told his brothers. "I swear to it."

Shannon didn't speak much about Kevin after he was killed, and when he did it was a funny story he remembered or good times they had shared. He seemed to want to remember his brother only in a happy-go-lucky way. For a while, Annette was concerned that Shannon was reluctant to talk about the murder because the gunman had thought he was aiming at him. Several times she reassured Shannon that his brother's murder wasn't his fault, but he never responded one way or another when she broached this most ticklish of subjects. He revealed feelings of guilt to Curtis—said he wished it *had* been him they were aiming at—but mainly Shannon avoided the topic altogether. He stayed off by himself, his face stony, as if brooding over something. Shannon was plainly angry, though whether at himself or the murderer, no one could say. When his parents weren't around, he too spoke of revenge.

Everyone except Dermmell danced around Shannon in those first weeks after Kevin's death. The first time Dermmell saw Shannon swaggering around like he wasn't to be messed with, he lost it. "Because of you," he yelled at him, "our little brother is gone." Shannon gave it right back to Dermmell, confronting him about all of the fights he had been in. They got into an argument that Dermmell was afraid would turn physical, but he was satisfied with himself for opening his mouth. Someone had to state the truth, no matter how painful.

Dermmell was as impenetrable as Shannon. He didn't say much while his brothers spoke about revenge. He didn't offer to help them in their plans, nor did he try to talk them out of it. Dermmell kept his thoughts to himself, no matter how dangerous and ill-conceived they might be.

By the time Thiem caught up with the murder weapon, it was in a police property room, in a box with other weapons slated to be destroyed. More than two weeks had passed since it had been confiscated. Too many people had handled the gun to even hope for a decent fingerprint.

Equally frustrating was that the clip had been removed. Killers generally remember to wipe their fingerprints from a gun, but they often forget about the prints they've left on the clip that slips into the handle of a semiautomatic. Or the shooter remembers to wear gloves during the actual shooting but not when loading the gun. The clip, a smooth metal surface, provides an ideal element for a good print.

According to the police report Thiem had retrieved, the pistol had been discovered at around six in the evening the day after the murder. The rumor on Ninety-second Avenue that the gun was discovered by a Housing clean-up crew was wrong. An anonymous tipster had called the police about a man brandishing a pistol in front of the turnkey on Ninety-second Avenue. Several cops rushed to the scene. They found no man with a gun, but they searched the area anyway. That's how they discovered a Colt .45 semiautomatic pistol stuffed into an easy chair.

Coincidentally, the cop who discovered the pistol had been at the murder scene the night before. He was the cop who spotted the empty .45 casings in the street across from where Kevin and London lay. But this same cop turned the confiscated pistol in to the property room without giving a thought to the previous night's murder.

Thiem was frustrated, but he couldn't be too angry. He might have made the same mistake. With so many weapons throughout East Oakland, he could forgive a cop who discovered a .45 a dozen blocks from a murder in which a .45 had been used, even if less than twenty-four hours had elapsed between the murder and its discovery. If prior to learning that Jones lived at the same locale, he asked himself, would *he* have done anything with the information?

Thiem sent the pistol to the lab to see if he had the actual murder weapon in his possession. He also asked the lab to run the gun for prints, without much hope. He also spoke to someone at communications to find out a name, an address, or at the very least a phone number for the person who had called about a man brandishing a gun.

A few days after Thiem learned about the pistol, Junebug was at the Oakland International Airport with two friends. One was a guy named Paul, the other Aaron's brother Anthony. They were licking ice-cream cones in the snack shop when a cop assigned to the airport detail approached them.

"What are you doing here?" he asked them. "Eating ice-cream cones," they said. The cop asked their names. "What's the matter, is it against the law for a black man to sit here?" Junebug asked him. Junebug was wearing sweatpants, sneakers, and a T-shirt. "We *paid* for these cones," Junebug told the cop. He pointed to a middle-aged white man sitting at another table. "Are you going to go ask that dude what he's doing here?" he asked.

Junebug assumed that the cop had them pegged as drug dealers, but in fact, a woman had complained to a security guard about two black teens harassing her in the parking lot. One of the teens, she said, was wearing a yellow jacket and a white hat, the other a gray denim jacket. That described Paul and Anthony's outfits.

The cop had cause to detain Paul and Anthony but not Junebug, but he hauled all three of them to an airport security office to run them for warrants. Junebug gave a false name—said his first name was John but used Fat 'Tone's last name—but the cop found something on Junebug identifying him as John Jones. The cop arrested him on the charge of falsely identifying himself to a peace officer.

The false identification charge would be dropped, but it would be there in his record when, a couple of weeks later, Thiem ran John Jones through the computer to see what his main suspect had been up to. He ran background checks on Anthony and Paul. Paul, sixteen, had twice been arrested on drug charges; Anthony had served time in a California Youth Authority facility for drug dealing. Thiem tried to restrain himself when he noticed the address Anthony had given the arresting officer. He lived down the block from John Jones, where the likely murder weapon had been found and the faded green car sighted.

19

NIGHTMARES

As he had feared, the news was nearly all bad when Brian Thiem called the police lab about the pistol. You've got the murder weapon, a tech told Thiem, but every print can be traced to police department personnel. Thiem cursed his rotten luck. If there was a bright side to the snafu, at least it was another clue pointing to Ninety-second Avenue and John Jones.

Assembling a list of possible coconspirators was Thiem's next big task. He walked to the basement to speak with someone working in the crime analysis unit. In theory, the department has the name and address of any kid working a drug hot spot for any length of time. When the posse or the beat cops detain someone for whatever reason, whether they make an arrest or just run a kid through the computer, a "field contact" sheet is supposed to be written up noting the name, date of birth, the location of the stop, and the make and year of a car, if appropriate. The field contact is something of a consolation prize short of an actual arrest, but at times it can be an invaluable tool in cracking crimes more serious than drug dealing.

Criminal analysis's computer spit out five names from the fifteen hundred block of Ninety-second Avenue. Twice Junebug had been arrested there, but his name wasn't on the list. Nor was Aaron's or even Tony's, even though the previous year he too had been busted on a dope charge in front of the Ninety-second Avenue turnkey. Thiem had five more names on his list of suspects, though he was no closer to cracking his case.

Thiem's next big hope was the car. Since he had first spotted it, the department's daily hot sheet included a description of the car and a license plate number. He mentioned that it was wanted in connection with a drive-by, but he stressed that under no circumstance were they to mention murder. He wanted the car stopped and its occupants identified, nothing more.

"There is not enough to arrest Jones at this time," Thiem wrote, "but I need to find out who he associates with and who drives/rides in the car." His dream was that when a cop stopped the car, Jones and his accomplices in the murder would be inside.

Meanwhile, Thiem dropped by to talk with Wilber White, the registered owner. White said he had sold his Chrysler Newport for $290 several months earlier, to a friend of one of his daughters. There was no paperwork consummating the deal, so White didn't have the buyer's exact name or address. But he said he thought the guy's name was something like Kenneth Boggans, and he gave an approximate address.

Thiem and his partner spent whatever free time they had over the next few days looking for Boggans, but there seemed to be no one by that name living in Oakland or any of the surrounding towns. That Friday was their week on call, during which time they picked up several new murders. Thiem's log for the Reed case revealed that he didn't make a single entry in it during the second half of August.

Junebug spent much of July and August trying to chase away thoughts of the murder. He avoided driving by the corner of Auseon and Dowling altogether, but someone only had to mention Eighty-seventh Street, or Bancroft, or he had only to catch a glimpse of a street sign for Auseon, and he'd be transported back to the night of the murder. Just seeing 'Tone or Aaron would do the same.

Junebug kept a copy of the *Tribune* article reporting Kevin's death in a dresser drawer. Even a corner of the newspaper peeking out from underneath his clothes would set his mind working. He'd hear the sound of the gun firing, he'd see the muzzle flash. He'd think, too, of the smiling, sweet-faced shot of Kevin in the newspaper. It was as if that picture had been branded onto his brain.

Junebug kept dreaming the same dream. He'd be running, though from no one or nothing specific. Somehow he'd end up at a house, standing among a group of people. The group is mourning the death of a boy, though no one knows why the boy has been killed or who killed him. Sometimes Kevin would be the first thing he thought of when he opened his eyes.

Junebug felt he was becoming more serious about life, though he hadn't decided to go straight. He was drinking and smoking less than before the murder, but if anything he was more heavily into dealing than ever. There was no connection to the murder, though; his increase was rooted in the bad blood between him and Fat 'Tone dating back to the carjacking. Weeks before he had heard the name Kevin Reed, he had decided to find a new supplier. He was now selling stuff he bought through his uncle Ben, whose products included crack but also powdered coke and heroin.

He sold drugs pretty much around the clock through much of the summer. He slept late in the mornings and gave himself Saturday nights off, and that was about it for breaks. Sometimes he'd sell on Ninety-second Avenue, but increasingly he sold over on Ninety-eighth with some guys he knew. Selling these other products raised the stakes, and he was that much more vulnerable to rivals, but he rationalized it this way: It doesn't matter, because I'm going to hell anyway.

Junebug was floored when his uncle Ben one day confronted him about the murder in which he was involved. "How do you know?" he stammered. "See, that's my point right there," Ben said. "I'm not supposed to know, but I do." Junebug didn't bother denying it. He told him the truth, or at least enough of the truth to make his culpability plain.

Junebug understood that he'd go to jail if he was caught, but he had been figuring that 'Tone would be the one serving heavy time. His heart nearly stopped when his uncle told him that the penal code allowed a

DA to slap a murder charge on *anyone* involved in a homicide; each person is equally culpable under California law. It makes no difference whether you pulled the trigger or shut your eyes when the shooting began. There are exceptions, of course, but not in a drive-by. In a drive-by, if the DA thinks he can prove that you had knowledge of the gun, then you're getting charged with murder one, premeditated murder.

Junebug also thought that if he wasn't caught by the day before his eighteenth birthday, he might turn himself in. As he understood it, if the cops caught you before you turned eighteen, you were automatically tried as a juvenile. Ben cleared up that misconception as well. For one thing, it's your age when you committed the crime, not when you're caught. For another, the only ones then automatically tried as a juvenile in California were kids fifteen or younger. If you're sixteen or seventeen (Junebug was sixteen), Ben told him, it's pretty much automatic nowadays that you're tried as an adult if the charge is murder.

Ben was at his sister's place watching the news when he told her that her son had been involved in a homicide—just blurted it out without any preamble.

Ann's brother was always inventing some crazy tale, especially when he was high or drunk—someone's out to kill him, or so and so was after him, but he pulled his piece and the guy won't dare show his face again—so she didn't give his comment a second thought. He had been drinking that day, and to her mind, this was just another of his cockamamy stories.

Junebug began the new school year thinking this might be the semester he turned over a new leaf. Yet his first day back ended with an experience that left him wondering if he ever wanted to show his face at Castlemont again.

After school a pair of girls Junebug recognized waved him over to a blue Suzuki. He sauntered over, feeling cocksure. When he reached the car, a kid he didn't recognize popped up from the backseat. Junebug's first thought was that he was a dead man.

"Didjoo know my brother Kevin?" The kid was bigger and older than he was. He had him dead to rights if revenge was his aim. He didn't know who the kid was, except he knew exactly what Kevin he was referring to. Later he found out that the guy's name was Curtis Reed.

"What you talking about?"

"You know who I'm talking 'bout."

Junebug froze. The episode probably lasted less than thirty seconds, but it felt like forever to Junebug. He said that he didn't know any Kevins. It wasn't much of a ploy, but he didn't know what else to say. He imagined himself lying in the gutter leaking blood from a bullet hole, but then the girl behind the wheel hit the gas and squealed away.

Once he stopped shaking, a serene feeling descended upon him. He felt strangely safe. Curtis had not made a move, but he had exposed himself. Junebug now had an advantage, if it ever got to that point. He knew what Curtis looked like and probably had a make on his car as well.

The thing Curtis couldn't get out of his head was how certain he was that the kid he was staring at was the same Junebug people were telling him had had something to do with his brother's murder. He had never laid eyes on him before, was just going by physical description alone, but he was certain this was the kid. Every fiber of his being told him so, even as he was still trying to make up his mind. A rage so fierce overcame him that he could barely speak. It took every bit of strength he could muster to ask one of the girls to call out "Junebug" to see if the kid came over to the car. Of course he did.

Curtis leaned close to the car door so Junebug couldn't see that he had a gun in his hand. He read the fear in Junebug as if he had suddenly been bestowed with a gift that allowed him to see into other people's souls. "Shoot. Don't shoot. Shoot. Don't shoot," he said to himself like he was playing a deadly version of "she loves me, she loves me not" inside his head. "Shoot. Don't shoot." He barked "drive off" to the girl behind the wheel and then wondered how he happened to make that choice. If he played the same scene over again, he figured he was as likely to shoot that second time as decide against it.

He asked the girl behind the wheel to drop him off at a friend's place. He told his friend Moosie what was up, and Moosie said he was game. Curtis removed his shirt and put on a wig. He got into the backseat of Moosie's car and headed off to where he had heard Junebug lived. He saw several guys hanging around outside at Ninety-second Avenue and Holly Street, but not Junebug. He thought about getting out of the car anyway and shooting every last one of them. This happened to him several times in the months after Kevin was killed. He would get so worked up about revenge he would start crying. The scary part is that when he got like that, he wanted to shoot anybody to silence the rage he felt inside himself.

This time common sense took hold of him. There would be a next time, though. Somehow he learned that the real culprit was a kid named Fat 'Tone. He'd keep an eye out for Junebug, but this big kid everyone called 'Tone would be his main target.

In the days after the murder, Fat 'Tone had moped around, as if in shock. He snapped out of it after a week or two, and then wished he could retreat back into the fog that had descended on him in the days after the murder. Kevin Reed was never far from his thoughts.

He tried convincing himself that he had been only remotely involved in Kevin's murder. It had been Junebug's business, so it was Junebug's fault. He didn't even know the kid. He couldn't have killed a thirteen-year-old boy, he told himself, because he wasn't *capable* of such an act. Sometimes he admitted to himself what he had done but tried rationalizing it away. He had been high and drunk that night, in no state to handle a gun. That had been the old 'Tone. The new 'Tone was smarter and more levelheaded in his approach to life.

He smoked less pot, because marijuana made him paranoid, but he seemed to be drinking more. He felt doomed. He kept thinking about his stupidity around the gun. Every day he expected Five-O to come crashing through his door with their pistols drawn.

He had always believed himself invincible when slangin' rock outside his grandmother's apartment; now he felt as if a bull's-eye had been painted on his chest. A blue Suzuki started cruising their corner. Word had it that the driver was one of the Reed brothers. He started hanging outside less, even though it cut into his profits. As much as

Tony feared the cops, he was more worried about the Reeds and retribution.

He took to carrying a gun whenever he left the house. In the past, he rarely walked around strapped because a turf gun seemed more prudent. One never knew when Five-O might surprise them, and a gun bust was worse than getting caught holding some rock. But a concealed weapon charge was the least of 'Tone's worries in the summer of 1990. Some days he felt so paranoid he kept his "nine"—a Tec-9—hidden beneath his jacket. Later he would admit it was crazy to be carrying a nine at the same time he was trying to convince himself that he was incapable of murder. Yet most people who kill somebody have long before convinced themselves that carrying a gun doesn't mean they are fit to *kill* anybody.

Aaron and Junebug, once the best of friends, drifted apart. Once inseparable, by mid-August they barely saw each other anymore. For Aaron, Junebug was a bad reminder of all that had happened.

Aaron was spending most of his time with a girl down the block named Regina. They truly cared for each other, Aaron would say later, but he confessed a tie between the murder and his blooming relationship. For one thing, he could no longer stand to be alone. For another, there was the advantage of geography. When about a month after the murder Regina moved downtown, Aaron jumped at the chance to place some miles between him and Ninety-second Avenue.

Regina and Aaron were practically living together by the start of that school year. For a while Aaron's mother, Doreatha, was none the wiser. When she wasn't at work, she was busy caring for her mother, who was suffering from Alzheimer's disease. Doreatha moved with Aaron's baby sister into her mother's house and left her sons on Ninety-second Avenue because there wasn't enough room at her mother's place. Also, she figured they were old enough to look after themselves.

When Doreatha was unsuccessful in reaching Aaron a few nights in a row, in a panic she called area hospitals and the police. Only then did she learn from one of her other sons that Aaron had been living downtown with his girlfriend for months.

■ ■ ■

Rick—the same Rick Bradley who had taken the fall for the carjacking that also landed Junebug in juvie for a month—knew there was something up with his friend Aaron. The happy-go-lucky kid he liked having around him was suddenly moody and preoccupied. "What's up with you?" he'd ask him. But Aaron would say something like, "I ain't tripping off nothin', man."

Rick was older than Aaron and something of a mentor to him. Rick shared with him the dos and don'ts of surviving the streets. Aaron could fool other people, but not Rick. Rick kept pushing; Aaron finally broke down. "Check this out," he began. On a long walk that lasted late into the night, Aaron told Rick everything that had happened.

After Aaron's confession, Rick rebuked him for letting all of this happen without ever making up his own mind how far he was willing to go. He also couldn't believe that Aaron had let himself get mixed up with Fat 'Tone. "You know if 'Tone gets caught, he's giving you up," he told Aaron.

Rick let his young friend know that he was down for him no matter what, but by then Aaron was too far gone into himself to take solace from his friend's offer. He kicked himself for getting messed up with the likes of Tony Davis. He hadn't done anything wrong, he had been telling himself, but then he hadn't acted right, either.

Not long after he had revealed the truth to Rick, Aaron confessed to his mother and to his two brothers. Aaron didn't so much blurt out the truth as own up to the clues that he and others were leaving.

Anthony's first hint came while he was hanging around on Ninety-second. John Banks handed him a back copy of the *Tribune* and told him to read the article reporting on Kevin Reed's murder. Anthony just looked at John, uncomprehending.

Other clues presented themselves. Anthony began noticing how people on Ninety-second were acting differently, not quite themselves. Everyone was buzzing about a blue Suzuki somehow connected to Fat 'Tone, Junebug, and Aaron. Anthony raised the subject with his brother when they were both at their grandmother's house.

"What?" Aaron was stunned. By that time he was no longer hanging around Ninety-second, so Anthony was telling him something he didn't know. As fate would have it, their mother happened to enter the room just as Anthony was saying that someone seemed to be looking for Aaron. Aaron tried sloughing them both off, but he ended up confessing to both that same day.

Doreatha Estill had figured that something was up ever since Anthony mentioned to her that Aaron hardly drove his old wreck of a car anymore. One day it was the most important thing in his life, the next it was a pile of junk. When she asked Aaron about it, he said he just didn't feel like driving it anymore. She didn't really care one way or another, but the illogic of it all gnawed at her.

Doreatha and Aaron were at a grocery store in San Leandro when her son told her what had happened. Her first thought was disbelief. She couldn't quite conceive of Fat 'Tone shooting the boy she had read about in the paper. She felt a great fatigue wash over her. "He actually shot somebody," she said. "That fool actually shot a thirteen-year-old?

"You're going to have to face up to what you did one way or another," Doreatha told Aaron. "You might as well do it now on your own and get it over with." Yet that was the last time she would discuss the murder with Aaron for months. She never thought of telling Ann Benjamin, she would say later, because she figured that was Junebug's business. She didn't really know 'Tone's grandmother except by sight, so she wasn't going to tell Vera what she knew. And, of course, although she knew that Aaron never took her up on her suggestion to turn himself in to the police, she said that with everything else going on in her life, "I didn't think anything more about it."

In early September, Annette Reed received a call from a friend who had always been especially fond of Kevin. She was calling with bad news of her own. Her thirteen-year-old nephew, Odell, had become Oakland's latest homicide victim.

Odell had been hanging around with a small group of kids down the street from his house the previous Saturday night. At around eight o'clock, someone walked up to Odell and shot him in the head with a .32. Odell's death was reported in a weekend roundup appearing on page five of Monday's newspaper. So many thirteen-year-olds were getting gunned down in Oakland that year, it seemed another's death was no longer page-one news, even in the Oakland *Tribune.*

"Oh, Annette, I know how hard it's been on you, but it would help my sister so much if you could call."

She knew what she was supposed to say, but Annette felt in no position to help anyone. Some mornings she considered it a victory if she could just get out of bed and get dressed. She had creditors on the phone and the fate of the house hanging over her head. Donald wanted to fight for the house, but Annette figured that foreclosure would be just as well. Losing it seemed the easiest solution.

Annette knew it would have been simpler to jot down the number and then never call, but she told her friend no, even though that meant letting down someone who had been there for her in the past couple of months. But the truth was this: about the only wisdom she could have imparted to Odell's mother was that you'll feel so lousy that the very idea of talking to a woman who just lost *her* baby frightens you to the point that you just want to stay in bed.

The thing that ate away at Dermmell was how easy it was to get a gun. He had avoided guns his entire life, but it was as if obtaining a piece in East Oakland was something you picked up without paying any attention. He paid fifty bucks for the thing, if that.

Dermmell wouldn't remember how he learned that a kid named Fat 'Tone had killed his brother. It might have been from his brothers or it could've been from his friend John Banks. That might have been how he found out where 'Tone lived. Banks had always been plugged in so that he knew stuff like that.

'Tone lived a half dozen blocks from the Reeds' house. Dermmell stashed the gun in the gym bag that was to be his ticket out of the inner city. He figured that the hardest part would be the wait, but it wasn't long before Fat 'Tone showed himself.

20

DERMMELL AT
THE CROSSROADS

Two months elapsed before Thiem could again take up his search for
the true owner of the 1967 Newport. He and his partner had caught
three new cases in the interim, including a messy love triangle involving
two ex-cons and a girlfriend who wouldn't cooperate with Thiem until
he threatened to charge her as an accessory to murder. On October 9,
after a quick bag lunch at his desk, he picked up where he had left off on
the Reed murder, with the approximate name and address of the car's
next owner after Wilber White.

On a hunch or maybe out of desperation, Thiem knocked on the
door of the older woman who lived at the address White had given him.
When he spoke to her before, she told Thiem that she'd lived there since
1980, but she knew no Kenneth Boggans or anyone by a similar name.
Since his last visit, though, she had received two pieces of mail
addressed to a Kenneth Boggans. The first was a notice for an unpaid
parking ticket. The second was a letter from Thiem's own department,
dated only a few weeks earlier. It notified Boggans that his car had been
towed as an abandoned vehicle.

Thiem might have cursed his luck again, but he was grateful that the
news wasn't worse. According to the notice, he had caught up with the
car less than two weeks before the police were scheduled to junk it as

scrap metal. So much for his hope that his coconspirators would reveal themselves driving around the neighborhood.

Thiem located the car at Rube and Dan's Towing in East Oakland. The car was missing three tires. The fourth was flat. The backseat was strewn with the balled-up leavings of numerous fast-food meals. About the only clue that seemed to jump out at Thiem was a phone message that read, "Rocky—from Cable Oakland for Tony to buy car." The message included a phone number, but that led to nothing but a few hours tracking down the wrong people.

Thiem requested that the car and its assorted leavings be dusted for prints, but he wasn't very optimistic. He was more likely to waste his time pursuing a fast-food worker with a criminal past than to add another suspect to his list.

Thiem figured that his next-best avenue for tracking down the car's owner was Wilber White's daughter Rosalind. Rosalind confirmed that she had hooked her father up with a man she knew as Kenny Boggans, but she could offer Thiem little more information than her father had already told him. She said she really only knew him through her cousin Erica. She had two numbers for Erica, both of which she gave to Thiem.

The woman who answered the first number said her sister Erica didn't live there and then hung up without so much as a good-bye. The second number proved to be the correct one. Erica said the man's name was Kenny Bogan, not Boggans. He was six feet seven inches tall (Wilber White had described him as five feet eleven) and around twenty-five years old. Erica said Bogan could be found living with either a sister on Ninth Avenue or his grandmother on Holly—the same address that White had given him.

Thiem tried Kenneth Bogan's name in every database he knew, but Bogan apparently had no criminal past, no driver's license, no telephone number, no anything. Suspecting that she was the grandmother that Erica referred to, Thiem again spoke with the woman who had given him the towing notice. For the third time she denied knowing him.

Meanwhile, Thiem turned his attention to a woman named Vivian Ferguson, who lived in the building next to John Jones's. Whoever had called 911 the day after the murder to report a kid with a gun had phoned from her apartment. (The 911 system registers a caller's phone number, even if that person requests anonymity, and then records the conversation.) Ferguson denied having made the call, saying that any number of people use her phone, so Thiem requested a tape of the 911 call. If the voice was distinctive enough, he'd have his caller. Five weeks after he put in his request, he would get his tape.

Vivian wasn't home when Thiem stopped by with a copy of the tape, but a woman in an adjoining apartment was. She told Thiem the voice on the tape sounded like Vivian to her. Thiem slipped a business card under Ferguson's door asking her to phone him immediately.

On his way back to his car, Thiem noticed two young men standing in the driveway in front of the Ninety-second Avenue turnkey. One told him his name was Patrick Jones, the other Tony Davis. Davis told Thiem he lived with his grandmother in the back unit. Thiem asked him about the faded green Chrysler parked in front of his building for a while. No, he had no idea who owned the car. Yes, he knew John Jones, lived a couple of doors down, but he hadn't seen him in a while. Thiem spoke to several other people, but none of them seemed to know any more than Tony had about the car.

Ferguson phoned Thiem the next morning. He played the tape for her, but she denied that it was her voice. "Sounds like my sister," Vivian said. She had been living with her at the time but had subsequently moved. No, she didn't have a phone number, but she assured Thiem that she'd track her sister down and get back to him with a number.

Thiem phoned her three days later. No luck, Vivian told him. He called again four days later. "Still trying," she said. This time Thiem didn't ask so much as order her to get him a phone number.

That was on October 23. Thiem's next log entry was dated December 20, and that was only to note a returned phone call from someone with the state's fingerprint-matching bureau. More than two months after Thiem had filled out the requisite paperwork, the state had found a match between a piece of paper in the abandoned 1967 Newport and

Anthony Torrence—Aaron's brother. The next notation in Thiem's log was from February 5, sixteen weeks after his last conversation with Ferguson. His case load in the interim included a triple homicide, a gang slaying, and a body found in a thicket of bushes along a busy Oakland street. During that time, he never heard back from Vivian Ferguson, but then he didn't call her again, either.

Leon was a guy on the block who scratched out a living working on cars. "You want to sell that car of yours?" he asked Aaron one day late in the summer. Aaron agreed without hesitation. "Do whatever you want with it," he said.

Leon parked the car around the corner. He had told Aaron he was buying it for the engine, but as it turned out, he needed an air jack to remove it. The car sat there until it was towed.

About a week after it had been removed, Leon asked Aaron, "You do something in that car?" A homicide cop had just been around asking about it. "You sell me a hot car, boy?"

"We did a little dirt in it," Aaron told him, cool but ambiguous.

"Well, what you want me to do?" Leon asked him. He owned the car, but it was Aaron's headache.

"Whatever you want, man," Aaron said. "As far as I'm concerned, you can burn the thing."

Junebug couldn't get out of his head something John Banks had said to him. Banks just sidled up to him one day and told him, "Somebody be looking around here for a tall skinny dark kid with high cheekbones." He was describing Junebug to a tee.

Junebug didn't let on that he much cared one way or another, reluctant to reveal even a trace of fear. Was homicide looking for him or was it one of Kevin's brothers? he wondered.

Signs of pending doom were everywhere. A friend told him about a couple of homicide cops showing his mug shot and asking about Aaron's car. He even heard from a guy he barely knew—someone who didn't real-

ize Junebug's involvement in the crime—that some fool named Fat 'Tone
had killed a thirteen-year-old boy in a drive-by that previous summer.

It was beginning to seem as if *everyone* in the neighborhood knew
that one or another of them had had a hand in the murder. Aaron figured they were on America's most wanted list. Junebug again contemplated turning himself in, but once more he told himself he'd deal with
whatever awaited him if and when the cops caught him.

One night around Halloween 1990, Curtis Reed and a couple of his
friends sat in a car parked outside Fat 'Tone's apartment building. Curtis
sat in the backseat, a gun by his side. He cursed his rotten luck when
'Tone appeared with his girlfriend and his girlfriend's baby (by a previous boyfriend). Curtis knew the girl from the neighborhood—Tonette
was her name. He calmed himself down; told himself to be patient. He
knew all too well the pain of killing an innocent bystander.

He told his friend to follow 'Tone and his small family as they drove
to a costume party maybe ten blocks away. 'Tone parked his car, apparently clueless that he was being followed. His back was to the street,
giving Curtis his chance. Curtis pulled out his gun. But as he was getting out of the car, a police car turned onto the street. It was as if the
police cruiser appeared at the very moment his foot touched the
ground. There had been a fight at the party and somebody had called
the cops.

Again Curtis was so pumped up with rage that he found himself crying. His friends tried talking him out of revenge, but he wasn't listening.
He fantasized about pumping so many bullets into 'Tone that 'Tone's
own mother wouldn't recognize him lying in the casket. He thought that
maybe he should forget about his friends and go cruising for 'Tone with
his brothers. He'd take 'Tone down first with a single shot, then they'd
each take a turn putting a bullet into him as he lay on the ground
writhing in pain.

Yet it seemed every chance Curtis got at 'Tone, somebody or something intervened. Like the time he was stopped at a traffic light and he
turned his head for a moment to see 'Tone at a nearby car wash. The

light turned green, the drivers behind him honked their horns, but Curtis couldn't hear anything, that's how stunned he was. Curtis usually had a gun on him back then, but of course he was without a piece on that afternoon. He made a U-turn and flew home to grab a pistol, but 'Tone was gone by the time he got back.

That's the way it went. After that, he told himself not to go anywhere without his piece, but he wouldn't get another chance at 'Tone. He'd get caught up in troubles of his own that would render Tony Davis the least of his worries.

In the fall of 1990, Junebug's sister Keisha was to enter the tenth grade at Skyline High, but a few weeks before her graduation from Bret Harte Junior High, a Castlemont counselor gathered together Keisha and about twenty other kids from the flatlands. She informed them that the district knew they were attending the wrong school, and every one of them would be attending Castlemont come fall.

Unlike Junebug, Keisha had been eager to attend classes at Skyline, which was created in the early 1960s so that parents in the hills had a high school of their own. Keisha had thrived at Bret Harte. Her grades had been good; she had found her social niche. Keisha would later describe that day the Castlemont counselor busted them as maybe the worst of her young life.

Keisha feared Castlemont even before she stepped foot in its hallways. The way people on the block spoke, the influences infecting the school were so bad that a decent education was impossible. Her first weeks at school didn't contradict her preconceptions. Every class was the same. Kids spoke nonstop, even as the teacher was trying to teach. They got up midclass and walked out without a word. Others lay there with a cheek against the desk, apparently asleep. She mainly kept to herself, because making friends brought about its own perils.

Some students spoke to the teachers without a trace of respect. She didn't know whether to blame the kids for their attitude or the teachers for putting up with it. Bret Harte's teachers were generally eager to teach; at Castlemont several of her teachers seemed to have given up.

It got so bad that Keisha would wake up dreading school. Some days she'd leave campus for lunch and not return. Other days she didn't go at all. This former honor student ended up with a report card filled with incompletes.

Anyone doubting the savage inequalities between districts would have to consider Keisha's performance once her mother arranged for her daughter to live with a friend in the suburban town of Vallejo. Back in a school with classrooms she would describe as "quiet and not chaotic," presided over by teachers who were "nice" and "attentive," she once again thrived.

For years Ann Benjamin thought about getting back into the church, but it always struck her as one more dilemma to solve. It wasn't just which church, but first which denomination—indeed, which religion. Not for all the money in the world would she join the church of her youth. Yet that left her with so many options she felt dizzy.

In the fall of 1990, Ann found herself on her knees in her bedroom, praying to God for guidance. It hadn't been an especially bad time, but there were very few good times in her life then. "I want to believe," she said aloud, "but I don't know where to turn." She was awaiting a sign.

The timing of the Seventh Day Adventist revival not far from where she lived might have proved enough to make her a true believer—the flyer announcing the event arrived within days of her plea. But the fact that the flyer quoted Revelation removed any doubt she might have had. She had always been intrigued by this book of the New Testament but its true meaning had eluded her.

Junebug didn't know what to make of his mother's sudden spiritual transformation. In a neighborhood where religion was paramount in so many people's lives, his mother had always stood out as an agnostic. Yet he was intrigued just the same. He joined his mother for services one Saturday and liked what he heard, especially the sermon. The preacher was a young man who spoke frankly of his drug use before he saw the light. Fate, Junebug believed, had drawn him to the church on this particular Saturday to hear this particular sermon.

There was a lot he'd never liked about grinding. It bothered him that they sold in the late afternoons and evenings even though there were always younger kids around. He couldn't stand his customers, whom he saw as beneath him. He treated them with respect because it made good business sense, but he felt like yelling, "Why don't you *do* something with your life?" And now he had a murder hanging over his head.

"If God could change around this guy's life," Junebug told himself, "I know God can change mine." Like that, he vowed to give up grinding for good. He'd live a righteous life, thereby atoning for his sins without the inconvenience of a long prison sentence.

Salvation of a different variety came into Ann Benjamin's life as 1990 was coming to an end. After years of working the second shift at the post office, she had saved enough money to move off Ninety-second Avenue. Moving meant another set of hassles when life already seemed overwhelming, but this was one headache she was happy to suffer through. That December, she and her four kids, including Junebug, moved into a little community tucked behind the eucalyptus trees that skirt Mills College. The house she rented was small for a family of five, but it was miles from the madness of East Oakland.

Junebug had always vowed that if his mother ever moved, he would rent his own place or move in with a friend. By December of 1990, though, he was eager to be far away from Ninety-second Avenue, and not just because of his sudden spiritual awakening. The truth was that between Kevin Reed's brothers and the cops, he felt like a sitting duck anytime he stood outside.

Ann felt happy and at peace for the first time in years. She had finally liberated herself from Ninety-second Avenue, finding a home to start building a new life. Her relationship with Junebug, after an extended and uneasy detente, was blossoming into something special. Every Saturday, Junebug joined Ann and his siblings for the church's regular services. He even became a semiregular at the church's Tuesday night prayer meetings. Among the thoughts she allowed herself in those heady first few months in their new home was that her perseverance may well have saved her eldest son from the fate of so many young black men in East Oakland.

Sometime in the fall of 1990, 'Tone awoke from the prolonged stupor that had descended on him in the months after the murder. Later he would date his reawakening to his repair of a 1972 Monte Carlo that he had bought around the time of the murder. As he would recall it, the time before he had the car was a black-and-white world darkened by dread and depression. After that he was somebody who at least resembled his old self.

The car had broken down while he was still in a fog over the murder. It sat in front of his aunt's apartment, a reminder of how lousy his life had become. The old 'Tone might have abandoned the thing, but instead he had the engine fixed, had the dents banged out, and brought it in to have it painted and pinstriped. He installed a phat stereo system that let you *feel* the music and lectured his friends against treating it like another hubba car. 'Tone felt no less proud than if he had saved his money one dollar at a time.

He'd get behind the wheel, his friends would pile in, and he would be the man in charge. To his mind, after months of trying to render himself invisible, with his fixed-up Monte Carlo, he was again someone to be noticed.

He continued to live in fear, of course—in fear of the Reeds and the fear born of knowing the cops were after him. The first time homicide came around, he was hanging around his grandmother's place with his friend Patrick. The cop was real straight, dressed in a sport jacket and tie, polite and formal but nosy and pushy just the same. He was with Patrick again when he saw this same cop drive by on Ninety-second Avenue. "Man, what's this pig want?" he asked Pat—but of course he knew exactly why Thiem would be asking about Junebug and about Aaron's car.

'Tone continued to slang rock on Ninety-second Avenue, but he told himself he was different now, more mature and more serious. No more stomping on customers, no matter what they did or what his mood. No more shooting a gun because he was stoned and wanted to feel the juice that came with watching everyone jump. He told himself he wouldn't be the same badass who refused to back down from anyone for any reason. The last thing he needed was a funk with a rival crew, forcing him to contemplate using a gun again.

'Tone thought about giving up grinding altogether, but that meant either going back to school or finding an honest job at chump wages. He never entertained the idea seriously.

'Tone felt a constant urge to confess to someone other than his aunt Paula, but the words always failed him. He wanted to tell two people in particular, his sister Angela and his girlfriend Tonette. The conversation with both went about the same:

"I may have to go to jail."

"What? What? Why?"

"Don't worry nothing about it."

"What you do?"

"Man, don't sweat it. It ain't nothing, just something I may have to do some time for."

And as abruptly as he had brought it up, he would drop it. 'Tone's vague hints didn't surprise his sister. While she didn't know what it was that was ailing him, she knew something was up.

Demmmell Reed stared at this kid they called Fat 'Tone, his mind a jumble of thoughts. He contemplated the life he might be taking and he thought about Kevin. He thought about the way his baby brother used to look up to him. Kevin had probably been his biggest fan when he was playing football. "My brother's going to end up in the NFL one day," Kevin would boast to all his friends. Demmmell knew that if he actually pulled the trigger, he'd never amount to anything but maybe the best defensive back in his cell block. He heard the voices of people bemoaning his fate: He could've been this, he could've been that.

Killing Fat 'Tone, he decided, would only double the pain his mother and the rest of the family were feeling. There on Ninetieth Avenue, across from Paula's apartment, he vowed he'd dedicate himself to schoolwork. "Kevin used to love school," he reasoned. "He's not getting a chance to go anymore. Why don't I finish up for him?"

■ ■ ■

Like a recovering cocaine addict who tells himself a couple of sociable toots couldn't hurt, Junebug reentered the world of grinding gradually, an hour or two at a time. He wasn't really getting back into it, he told himself, just earning a bit of pocket money, but it wasn't long before slangin' rock became an all-night thing again. He fell back into it as deeply as ever.

He attended Saturday services with his family as if nothing had changed. He wasn't the same gung-ho believer he had been for a time, but he did continue to read his Bible. Deep down he recognized that he was a hypocrite, but he told himself that he knew plenty of other kids were no better.

Like 'Tone, Junebug told himself he would approach his selling in a more adult fashion. He now had a plan, inspired by a conversation with his uncle Ben. Ben was encouraging him to think about grinding as his ticket out of East Oakland. Junebug had always dreamed of work as a rap producer, so he told himself that when he put away twenty thousand dollars, *then* he'd give up dealing for good.

Early in 1991, Junebug moved in with his mother's friend so that he, like his sister, could attend school in Vallejo. He didn't have much choice— he had been suspended from Castlemont after intentionally bumping into a teacher in a crowded hallway—but he believed that the move was for the best. Like Aaron, he seized this chance to escape the life he had been living.

It felt good being in Vallejo. Life seemed calmer than it had at any point since the murder. He quit grinding. He started taking school seriously again. This sprawling suburb forty minutes from Oakland was the kind of place where bad things happened, but it was also a community in which trouble found you only if you were looking for it. It was quieter and more peaceful than Oakland, a simpler world to negotiate.

His urban credentials won him the instant respect of his fellow students. But he fell back into his old habits about a month after moving to Vallejo, on the occasion of his seventeenth birthday.

He hadn't been on Ninety-second Avenue in about a month, but he figured he'd commemorate the day in the proper fashion. They were drinking and smoking and they got to laughing hard, and suddenly Junebug missed his days kicking it on the corner. He had been considering applying for a job at a McDonald's in Vallejo. But now, back on Ninety-second Avenue, he asked himself why he would want to slave away at $4.25 an hour when money could be had so much more easily.

And so in April of 1991, almost one year to the day that 'Tone had squealed to the cops about the carjacking, Junebug was again hanging around with Fat 'Tone and the rest of the nine-deuce crew. Life was funny, Junebug said to himself. So much had happened in the intervening twelve months, yet here they were, pretty much back to the way things had been.

The day after he picked up the case of a forty-one-year-old Oakland woman found strangled to death in some bushes, Brian Thiem took his first serious look at the Reed file in more than three months. Thiem began by checking in on his prime suspects. "Let's see what Mr. John Jones has been up to lately," he said to himself, sitting at the computer terminal at the back of the homicide room. He typed in Anthony Torrence's name and, while he was at the keyboard, typed in Kenneth Boggans and Kenneth Bogan. Then he tried Kenneth Bogans. The sound in his head was something like a cash register ringing when a police record flashed on his computer screen.

Bogans was on parole after serving time on an auto theft, which meant that a parole agent would have a current address. Bogans wasn't at home when Thiem and his partner stopped by, but his mother was. She told them, yes, her son was driving a big green car at the start of last summer. They were barely back in their office when Bogans himself was on the phone. He promised to make it downtown as fast as he could.

Bogans said he'd bought the car in May, for $280, but then sold it sometime in June to a guy named Lance. Thiem, of course, wasn't surprised when Bogans told him he didn't have a last name or an address. What Bogans could tell him—that Lance hung out with a small crew at Eighty-seventh and MacArthur—made Thiem wonder if he hadn't wasted a lot of time focusing exclusively on Ninety-second Avenue, despite the anonymous tipster who'd said the kids responsible for the shooting hung around on MacArthur across from Castlemont High.

The Oakland Police Department's field contact system proved far more helpful in pointing Thiem to Lance than it had when he was looking for a listing of John Jones's potential cohorts. A printout of those operating around Eighty-seventh and MacArthur revealed a twenty-year-old named Lance who had been arrested on a dope-dealing charge several months before the murder. Thiem and his partner took two weeks tracking Lance to an apartment at Ninety-fourth and MacArthur.

Lance told Thiem he had bought the car for $150 the previous summer from a guy his sister knew. He probably hadn't owned it but a few weeks before this kid named Aaron offered him two hundred dollars. He didn't know Aaron's last name, he said, but he knew where he lived because Aaron's brother Anthony was a friend of his. Lance took them there, and Thiem's heart started racing.

Back at his office, Thiem grabbed Anthony Torrence's police record. There was no Aaron Torrence in his records, but Anthony's file revealed that his mother's last name was Estill. Thiem typed in Aaron Estill and found a match. Same address, same mother. He even allowed himself to think that he might have just tracked down the true owner of the car the night Kevin Reed was killed.

21

THROW AWAY
THE KEY

On March 21, 1991, more than eight months after he first heard the name John "Junebug" Jones, Brian Thiem rang the buzzer to Aaron Estill's apartment. No one was home, so Thiem stuck a business card through the mail slot. He didn't bother with a note because he'd found that his title alone was usually sufficient. Aaron found the card and crumpled it up, but Anthony saw it lying around. He gave it to his mother the next time he saw her.

Doreatha Estill's first thought was, Lord have mercy, who's been found dead with my name in their pocket. She didn't think it concerned Aaron because, as she said later, that "incident" the previous summer "had completely slipped my mind." She called Thiem immediately but was told he was on vacation until the second week in April. That left two weeks for Doreatha to stew anxiously.

For months Aaron had been letting on to his girlfriend Regina that he was in some deep trouble, but he always dropped only vague hints. "I'm going to be leaving and don't know when I'll be getting back" was about as specific as he ever got. After Thiem's visit to his apartment, he swallowed hard and told her what had happened the previous summer.

Regina was angry at first, but she came around. "We're going to get through this," she assured Aaron. They even spoke of running away together. From his mother and others he had gotten a speech; Regina, Aaron told himself, was acting more like family than his own family.

All of which made him damn the rotten timing of the murder. He had caught this case just as he was getting into something special with a girl for the first time in his life.

Thiem didn't mince his words when he finally hooked up with Doreatha over the phone. He wanted to talk to Anthony and Aaron about Aaron's car because he was pretty certain it had been used in a drive-by shooting the previous summer. Doreatha was equally frank. She told him that Aaron had admitted to her that he and the car had been involved in a shooting.

Thiem motioned to one of his cohorts to start the tape recorder that homicide keeps plugged into its phone lines. Tape recorders are to homicide investigators what service revolvers are to patrol cops: their main weapon for catching people. Thiem didn't let Doreatha know he was recording their conversation. The tape would be useless in court, but Thiem figured it might come in handy during the interrogation of her sons.

Doreatha told Thiem pretty much the story Aaron had told her: Her son was driving the car that night, but he swore he didn't know the other two had a gun with them. The other two kids involved were named Fat 'Tone and Junebug. According to her son, 'Tone was the shooter.

"If Aaron can come down here and tell me what happened and tell me the whole truth, he's gonna be a lot better off," Thiem said. "If Aaron doesn't cooperate, we might end up holding him equally responsible for the murder."

Doreatha readily agreed to bring both boys to police headquarters the next morning. Thiem asked her not to let on where they were headed because otherwise they'd have a chance to square their stories with the other suspects.

"I'll just tell them I got somewhere that I want them to go," she told Thiem.

■　■　■

Anthony woke Aaron from a dead sleep. "Mama wants you," he said.

"What?"

"She wants both of us. I don't know."

"Awright."

Doreatha Estill played it coy in the car ride down to police head-quarters. When they asked where they were going, she told them it was a surprise. Aaron's first guess was that they were going to Reno for the day. When it was obvious that they were heading downtown, Aaron said, "Tony, she's probably taking us to jail." All three of them laughed, but then Doreatha said, "I don't know about all that, but I am taking you to the police station."

"I ain't going in there," Aaron said when they pulled up in front of the police headquarters. "I ain't talking to nobody." His mother didn't put up much of an argument. She just said, "Aaron, they're on to you. You're going to have to talk to these people sooner or later, so you might as well do it now."

"Awright."

Thiem and his partner spoke with Anthony while Aaron and his mother fidgeted on some plastic chairs down the hall from the homicide room. Aaron kept thinking about his conversation with Rick. "You know if Fat 'Tone gets caught, he's gonna give you up," Rick had told him. Tony had already ratted out his friends Rick and Junebug. Why should he risk himself to save Fat 'Tone?

The two detectives spoke to Anthony for a couple of hours. They taped the last twenty minutes of their interrogation. He told them what little he knew—that someone or some kids had jumped Junebug; that Junebug enlisted Aaron and 'Tone so they could fight them; that the next thing Aaron knows, a gun's going off.

"Who did Aaron say started shooting?" Thiem asked him.

"Fat 'Tone," Anthony said.

"What did Aaron say Junebug wanted to do?"

"He was gonna get out and fight. Fight the dude that jumped him." Aaron hadn't told him much more than that, Anthony said, except that he felt bad because a "little boy and a girl" had been shot. He said that neither Junebug nor 'Tone had confided in him about the murder, although Junebug had warned him that he might not want to drive Aaron's car, because it was hot.

Thiem placed Aaron in the interrogation room. He sent Anthony and Doreatha home with the promise that he'd drive Aaron back to Ninety-second Avenue himself. Thiem and his partner sweated Aaron for a couple of hours before they started talking to him. Nearly two hours later, Thiem turned on a recorder so Aaron could give a taped statement.

Thiem began the recording the way he always does, with the Miranda drill, so he'll have on tape his suspect waiving his right to an attorney and his right to remain silent. Yes, he owned the Newport, Aaron said. Yes, he was driving it the night of the murder. At first it was just him and Junebug alone, but there were too many people to fight, so they drove over to 'Tone's. They went over to get Tony, he said, and also "some kind of stick or something."

Aaron denied that they went to 'Tone's place to get a gun. He said he had no idea that 'Tone had a gun in his pocket. Junebug, he said, told him and 'Tone that they were there only as a backup should anyone jump in while he was fighting. But the next thing he knows, 'Tone's ordering him to keep driving straight and he hears something like seven shots from the back of the car.

"I was just shocked," Aaron said. "I asked him why—why did you just do that? I was calling him names. I said, 'You's stupid for doing that.'" According to Aaron, 'Tone said nothing in response except, "Don't tell nobody."

Thiem didn't hold Aaron, despite his confession. He didn't believe Aaron when he said he didn't know about the gun, but arresting him meant he'd be assigned a lawyer. Once an attorney was involved, Thiem would never get Aaron to admit to knowledge of the gun. Be patient, Thiem told himself. He would talk to John Jones, then Tony Davis. He'd see what he could get from each kid to use against the other two.

About a week before he spoke with Thiem, Aaron ran into Junebug on Ninety-second Avenue. Aaron pulled him aside to pass along a message.

"Homicide's looking for us," he began. He told Junebug about the business card he had intercepted and then asked his friend for advice.

Junebug was more annoyed than thankful. He was working hard to chase away thoughts about the murder, and here Aaron was burdening him with his problems. Junebug shot his friend a disgusted look, as if to say, "Do I got to spell this out for you?" They had spoken several times about copping to the truth if the cops caught up with them, but Junebug was now intent on earning the twenty thousand dollars he figured he needed to become a rap producer. If a cop asks you a question, you deny everything. You offer as little as possible. You assume a silent pose or you make up a story, but the bottom line is you don't tell the truth.

Aaron didn't bother letting Junebug or 'Tone know that he had spoken to homicide. He knew it was only a matter of time before Thiem returned to arrest him, but he didn't go on a final binge. Instead he retreated even more into his life with Regina. He was feeling melancholy and interested in nothing except time alone with the girl he thought he might love. In a way, he felt more at ease than he had in months. The inevitable, it seemed, had released something within him resembling relief.

The day after talking to Aaron, Thiem knocked on the door to Ann Benjamin's new house. He introduced himself as a homicide detective, and Ann crossed her heart, bracing herself against tragic news. Thiem told her there was nothing to worry about, they were just there to speak with her son. Her eyes about popped out of her head. "No, no, no, ma'am, we just want to talk with him," Thiem assured her. "We know he didn't kill anybody, but we think he knows who did it."

The typical mother Thiem encounters tells him she hasn't seen her son for weeks when the truth is he's asleep in the back room. Ann, however, was as cooperative as Doreatha had been. John wasn't home, she said, but she promised to make sure he stayed home the next day.

Ironically, before coming home that night, Junebug stopped by for his regular Tuesday night Bible session. "If you end up in jail," the pastor said to the group that night, "it will still be alright." Junebug could have sworn the pastor was looking straight at him while he uttered that line.

Ann pleaded with Junebug the next morning not to go out, but Junebug was intent on visiting a girl he had just met and 'Tone was already on his way to pick him up. They headed over to Castlemont, but the girl wasn't there. Junebug asked 'Tone for a ride home, but 'Tone said he first needed to pick something up at his grandmother's place. Two cops from the posse were on them as soon as 'Tone pulled up in front of the turnkey. 'Tone never felt so relieved in his whole life when one of the cops said they were looking for John Jones on a probation violation.

The cops put Junebug in one of the sweat rooms, where he sat from three to seven o'clock. Thiem had no grand plan when he began his interrogation. He was dealing with kids. He figured they'd say whatever they chose to on tape and then he'd use his intellect to outwit them.

"Aaron's told us everything, so you might as well be honest with us, John," Thiem began.

Thiem and his partner spoke with Junebug for a couple of hours before taking a short break while Junebug went to the bathroom and drank a root beer. They turned on the tape recorder at 9:00 P.M.

Junebug told the story pretty much as Aaron had: He and Aaron drove by the corner of Auseon and Dowling, to fight two kids who had jumped him. There were too many of them, so they fetched Fat 'Tone. Junebug claimed he had no idea that Tony had a gun on him—never asked him to bring one, didn't know he had it until 'Tone was actually shooting. They drove past Auseon and Dowling once, and then again. On their second pass through, 'Tone asked if that was them right there. The next thing he knew, 'Tone was blasting from the backseat.

"I was in shock," Junebug said. "I said, 'Let's go, let's go. Let's get out of here.'" He said he heard between five and seven shots and saw one of the kids fall to the ground.

"Why didn't you stop and try to help that person, or go call an ambulance or something?" Thiem asked.

"'Cause everything happened so fast that—the first thing I wanted to do is just leave," Junebug said. "I just didn't want to be around everything. Then we didn't call the ambulances or nothing. I really don't know why we didn't call it in."

When Thiem asked him why he thought 'Tone might have started shooting, Junebug said, "He wanted to make it up to me because of an earlier incident. He said he did it to prove to me that he was still my friend."

Junebug claimed that he and Aaron had waited in the car when 'Tone went inside, presumably to get his gun, but Aaron had told them that Junebug had gone inside with 'Tone. Junebug said that Aaron must be mixed up, and Thiem dropped the point. He didn't press Junebug too hard because he didn't figure he needed to yet.

The first thing 'Tone noticed were the gun barrels pointed at his head. His first thought was that the Reed brothers were about to waste him. He was sitting in his car, letting it warm up, and thought this would be his inglorious final act. Then he noticed the uniforms. The cops made up some business about his car being involved in an accident, but the way they were pointing their .357s and .45s at him, he knew it wasn't about any hit and run.

Thiem had ordered his four-officer arrest detail to approach Fat 'Tone with their weapons drawn — routine procedure when arresting a suspect accused of a shooting. But after seeing his man in handcuffs, Thiem realized that he could have arrested him by himself.

"I could have walked right up to that guy and said, 'Tony, I'm the police, you're under arrest,' " Thiem said to his partner, "and he would have gone right along."

'Tone denied everything. He wasn't in the car the night of the murder. He didn't know of any drive-by shooting at Auseon and Dowling. But then Thiem told 'Tone that Aaron and Junebug had already told him what had happened. Thiem also fibbed, telling 'Tone that his fingerprints had been all over the gun. 'Tone revised his story.

Yes, he had been in the car that night, but he hadn't done the shooting. There was a fourth person in the car with them, a guy named Steve. Steve pulled the trigger. 'Tone couldn't tell them much about Steve — not his last name, not where he lived, only that he was a bad apple who had done some time in juvie for a stabbing the previous year. 'Tone said he was stunned when Steve suddenly started shooting.

On tape 'Tone described the shooting this way: "I didn't see anything, but I heard a girl scream. I said, 'What you doing? What you doing, man?' And he said, 'I didn't hit nobody.' " 'Tone said no one really liked Steve.

To account for his fingerprints on the gun, 'Tone said he had handled the .45 just before he, Steve, Junebug, and Aaron headed over to Auseon and Dowling. He'd held it without firing it, just to see what it felt like.

"What do you think Aaron would have said happened?" Thiem asked him.

"I don't think he would have told on Steve," 'Tone told the two detectives.

"Why?"

"'Cause I think he kind of like scared of Steve." Junebug would tell the truth about Steve, 'Tone said, because he wasn't frightened like Aaron.

'Tone was obviously lying, but Thiem still couldn't believe that this was his murderer. He kept asking 'Tone to speak up, he spoke so softly. 'Tone struck Thiem as an oversize and frightened kid, pathetic rather than aggressive or coldhearted. Most of the people he arrests for murder aren't murderers to his mind so much as people who've killed someone in a murderous moment. Only one in twenty of his suspects, he figures, are cold-blooded killers. 'Tone seemed as docile and unlikely a killer as he had came across.

Thiem left 'Tone alone to stare at the walls awhile. When he returned around two hours later, at 1:45 P.M., he was far more aggressive. He confronted 'Tone about the more obvious inconsistencies between his version of the event and Aaron's and Junebug's. In his log, Thiem wrote, "We told Davis that we knew that the shooting was from the right rear of the car while he said it was from the left rear, and that both Jones and Estill said he was the shooter. At about 1403 hours, he began crying, asking what was going to happen to him. He then said he would tell them the truth."

The cops don't keep the tape machine running throughout an interrogation, so what might have occurred to change 'Tone's mind is a matter of 'Tone's word against Thiem and his partner's. Thiem confessed that he'll employ just about any bluff to get the job done. He'll cajole, he'll raise his voice, he'll make claims he knows aren't true. "You'll make it easier on yourself if you tell the truth," he'll say, even though he knows that confessions make it easier only on the cops and the prosecutors.

He'll hint at the leniency a suspect will be granted if he confesses to his sins, although in reality, a confession weakens a defense attorney's bargaining power and therefore increases the likelihood that a defendant will receive a stiffer sentence.

To Thiem, any lie is permissible as long as it doesn't induce an otherwise innocent man to confess to a crime he did not commit. In his reading of the pertinent case law, telling someone that his prints were found on the murder weapon is OK because an innocent man would say bullshit, I never touched the gun. But telling a man it'll be the death penalty if he doesn't confess is forbidden, because when staring at the possibility of death row, fifteen to life might sway an innocent man to tell the cops what they want to hear. Thiem's other hard-and-fast rule is that an interview is over the moment a suspect requests a lawyer.

In 'Tone's version of those sixty-six minutes preceding his second taped statement, Thiem broke both of his cardinal rules. None of the twenty-some-odd "special circumstances" that allow a district attorney to seek the death penalty applied in this case. 'Tone didn't kill two or more people, nor did he commit the murder during the carrying out of a felony, such as a robbery or a rape. He didn't kill a police officer, use a mail bomb, or poison his victim. Yet 'Tone quotes Thiem telling him that confessing now might be the only way he would spare himself a death penalty conviction later. 'Tone also claimed that every time he asked for an attorney, Thiem would say something like, "Don't make this harder on yourself than you have to. We only want the truth."

Thiem, of course, denied ever mentioning the death penalty during his interview. He denied refusing 'Tone an attorney as well. "There's no way we would've kept talking to him if he asked for a lawyer," he said. "That's a clear violation of Miranda. If you ask for a lawyer, the interview is over." When pressed, he would say only that it was his word and his partner's against someone who had confessed to a murder.

Whatever happened in the preceding hour, 'Tone admitted in his second taped statement that there was no Steve in the car. I pulled the trigger, he admitted, I killed Kevin Reed. If anything, his voice sounded even smaller and thinner than it had during his first statement. The tape is full of slurping, as if 'Tone had been crying.

'Tone pointed an accusing finger at Junebug. Junebug had asked him to get the gun. He gave Junebug the gun when he got inside the car, but Junebug handed it back as they approached Auseon and Dowling. He says Junebug told him the gun had only a single bullet. "We ain't gonna kill nobody," he quoted Junebug as saying, "we just gonna scare 'em."

'Tone said he had meant to squeeze off one shot. He was aiming over everyone's head, but the gun jammed, so he squeezed it harder and then it was like he lost all control over the weapon. He squeezed the trigger only three times, although he heard the gun go off five or six times.

Thiem explained to 'Tone that a .45 semiautomatic pistol discharges a bullet only when you pull the trigger. It's not like an automatic, where if you simply keep the trigger depressed, the gun keeps firing until it's out of bullets.

"I was trying to jerk it back in the window, and it kept going off," 'Tone said in a pleading voice. "It was just going off. I pulled the gun—like as it was going off, I heard somebody scream, and was pulling the gun in the window, and I thought, 'Thought you said it only had one bullet.'

"You see, what it was is, when I heard this girl screaming, I like panicked, and I was just trying—seeing what was up with the gun, and it kept going off." So preoccupied was he with regaining control over the gun, he claimed, that he was no longer aiming after that first shot.

"You know that you hit three people out there," Thiem said. "I mean, that's pretty good shooting for someone that isn't aiming."

"I—I wasn't aiming. I was not aiming. I was not aiming. I—I'm—I told you all the truth, and I'm not fit to start lying now. I was not aiming. I was not aiming."

Thiem said, "Tony, I believe you, I just have to ask those difficult questions sometimes. 'Cause that's what some people might ask me, OK? Is there anything else here that we didn't ask you that you feel might be important?"

"That I didn't want no—I didn't—I didn't want nobody dead."

"OK."

"I didn't want nobody dead."

All told, 'Tone spent somewhere around twelve hours in the homicide interrogation room, most of the time by himself. Several times Thiem asked if he wanted something to eat or drink, but 'Tone declined every offer. A deputy district attorney arrived to read through Thiem's reports and listen to the tapes. Five hours after that, at 8:40 P.M., the deputy DA conducted his own taped interview. 'Tone was then brought to lockup and a formal indictment was entered the next day.

At 5:00 P.M., 'Tone was allowed his one phone call. Thiem surreptitiously recorded the conversation. If 'Tone made any further admissions to his family, he wanted it on tape.

'Tone revealed no secrets in the fifteen minutes he talked with his family and friends. The tape was nothing more than a voyeuristic peek at a nineteen-year-old a couple of hours after he confessed to a murder. Carol, 'Tone's mother, alternated between hysterics and rage. The conversation began with the jarring sound of Carol sobbing and 'Tone pleading with her to stop. "Quit crying, Mama." And then louder, "Mama, quit crying!" In the background, 'Tone's aunt Paula can be heard chiding her sister: "You're going to make him—he's in jail, girl!"

Later in the conversation, Carol launched into a high-speed invective aimed at Junebug and Aaron: "Those motherfuckers cross you like that? You don't got no right—you don't go to jail for—sit in jail for no motherfucker."

'Tone didn't take the bait. Instead he told her that the best thing she could do for him was to get herself into a detox program and straighten herself out.

Paula tried to be a calming influence, though she too would express her anger at Aaron and Junebug. "It was an accident," 'Tone told her. "I know that," Paula said. "I know it was an accident. Don't worry about it. Don't even worry about it, OK?"

Paula put 'Tone's new girlfriend, Dana, on the phone while she ran to get a pencil and paper. Dana asked 'Tone what was up and he said, "Nothing." With Thiem standing no more than five feet away, he tried whispering to her, "They snitched on me." He repeated himself several times, but Dana still couldn't make out what he was saying. He then asked Dana to put Paula back on the phone.

"Tell Mama, 'don't worry,' " he told Paula.

Paula said, "I know you don't want to be no snitch to them motherfuckers, but you heard what they had to say, now you let them hear what you got to say, you know? You be very cooperative with them Tony, OK?"

Much of the conversation was taken up by the mundane, like phone numbers and the logistics of picking up the keys to 'Tone's car. Near the end of 'Tone's fifteen minutes, only 'Tone and Paula were on the phone. "I love you all," he said between sniffles. "I love you. Tell everybody I said I love them. I gotta go." The conversation ended with Paula assuring 'Tone that she'd take care of his car. She had taken his tapes out of his car because he had left the sunroof open that morning and she was worried about what the elements might do to his music.

That night in lockup, 'Tone ran into a guy he knew from the neighborhood. The guy told him he was in on a dope possession charge. "What you in for?" he asked.

"They're trying to get me on a 187."

The guy looked at him. "You know they can't get you without a murder weapon and a statement. Whatever you do, don't sign a statement."

'Tone thanked him for the advice and told him not to worry, he was cool.

'Tone spoke to his grandmother the next day. Of course she would know the truth by then, but he dreaded hearing her voice more than any other. Yet as 'Tone would recall it, they didn't really have much of a conversation.

"You really do it?" Vera asked.

"Yah."

"Well, you gotta ride it out," she said. And that was that.

Two days after inducing a confession from 'Tone, Brian Thiem called Doreatha Estill at her mother's house on Eighty-eighth. He wanted to speak to Aaron again—was he around? Doreatha told Thiem to look for him over on Ninety-second Avenue. She rushed over there, catching Aaron as he and Regina were about to leave. Aaron thought about fleeing but then figured it was too late to run.

This time Thiem and his partner weren't as matter-of-fact as the first time. They spoke to Aaron for around two hours before turning on the tape. Aaron sat while the detectives hovered above him, firing questions, one right after another, allowing him barely any time to answer one before posing another. They called him a liar, they yelled at him, they slapped the table. They pushed him especially hard about his claim that he hadn't known that Fat 'Tone had a gun. If Aaron confessed knowledge of the gun, Thiem knew the DA would charge him with murder one—despite what he had told Aaron's mother about her son getting a deal if he cooperated.

As Aaron would remember it, he told the two detectives, "You all are trying to pressure me into saying something I don't want to say"—a charge Thiem denied. "I want to call my mama." By law, the police must allow a parent or guardian in the interrogation room if a juvenile demands it. But Aaron said they wouldn't allow him to phone his mother right then. According to Aaron, when he finally told them, "Yah, I seen the gun," they turned on the recorder.

On tape Aaron sounded even younger than sixteen as Thiem walked him through the differences between his first statement and his admissions in the preceding hours. Besides admitting to having seen the gun, the other major difference between the two statements was his portrayal of Junebug. He had quoted Junebug as telling him to drive over to 'Tone's to "get a bat or a gun."

"Junebug was pretty angry at this point, wasn't he?" Thiem asked.

"Yah," Aaron said.

"And what did he say—maybe it was an emotional thing—but what did he say he wanted to do to these boys?"

"He said he wanted to kill them."

"He wanted to kill them?"

"Yah."

Aaron said he saw 'Tone pull out the gun when they were parked a few blocks from Auseon and Dowling. He heard 'Tone jack a round into the chamber. Then he saw him adjust his jacket collar so it covered the lower part of his face. There wasn't much conversation, as he remembered it. 'Tone asked, "What we gonna do?" or something to that effect, and Junebug said, "Let's go get 'em."

Later Aaron would claim that it was nine months after the fact and he couldn't remember what was said, but the cops were demanding specifics, and that's what he offered.

"When we talked before, you said something like Junebug was saying, 'I want to pop them fools.' Did Junebug say that?"

"Yah."

Aaron told the detectives that he had asked 'Tone straight out, "You gonna blast 'em?" 'Tone had said "yah," but Aaron said he still didn't think 'Tone was going to shoot anybody, despite the gun in his hand. "I didn't think he had no heart to do it," Aaron said. "I ain't known them to be like that. I was trying to play it off or something."

Aaron said no one had touched the gun but Tony. Junebug never passed it to him, nor did he say anything about only a single bullet in the clip.

Aaron thought that by cooperating, he'd be slapped with a reduced charge. But the interview ended and he overheard Thiem talking with a DA. They were talking about charging him with murder one.

By the time Thiem knocked on Ann Benjamin's door again, her life had taken a horrible turn for the worse. This time the culprit was a drunk driver. She was driving home when a car jumped a barrier on the highway and totaled her car. She didn't suffer any serious injuries, but she was looking and feeling pretty banged up. A cop on the scene told her she was lucky to be alive. When Thiem showed up at her home three days later, he did a double take: "Whoa, what happened to you?" He was thinking the worst, given his occupation.

This time Junebug was home. In fact, he had answered the door because his mother couldn't get out of bed without great effort.

"Will he be coming back home?" Ann asked Thiem.

"Once we're done talking, the DA will review the case and he'll make the decision. I can't make any promises."

"If I want a lawyer, can I get one when I'm down there?" Junebug asked.

Thiem weighed his words carefully. "Just like last time, when we get down there, I'll advise you of your rights and you can make a decision then." Thiem added, "You don't have to come down now. But if you don't, I'll talk to the DA, and if he wants to issue a warrant, then I'll be back."

Ann scoffed at Thiem's suggestion. They wouldn't need a warrant to bring Junebug in, nor did her son need a lawyer. She knew the truth by then, but in her mind Junebug hadn't killed anybody.

"Go and get it over with," she told Junebug. "Just tell them the truth."

Junebug would later claim that he asked for a lawyer at police head-quarters—a charge Thiem denies. Junebug said Thiem and his partner responded to his request by walking out of the room without a word.

"It's going to be the same as the first time," he would quote Thiem as saying upon their return. "We're just going to ask you some questions to clear a few things up."

"I want to go back to my mama," Junebug said. "She was just in an accident. I need to take care of her."

"No promises," Thiem supposedly told him. "But we'll see what we can do."

When, hours later, he overheard Thiem tell a DA that he was confi-dent that they had more than enough to charge Jones, Junebug chided himself for having been so foolish as to believe that he would get to go home if he agreed to talk with them again.

"Why you arresting me?" he asked. "I didn't pull the trigger."

Junebug called his mother to tell her what was up, but she had already figured it out. After Thiem had taken him away, it registered with Ann how Junebug had sounded when he asked for a lawyer. He'd spoken the words an octave or two higher than his normal speaking voice. It had been the voice of fear, she thought to herself. It was then that she knew her son would not be coming back home for a long, long time.

PART THREE
TWO YEARS LATER

22

"JUST ONE OF THOSE THINGS"

A young man, maybe twenty years old, lay sprawled across the front seat of a black Monte Carlo parked by the turnkey on Ninety-second near Holly. The passenger door was flung open, his legs spilled out onto the curb. The car rumbled and shook with the sounds of Too Short, a slightly gangsterish-sounding rapper who was all the rage among the young men of East Oakland in 1993, if for no other reason than the phat, brain-rattling bass lines he laid down.

Several others stood around the car, nodding in rhythm. They were laughing as I walked up. They caught sight of me and their faces snapped shut. Not even vestiges of a single smile remained. One young man's chin was thrust defiantly forward, and another worked his jaw muscles, but otherwise their poses suggested casual indifference.

From all outward appearances, they were just five guys hanging out on a warm, listless June afternoon, listening to music, no different from the old men on East Fourteenth Street who whiled away their days sitting on crates and discarded kitchen chairs with rusted legs and ripped vinyl upholstery. That they were breaking the law was obvious (just ask the cops, their neighbors, or some of their former associates), yet difficult as ever to prove. Two years after Fat 'Tone, Junebug, and Aaron were arrested for the murder of Kevin Reed, nothing had really changed on the corner of Ninety-second and Holly except some of the names and the fact that a twenty didn't buy you as much rock as had in the past.

Vera Clay was still living in the Ninety-second Avenue turnkey, twenty-four years after she first moved in. The Reagan era had forced local housing authorities around the country to slash their already meager maintenance budgets, so of course the building was a shambles both inside and out. Large patches of stucco siding had fallen away from its exterior. The staircase leading to the second floor was rotting away, a tragedy waiting to happen. Vera's apartment appeared as if it hadn't been painted since she first moved in. Squares of sheetrock had been tacked up where patches of ceiling had fallen down.

Vera was a stout woman with large, drooping features. Her face sagged in a perpetual frown. She had thick arms, an ample chest, and a behind like a caboose trailing behind the rest of her. She was prone to shouting out orders for anyone who might be within earshot. "Get me my cigarettes!" "Answer the phone!" "Grab Tony's address off my dresser!" Every order was summarily carried out: a pack of cigarettes appeared, the phone stopped ringing, there was an envelope written in Tony's hand.

Over the phone she had expressed a "don't mind if you do, don't mind if you don't" attitude when I first suggested an interview. The television blared, even when there was no one watching it. The phone rang constantly and people walked in and out so often I couldn't keep track of everyone. Four generations still called her apartment home, or at least home base; one more person, even a stranger, wasn't going to affect her one way or another.

She seemed to have adopted a similar attitude upon Tony's arrival years earlier. "What was 'Tone like as a boy?" I asked. "He was heavy." "No, no—what kind of child was he, what kind of personality did he have?" "I guess he just played like other kids. I don't know. I can't say." She offered a similar answer when I asked her about the impact on Tony of his mother's absence: "I don't know," she said. "He never said anything to me about it."

She summed up her grandson this way: "I knew Tony was no angel, but my kids always kept things from me. My instincts told me that something was going on, but I didn't know what. I never seen him do anything. That's what I often say."

Vera expressed considerable bitterness about the lawyer who was assigned to Tony's case, a public defender named Al Hymer. ("Would have hired a *real* lawyer if I had the money," she said.) Hymer, though, was just about the best lawyer she could have gotten, no matter how much money she was willing to spend. Among the legal community that meets informally before and after court or in the steam room of the Oakland Athletic Club, Hymer makes just about everyone's list of top local defense attorneys. A Stanford graduate with nearly thirty years of trial experience, he figures he's represented somewhere between two hundred and three hundred defendants accused of murder.

Hymer's signature is his homey, aw-shucks style. Born and raised on a cattle ranch in a desolate stretch of northern California, by appearances he looks strictly Iowa farm belt. He has an open and honest face and deep blue eyes that invite you to trust him. Except when he's working a jury trial, he wears his hair in an unkempt and unruly style. For a jury, he slicks his hair down and keeps it carefully combed, lending him the look of a kid dressed up in his Sunday best.

Hymer first met Tony a few days after his arrest. Tony struck him as a scared kid clinging to his claim that although he had squeezed the trigger only once, the gun had fired six times. Tony struck him as no better than his typical client, wholly unrealistic about his situation. Between his sorry alibi and a taped confession, Tony hadn't left his lawyer many options, but he nonetheless expected Hymer to get him off, like lawyers on TV do on behalf of their clients.

Hymer's biggest hurdle would be Tony's admission, corroborated by his two coconspirators, that they had passed by the corner of Auseon and Dowling, stopped to confer a few blocks away, and *then* he shot the gun. That would be the linchpin to the DA's claim that this was a premeditated murder—murder in the first degree—carrying a sentence of twenty-five years to life plus an additional three years for having used a gun to kill Kevin Reed.

Still, Tony offered enough during that first interview to start Hymer thinking about a potential defense. Hymer asked a law clerk to work on a motion to suppress the confession, based on Tony's claims that the police had ignored his requests for an attorney and dangled the death penalty over his head. His only other hope was trying to prove that Tony had been as wasted the night of the shooting as he claimed—so drunk and stoned that he was guilty of manslaughter, with no notion that he was endangering human life.

Getting the DA to agree to a voluntary manslaughter plea rather than the standard second-degree murder offer would be a stretch, but it would mean the difference between ten years in jail (a twenty-year sentence cut in half, assuming time for good behavior in prison) and the eighteen-to-life sentence Tony would serve if he agreed to a murder two plea. (The typical murder two inmate served between fifteen and eighteen years, at least back in 1991.) Hymer wasn't optimistic, but he made his pitch just the same, appealing to the DA assigned to the Reed murder to consider Tony's age and also his life circumstances.

Hymer is certain that his adversary on this case was a deputy district attorney named Jack Quatman. Quatman, however, claims not to recall a thing about the case. "Doesn't ring even the faintest bell," he says, despite the ages of those on either side of this case.

In 1991 Quatman headed one of the DA's three trial teams specializing in serious felonies. Quatman began with ten trial attorneys but two years later was down to six. Handling a swelling caseload with fewer bodies meant that the lawyers under his charge often worked late into the night and on weekends. "The reality is that you try more and more cases until you drop in the courtroom," Quatman says. He suggests that if he can't recall a particular case a couple of years after the fact, that's because some days he leaves the office barely remembering the case he worked on the week before.

"It used to be, when I first started in this office, you worked your way up slowly to handling a 187 [a murder]," he says. "It'd be years before you handled your first murder trial. Now, when a new deputy is transferred from muni [municipal] court, they'll try one nonmurder case and the next one's a 187."

He can't recall the details of this case, but Quatman says he cannot imagine agreeing to manslaughter on a drive-by that killed an innocent thirteen-year-old and put two fourteen-year-olds in the hospital. Which is exactly what Hymer recalls Quatman telling him. The deal was murder two, take it or leave it.

Hymer figured that Tony would be like most of his clients. He'd complain that fifteen or eighteen years in prison was too many because some guy in jail had told him that anything over five years, or eight years, or ten years—who knew what was being taken for gospel in the jails at any given moment?—on a murder beef was a bad deal. He'd never offer anything remotely resembling remorse, at least not in Hymer's presence. He'd want to know only what Hymer could do for him, and why it wasn't more.

Yet Tony proved the exception to the rule. Sometime shortly after his preliminary hearing, in which he was bound over to superior court to stand trial, Tony initiated conversations with Hymer about the terrible act he had committed and the pain he had caused so many people. Tony even pressed Hymer about accepting the DA's offer of murder two, even though Hymer had yet to argue a couple of motions he was planning to file—and even though eighteen to life was no deal. Hymer didn't think there was much chance he'd get anywhere with any of his gambits, but he at least wanted to give it a try.

"He was against my doing it," Hymer says. "His attitude was he had done something wrong and believed he had it coming to him. He just wanted to take the deal."

The county probation officer who interviewed Tony expressed a similar sentiment. "We are touched by the fact that this defendant spoke to us openly and freely about his conduct in the shooting," he wrote in the report required whenever a defendant pleads guilty or is found guilty of a felony. "He spoke candidly about his marijuana habit and his years of selling cocaine. He seemingly made no attempt to hide the truth from us; the shame and the remorse that he displayed appeared genuine."

Hymer pushed for a sentence that would allow Tony to begin serving his sentence in a California Youth Authority facility. Under that plan, endorsed by the presiding judge and the probation officer, he would be a ward of the CYA until he turned twenty-five and then he'd be transferred to a state penitentiary to serve out the remainder of his sentence. "We view the defendant as unsophisticated and lacking in callousness and [believe that he] might experience undue hardship in protecting himself in the adult facilities," according to the probation officer's report.

The CYA, however, rejected Tony. "We don't believe the proper security exists," the CYA wrote in a form letter addressed to the presiding judge on the case. No further explanation was provided. 'Tone pleaded guilty to second-degree murder and, in September 1991, became the responsibility of the California Department of Corrections for anywhere between twelve years (the minimum time someone can serve on an eighteen-to-life sentence) and the rest of his natural life.

Incredibly, nearly two years into 'Tone's term, Vera had no idea how stiff a sentence her grandson had received. Vera thought 'Tone would be out after seven years. His sister Angela was under the impression that he'd serve about four years. Paula was similarly misinformed. Paula would have figured out the truth, but by the time her nephew was sentenced, she had married a man in the military and was living in Honolulu, where she worked for a catering company.

Vera attended Tony's preliminary hearing, but she never returned to court. The presence of the Reed family, she said, proved too great a burden to endure. She remembered reading about Kevin's murder when it happened—remembered feeling terribly sad that so young a life had been taken. She thought about telling Annette Reed how sorry she was for what had happened, but she couldn't do it. Instead she told herself, "He's gone and ain't nothing I can say will bring him back."

Two years later, she was still kicking herself for her lack of courage that day.

Vera knew little about the case prior to attending the preliminary hearing. Tony had told her nothing about the murder except that it had been an accident and that he hadn't meant to kill anybody. Paula knew enough to tell Vera that somehow the whole thing was Junebug's fault, but the truth was that she didn't know much more than that until the prelim.

Vera felt immensely relieved when the pathologist testified that Kevin was most likely killed by a ricochet off the street. "See, that proves right there that it was all an accident," she said, ignoring, at least for the moment, that Tony had also shot a girl in the face and a boy in the thigh. She also took great solace in 'Tone's claim that the gun had kept going off as he tried to pull it back inside the car.

Vera was dumbfounded when I inadvertently let slip that Tony was serving an eighteen-to-life sentence. "I know he done wrong," she said. "I know he should be paying a price for what he did. But I don't know why he should get all this time when he didn't intend on doing this. He wasn't a cold-blooded murderer; it was an accident.

"It was just one of those things."

One month after we met for what was to be the first of several interviews, Vera died at the age of fifty-seven, from complications following a thyroid operation. Her death left the family feeling bitter, full of recriminations about the supposedly shoddy medical care she had received. It also left them without the glue that bound everyone together. "For a while there, it was like I was living everywhere but nowhere," Tony's sister Angela said when I finally found her after several months of searching. She said that with Tony locked away and Vera gone, it was like the family had scattered to the wind.

23

THE PRICE
OF PRIDE

Two years after Junebug's arrest, Ann Benjamin was still beating herself up over the way she'd handled her difficult eldest son. Why had she worked so hard when her son so obviously needed more of her attention? If she had been around in the evenings instead of at work, she told herself, he couldn't have gotten away with as much as he did. She harassed herself for having spent too much time thinking about Keisha at Junebug's expense because she understood girls so much better than boys. She even wrote to her son while he was awaiting trial to ask him for forgiveness.

Ann was also kicking herself for her handling of the police. She believed she had let Junebug down in her dealings with Brian Thiem. She couldn't believe she had been so naive as to buy his "I just want to talk to him" line. Between the first and second time Thiem had come to speak to Junebug, her son had told her about those two fateful days in the summer of 1990. She demanded no less than the entire truth and Junebug pretty much complied. She tried listening to his every word, but she found herself distracted by emotions. She was overcome by sadness, not for herself, not for her son, but for Annette and Kevin Reed. So preoccupied was she by empathy for Annette Reed that she temporarily lost sight of her own and her son's interests.

Only once it was too late did she realize that she should have first consulted with a lawyer before allowing Junebug to speak with the police. I didn't help matters any when I mentioned something Thiem had told me, that he didn't think the DA would have had much of a case unless all three suspects confessed to the murder.

Junebug was assigned a private attorney named Bill Daley. The local public defender's office considers it a conflict of interest to represent more than one client in a case in which there are multiple defendants, so lawyers like Daley are appointed by the court to represent the indigent, with the county picking up the bill.

Ann expressed feelings of bitterness toward Daley, much as Vera had done when talking about Al Hymer. Ann, however, had more cause for complaint, if for no other reason than Daley's inexperience. Daley had handled only one murder case prior to representing Junebug, and in that case his defendant had not fared well. Two young men had been arrested for the shooting death of a fifteen-year-old kid—an innocent bystander—at a birthday party. Both defendants were equally culpable as each had fired a shotgun, and it was a shotgun blast or blasts that had killed the boy. Daley's client was convicted of first-degree murder and sentenced to twenty-eight to life. His codefendant was found guilty of voluntary manslaughter, which carries a sentence of six to sixteen years.

Where Hymer has specialized in murder throughout a long and distinguished career, Daley advertised himself as a generalist. He was a solo practitioner who rented cheap office space in a building downtown. He took anything that came his way, whether criminal or civil law. He preferred civil cases, but he put his name on the bar's court-appointed list because solo practitioners invariably need the work. In short order, the drug busts and the burglaries that every court-appointed attorney starts with became the bread and butter of his practice. The more criminal cases he tried, the more he seemed to enjoy the work; eventually he became one of a small circle of private attorneys who make up the criminal bar in Oakland.

Daley met with Junebug for the first time only minutes before the two of them stood before a judge at a juvenile detention hearing—the equivalent of a bail hearing in the adult courts. (It's typical that a court-appointed lawyer will be called to handle a case without so much as twenty-four-hours' notice.) Daley didn't bother arguing for Junebug's release pending a verdict because he knew that his motion would have been denied.

The outcome of Junebug's next hearing—where it was determined that he would be tried as an adult rather than as a juvenile—was equally preordained. In some states, juveniles charged with a serious felony are automatically tried as adults. In California, there are still what are called 707 hearings, even though juveniles aged sixteen or seventeen who are charged with murder are almost automatically tried as adults. Daley made his case, stressing that Junebug was neither the driver nor the shooter and that he had experienced a religious reformation following the murder. The district attorney, in turn, characterized Junebug as the mastermind behind a shooting that left a thirteen-year-old dead. To no one's surprise, Junebug was sitting beside Tony at the preliminary hearing in an adult courtroom one month later.

The first time Ann came face-to-face with Annette Reed was at Junebug's 707 hearing. Ann was waiting for the hearing to begin when she saw a man tap his wife on the leg and point to her. As she was wondering who these people could be, it became obvious to her.

"She was giving me the cold stare throughout the entire hearing," Ann said. "I mean, the kind of stare where someone doesn't blink their eyes, doesn't turn when you look their way."

The staring stopped the next time they were all in court, at Junebug and Tony's preliminary hearing. "That's where it came out that *her* son hit my son for saying he wasn't so-and-so," Ann told me. "Then I looked at her and gave *her* that look." Still, Ann felt guilty every time she saw Annette at a hearing or when she ran into her around town, which happened several times. They spoke only once, and that was brief. As both would remember it, the conversation went something like this:

"Are you Tony's mother?"

"No, John Jones's."

"That was tragic what he did to my son."

"Yah, the whole case was tragic."

Annette burst into tears and Ann didn't know what else to say, so she said that she was sorry and walked away.

"My heart goes out to her," Ann says. "She loved her son and he's no longer here, and the one who was killed didn't even have anything to do with what went on. He was just an innocent.

"I can't say I understand how she feels, because my son is still here, and hers is gone, but the situation could have been turned around. *My* son could have been gone instead of her son if he hadn't blocked that pipe with his arm."

Ann visited Junebug faithfully three times a week—the maximum permitted—while he was locked in juvie awaiting the disposition of his case. Incarceration had made Junebug more introspective; the two of them would often engage in what both characterized as intimate, heart-to-heart conversations. They never felt closer than in those months following his arrest.

Ann didn't miss a single hearing, no matter how routine. Never was it easy. Her neck was in a brace for months after her auto accident; she ached all over. Brown-shirted sheriffs would escort Junebug into court wearing a yellow cotton jumpsuit. (Yellow is the color assigned to those housed in the county's maximum security lockup.) He was manacled around his ankles and his wrists were bound to a chain secured around his waist.

Junebug often told his mother how bad he felt putting her through such hell. Ann appreciated the sentiment, but it only deepened her resolve never to allow him see her cry. She'd dam up her tear ducts through the hearing and then cry that much harder later.

Bill Daley was another source of irritation. He would never speak with her except in the minutes before a hearing was about to start. He'd invite her to call him at his office but then wouldn't return the messages she left. Worse, Junebug complained that Daley never spoke to *him* either, except under those same rushed circumstances.

Ann would sit in court staring at Daley, making herself sick with worry. His every tic, his every mannerism drove her crazy. He sat there nearly silent during the preliminary hearing. Daley's deference made sense—Hymer was far more experienced, and there are countless stories of cocounsel who destroy each other's case with conflicting strategies—

but Ann was convinced that it only underscored how ill prepared he was to represent her son.

"Thank God Junebug and Tony were tried together," she says. "It was like my son's lawyer was there in body alone."

From Daley's perspective, his relationship with the DA trying the case was the only one that counted. His goal was getting Junebug a Youth Authority commitment, thereby guaranteeing his release by the age of twenty-five. To him, the case was going well because the DA was open to his proposal.

As a court-appointed attorney, Daley was paid a flat fee of $425 for representing Junebug in two juvenile court hearings. He was paid another $1,000 when his client's case was remanded to the adult court, plus $150 a day for his trial work during a two-day preliminary hearing. He was paid $100 for the single motion he filed and another $75 for arguing it in court. Daley says he long ago stopped trying to calculate his hourly rate on court-appointed cases because the bottom-line figure is too depressing to contemplate.

Sure, he probably ignored some phone messages. And he probably was rushed every time he spoke to either Junebug or Ann, because that, he says, is life as a solo practitioner. It seems you never have time for anything except those things that require your immediate attention.

In April of 1992, John Jones stood in court to plead guilty to murder in the first degree. Daley had convinced the DA to sign off on a Youth Authority commitment, but the Youth Authority hadn't agreed to take Junebug. Daley showed his inexperience, his colleague Al Hymer said, by failing to stipulate that his client's plea was conditional on the Youth Authority's acceptance. The Youth Authority was always rejecting deals cooked up by a DA and a defense attorney—as had happened with Tony. If the Youth Authority rejected Junebug, he'd be sentenced to twenty-eight to life in an adult penitentiary—the maximum that he would get if a jury had found him guilty. The judge might let Junebug retract his plea, given that a Youth Authority commitment was implicit in his acceptance of the deal, but not necessarily.

A probation officer, as is customary, had met with Junebug before he made his plea in open court, to ensure that he understood what was going to happen. "Are you sure you want this, son?" the woman asked him. Before court, Junebug told Daley about the conversation, but his lawyer waved him off. "Don't worry," he told him, "it's all taken care of."

The first time the Youth Authority rejected Junebug, Daley told his client that it was merely a paperwork gaffe. After the second rejection, Ann called Daley. "He told me not to worry, that Junebug's out at the YA center in Sacramento getting processed," Ann says. "So I had to tell him, 'No, he's not, I just got back from visiting him at Santa Rita [the county jail he was transferred to after he turned eighteen].'"

Finally, seven months after Junebug had first entered his plea, he and his mother learned that he had been accepted by the Youth Authority.

Daley himself apparently never shared their anxiety. "I was never quite sure what was going on with YA," Daley says, "other than maybe they were overworked or they didn't want him. They eventually had to have accepted him, or I would have heard otherwise. I never heard they finally rejected him, or I would have been called back to court. So I assume that's where he ended up—in YA."

Ann was still living in the same house she had escaped to after Ninety-second Avenue when I first met her in the spring of 1993. Her home looked underdressed, as if they had moved in only a few months earlier. Ann blamed the repeated burglaries she had suffered on Ninety-second Avenue. Owning something like a stereo wasn't worth the potential pain and aggravation of having it stolen. "I don't much care about material things anymore," she said.

Ann was a remarkably upbeat woman with a demeanor that belied the hard life she'd lived. She laughed frequently, even when discussing the more tragic moments of her life. The harsher the reality she was describing, the more defensive she'd feel about her inherent good cheer, as if her ability to retain her spirits was not a strength but a sign that there was something wrong with her. She would say frequently, "Trust me, I was crying then." But her sunny disposition would break through yet again as she followed up her assurances with a hearty, full-throated laugh.

It turned out that I was virtually the first person other than Junebug and Keisha with whom she spoke about the murder. She said she feared what people might think of her as a mother, so she generally avoided talking about Junebug. The extended family knew he was away on a murder charge, of course, but that was about all they knew. Ann confided in God and with the single girlfriend with whom she felt she shared a close bond, but no one else. She was never the type who revealed her problems to others, she said.

I would tell her that she had done the best she could given the circumstances and then feel awkward about overstepping some kind of boundary. Yet eventually I became something of a sounding board for her, a way to relieve the pressures born of a son locked behind barbed wire in a facility two hours away. Junebug was permitted to call her collect several times a month—no small economic burden. Every time she and the kids made the trip out, she seemed to spend another thirty to fifty dollars—on gas, on lunch, in the vending machines, and on gifts for Junebug like soft toilet tissue and lotions. She'd try to make it there every other weekend, but Junebug pushed her to come more often.

"I'm doing all I can, but I don't think he understands that," she said.

Ann wished her ex would relieve some of the pressure by occasionally visiting his son. He claimed, she said, that he couldn't see Junebug because he was on parole after serving time for a felony conviction. The Youth Authority, however, has no steadfast rule forbidding a father on parole from visiting his son.

Countless times Ann had considered what happened the night before the murder and how Junebug might have handled things differently. Had he turned to her for help, she would have told him to let it go or, at the very least, leave 'Tone—and a gun—out of it. Yet she recognized that the life of a teen is a lot more complicated than when she was that age. You're a "punk" if you allow a pair of younger kids to play you like a chump. Too, one never knows nowadays who might be packing a pistol. Going to a fight with a gun tucked in your pants is idiotic, but walking into a fight with nothing but your wits and your fists might be equally foolish.

Pride, she figured, had been Junebug's downfall—and by extension Kevin's. He couldn't simply walk away because he was too preoccupied by how his friends might be looking at him.

As we talked, Ann would tend to a toddler named Rasheed, her brother's son. Rasheed's mother, she said, was hooked on drugs, and her brother was in no position to raise the boy on his own. She had taken Rasheed in when he was just three days old. She views caring for him not as an obligation but as a gift.

"God took one son from me," she says, "and I inherited another."

In the summer of 1993, Ann visited a friend, a deacon from the church, who had moved to Montana. She had dreamed of returning to the South, but after seeing Montana, she realized that she actually longed to live in a small town, whether north or south of the Mason-Dixon line.

"It reminded me of back home," she said of her friend's new community. "They had a big garden, chickens walking around, lots of space." The town was home to fewer than three thousand people. She set the spring of 1994 as her date to move but then pushed back her deadline several times. She finally escaped in November of that year.

The move tortured her because it placed so much distance between her and Junebug—visiting him more often than once or twice a year would now be impossible. But she had Keisha and her other two sons to worry about, and also Rasheed. Her middle son was doing fine, but her youngest reminded her of Junebug at his age, so much so that she shuddered when she contemplated his adolescence living in Oakland. The streets had already taken one son. She wasn't ready to lose another.

24

ANNETTE

In April of 1993, Annette Reed's photograph appeared on page one of the Oakland *Tribune*. The expression on her face and the faraway look in her eyes suggested a despair and resignation so deep it might never lift. Below the picture of Annette was a small snapshot of her son Shannon, his hat turned backward and a smile on his face. The caption to this second photo read, "Shannon Reed, who accidentally shot and killed himself, was the second child in the Reed family to die by gunshot." Shannon, seventeen, had fatally shot himself in the head while messing around with a .38.

The Reeds were not the first Oakland family to lose more than one child to street violence—one woman, in fact, had buried three of her four children, all victims of guns—but the increasing frequency with which it occurred made it no less tragic. "I cried as soon as it happened," Bridget Reed was quoted as saying, "and then I couldn't cry any more because it's just so unbelievable." Bridget, nineteen, was suddenly the baby of the family.

Ann Benjamin read the *Trib* article and cried. So, too, did Vera Clay read the news with a heavy heart. Both contemplated sending a check—there was the same appeal for funds that had accompanied the news story reporting on Kevin's murder—or at least a condolence note, but they each got stuck on one paragraph up high in the story: "Reed had attended the trial and was awed by the cavalier attitude of the assailants. 'It was like they didn't care about taking my son's life,' she said."

Seven months after Kevin's murder, the Reeds' erstwhile dream house became the property of the DD and D Real Estate Company. The family didn't look for a new home, but instead everyone was left to fend for himself or herself, clinging as best one could to whatever shard of wreckage floated by.

Annette moved several times before finally ending up in a two-bedroom apartment on a busy street in East Oakland, across from Highland Hospital. She said one grew accustomed to the sirens of the incoming ambulances, like people who live by railroad tracks can eventually tune out passing trains. Violent crime wasn't nearly as rampant in her new neighborhood as it was in her old one, but it was still considered a high-crime area.

Adornments inside the apartment were few. There were a few pieces of furniture in the living room, but no couch. On opposite walls hung a pair of matching paintings depicting the same serene river scene. There was also a blown-up picture of Shannon, a gift from her son Curtis. Framed photographs of her children, Kevin and Shannon especially, were scattered around the room: Kevin wearing a gold-colored football uniform; a shot of Shannon draped across Kevin's shoulder at Kevin's elementary school graduation. A well-worn Bible sat on a mantel. "A good friend," Annette said.

By the time I met Annette Reed, she was forty-four years old, a once-energetic woman who believed she had hit rock bottom in July 1990—but in the intervening years, she had lost another son, been evicted from her house, gotten a divorce, and had a car accident that shattered her ankle. Some days, she admitted, she felt like lying down and never getting up.

A daunting stack of forms lay on a coffee table, beside the official resolution passed by the Oakland City Council in Kevin's honor. That morning Annette had been to the county's social service office to see about getting on General Assistance. She had received public assistance in the past—Aid to Families with Dependent Children—but she hated the idea that she'd again be resorting to the welfare system to pay her monthly bills.

While Shannon was alive, she had worked part time when she could find the work. It was nothing steady, but she had survived. Since Shannon's death, she had gotten a job as a clerk in a factory in Hayward, a suburb twenty minutes to the south, but she hadn't owned a car, and public transportation had proved so time-consuming and expensive that she'd given up. She chided herself about self-pity, but beating herself up about her supposed lack of strength only added to her burdens. The monthly three hundred dollars from General Assistance wasn't much, but she was feeling desperate.

"The mornings are the toughest," she told me in a quiet but husky voice that made her sound perpetually hoarse. She'd see the pictures of Kevin and Shannon propped around her living room and her day would be ruined. She'd be rendered paralyzed, unable to walk outside even to pick up something at the corner store. She'd cry until she couldn't cry anymore. In a mirror she'd catch a glimpse of her swollen face, her eyes blotted red. On days like that she could only pray that tomorrow wouldn't be quite so bad.

It had been two and a half months since Shannon died, and Annette said she had experienced some good days in recent weeks. There had been two or three days in a row when she didn't remember crying even once. "But when I realize I didn't cry, then I feel guilty to some degree, like I'm forgetting about my sons," Annette said. She would tell herself that she was only struggling to move on with her life, but of course the words were easier to say than to believe.

She felt desperate for professional help, but she didn't have the money for a therapist. She availed herself of the free clinic at Highland, but she was assigned a different counselor each time. That meant telling her story from scratch every time she went in, so she stopped going.

"There's just no remedy," she said. "You can't do anything. You just have to live it. Drinking's not going to help. Not drugs. Nothing.

"You just have to live with it, cold turkey, point blank, stare it in the eye."

Annette had attended just about every court hearing concerning her son's case. The toughest couple of days were the preliminary hearing, when the DA put Brian Thiem, the medical examiner, and also London and Natasha on the stand. It was at the preliminary hearing that she learned that her son's murder was in large part about Fat 'Tone wanting to get back into Junebug's good graces. That revelation left her feeling cold. Thinking she had lost her son in a fight over a stolen bike was difficult enough, but this was more than her mind could comprehend.

Annette was bitter that none of the mothers had offered her condolences in court. "If it had been my son on trial, I would have wanted to let that parent know that I am ultimately sorry and hurt about what happened," she said.

"I'm sure John Jones's mother feels bad about what happened, is wondering what went wrong, what caused him to do such a crime, because I'm sure she didn't teach him to do that," Annette said. "I'm certain she's hurting in so many ways, even though her son is still living. But I feel anger towards her just the same, because the fact is that her son is alive and mine is dead."

She hadn't anticipated anything like a verbal apology from any of the three defendants, but she had expected to see *something* that at least revealed regret. "All three of them just sat there," she said. "I didn't see any remorse on their faces. It made me so angry to sit there and look at this big, stupid-looking kid and think that he had gone out there and mowed down children in the street. He was bigger than my son. He just sat there.

"The other one [Junebug], his mother tried to get a minister to say that now he's been saved, to say this, that, and the other. But he instigated and planned and sought out these kids to shoot them and kill them. This was premeditated."

To her mind, Junebug was the "mastermind" who had put the plan in motion, and Tony the "assassin" who had willingly carried out the "execution."

Annette expressed something approaching sympathy for Aaron. "He just got caught up in a stupid, foolish thing he had nothing to do with," she said.

From the beginning, Annette understood that I would be speaking at length with her son's killers and their family members. "People should know the other side of it," she said. "I have no problem with that." She thought the story of the three young men who murdered her son might be salutary. "In a way, you can't blame the kids for the trouble they get into, given that they don't see a future for themselves," she said.

Still, she was disappointed that Junebug and Tony both received sentences short of life in jail with no possibility of parole. "I hope something goes wrong that they never get out," she said. "I really do. They need to think about this for a lifetime like I have to think about this for a lifetime. If I could get off this boat in seven years, it'd be nice. But I have to think about this for the rest of my life."

Whenever Annette spoke of Kevin or Shannon, her eyes would shine as if her two sons were a spectral vision standing there in her presence. She would gaze into space with a serene smile across her face. Sometimes she spoke of her two sons in the present tense. "Kevin is a little flirt," she said. Shannon, in contrast, "has a real clowny personality."

Enduring Kevin's murder was awful, but the time after Shannon's death was even worse. She told people that she and Shannon had been close. He'd talk to her about girlfriends, about his day at school, about his friends.

Yet in the weeks leading up to his death, Shannon had apparently been messing with the Smith and Wesson .38 with which he shot himself. She had had no clue that he owned a gun. On the day he died, he was hanging around inside with a few friends and his brother Curtis. He pulled out the gun and started twirling it like an outlaw from the movies. He opened the cylinder, spun it, and then closed it. He put the gun to his skull. A friend called to him and the gun went off as he was turning his head. He was pronounced dead on arrival.

In a million years, Annette wouldn't have guessed that her son's life could possibly have ended like that. "I guess we weren't nearly close enough," she said.

Two of her three surviving sons, Donald and Dermmell, she said, were like their father, prone to yeses and nos, although you knew there was much more going on inside their heads. Her son Curtis, though, would go through the same ritual every time he visited her. He'd walk over to her gallery of photos, pick one up, and then start talking about whatever popped into his head.

"With Curtis," Annette said, "we'll talk and laugh and then I'll boohoo a bit, and he'll say, 'Aw, Mama, don't get like that.'"

Curtis was standing outside on the porch talking on the phone when he heard the gunshot that took Shannon's life. He ran inside and knew immediately that the prognosis was grim. In the movies, a guy cradles his brother's head in his arms. Curtis couldn't bring himself to touch Shannon, though. He walked outside because he couldn't stand to see his brother like that, a bullet wound to the head.

Curtis had just finished serving a seventeen-month stint in prison. He had been arrested on a kidnapping charge at around the same time that Brian Thiem caught up with 'Tone, Junebug, and Aaron. A supplier had just taken him for $38,000—his entire stash—and he was crazy to get his money back. First he was enraged, then impressed. He couldn't believe that someone had taken him for so much money with so little effort. He was in the wrong line of work, he told himself. And like that he decided to give up drug dealing, at least for the moment.

A former customer who owed him some money gave him a line on a couple of dealers supposedly making big money in a town forty-five minutes from Oakland. Curtis and two other guys kidnapped the dealer and his girl at gunpoint, then held them for ransom. But the dealer's partner called in the cops. One of the guys in on the job with Curtis spilled everything to the police, portraying Curtis as the mastermind. Curtis figured he was looking at thirty years and counted himself lucky to have gotten a three-year sentence. "My understanding level at that point, man, was below zero," he said. "I had no knowledge of myself. I was lost."

Just as he'll hear until his dying day the gunshot that took Shannon's life, Curtis will never forget his first hours at San Quentin prison. "They walk you through there buck naked," he said. "You hear these gates closing one after another and you're thinking, 'Ain't no way out of here.' You serve your time or you die in there, that's it.

"They're walking us through the yard and everyone's looking, and I'm thinking to myself, 'Who do I know and what have I've done to who? What have I have done that's gonna come back to haunt me in here?'

"They put me in front of the cell and said, 'OK, you can get in now.' And I looked in there and I'm like, 'What, I'm supposed to go in there?' He says, 'Yeah.' So I ask if they're just holding me there and he says, 'No, this is where you're gonna be housed at.' So I says, 'You're kidding me.' And he says, 'Man, get in the fucking cell.'

"I threw my bag on the bed, turned around, and it was like a magnet. Everybody does it. You grab the cell bars. I'm grabbing the door, looking out. I couldn't see much of anything, but it was like I couldn't let go of those bars.

"It was the warehousing of human beings. You're just something they put on a shelf. It was like a five-floor kennel in there. You know how when you walk in a kennel, all the dogs are barking because they want to get out? That's prison. Ain't no peace."

Ultimately, he was transferred to a medium-security facility in northern California, the California State Correctional Facility at Susanville, six hours from Oakland. "No one visited me out there," he said. "I felt dead. I felt like I was in the ground and no one was even around to throw a rose on me. Nobody put money on my books. I would see ex–drug addicts who I used to sell drugs to on the street in there living better than me. I knew my family had problems of their own, but at that point I didn't care, I was just thinking about me, me, me."

Curtis returned from the penitentiary with a much harder edge. He was quieter (though never quiet), moodier, and more introspective. "Curt, you too serious," friends told him. "Try smilin' sometimes." But he couldn't or wouldn't because to him there was nothing worth grinning about. He would go to job interviews, but they would always end the same way. A prospective employer would ask him about his record, and that'd be the beginning of the end. Several times he stalked out of a job interview. "I don't need your damn job anyway," he would yell.

"It's like I had an attitude back then that stuck with me that I couldn't get rid of," he said. "I don't like the way you talk to me, or the way you're staring at me, so I'm going to fight you." He told himself he had grown up in the pen, but it wasn't long after his release that he took up dealing again. The quick money again proved too seductive. Not surprisingly, he caught another twelve months at San Quentin for violating parole.

I first spoke with Curtis while he was serving out his parole violation. He was mistrustful and harsh over the phone; ultimately, he decided against my coming out to interview him. The day after his release, however, he called me, his voice eager and upbeat. He was a completely different person from the hardened inmate I had spoken to several months earlier.

Curtis was a smooth-faced, soft-spoken young man of twenty-four who seemed intent on living his life differently. He was married and back in the church. While locked away, he had secured a scholarship to help him go to college. If all went as planned, he said, he'd be starting at a local community college in the fall of 1995.

During that first meeting, he told me about a day he'd never forget, when he met a prisoner at Susanville with long dreadlocks and a near-encyclopedic knowledge of African and African-American history—"Roots," everyone called him. "He's this skinny dude, with a ring in his nose, always smiling," Curtis said. "I'm sitting there waiting to get my hair cut and he's talking with these other brothers about Africa and ancient civilizations, about philosophy, about AIDS, about oppression. Everything. I'm hanging on his every word, practically in his face in a place where people tell you to keep your distance. But I don't care, and he didn't mind. I realized after a while that there was no one around anymore but me and him. I'm firing question after question," Curtis said. "At first I'm trying to trip him up—like, you talk good but let me see how good you really are—but eventually I'm asking because I want to hear everything this brother has to say."

Some inmates had the weight pit. Others would run, or get stoned on whatever contraband they could lay their hands on. Curtis found his solace in books. After hooking up with Roots, Curtis read anything he could get his hands on. The sensation of learning was sometimes so intense that he would find himself crying in his cell.

Curtis said he discovered himself at Susanville, even if it took him several more years to straighten out his life. "Back then, I couldn't say I was a man," he said. "I didn't understand. I *feared* work. Now I tell myself to be patient, to act responsibly, to be a man.

"I feel still I have a lot of growth I need to do," Curtis said. "But the thing is, I don't want to just try anymore. I don't want to be some guy they say has promise. I want to be a doer."

The Buckner family didn't suffer like the Reeds did, but they had heartaches just the same. After the shooting, Natasha Buckner no longer felt safe taking a city bus home from school, so her father, Greg, started picking her up after school. His employer objected but Greg felt he had no choice. Suddenly he was without a job.

Her mother, Sheila, worked for an employer more understanding of their situation, so they weren't without money. But the mortgage became that much tougher to make each month. It didn't help that Natasha's orthodontia alone required three thousand dollars out of pocket. The state's victim assistance fund, it turned out, was something the politicians talked about but nothing that this victim, at least, could use.

"I've stopped going to church," Sheila Buckner told a columnist for the Oakland *Tribune* one year after the shooting. She also stopped spending time with friends. "I can't explain what happened to me, but I just cut everybody off," she said. "All I can do is get up, go to work, do my job, and come home." Greg and Sheila Buckner didn't want much to do with this book—"We've really put all this behind us," Sheila told me—but Natasha was anxious to talk with me. She had graduated from high school in June 1994, and began her studies at a four-year college back east that fall. She declared herself a psychology major because she thought she might one day become a psychologist.

Natasha has only the faintest of scars where the bullet entered and exited her cheeks. Few of her university classmates even know that she had been shot, she says. She may be less trusting and a bit more fatalistic because of the psychological scars she endured but, if anything, Natasha feels stronger and more mature for having endured so great a trauma at so young an age. "I'm not stressed about it," she said. "I don't think about the guys who did this to me. I don't live with hate. I hate the fact they killed someone and that I was injured, but I could also see it from their perspective.

"I've moved on. It's just a part of me."

■ ■ ■

Annette and I had gotten together once at the start of the summer of 1993 and then again in August. Her feelings of resentment were running high around the time of our second meeting. That week, a man armed with a pair of Mac-10 semiautomatics had walked into a law office in downtown San Francisco and killed eight people. The local media were playing the story as if there were no news other than this killer's mad dog dance.

The newspapers included schematics depicting the "killer's route." For days the TV anchors waxed foolish about a range of serious topics the killings raised, from the ease of obtaining nasty weapons like the Mac-10 to the pain we all feel when confronted with murder. There were in-depth articles about each of the deceased and ad nauseam accounts of the killer.

Kevin's murder had merited barely a mention in either the *Chronicle* or the *Examiner*, the Bay Area's two main daily newspapers.

"When one of my kids or someone else's child gets killed, it's the same hurt," Annette said. "There's no difference in the hurt or the loss or the pain. You know more teenagers are killed in a month in Oakland than were killed at that law firm, but why does it have to happen in a big official building for people to pay attention to the pain? Why does it take something like that to get people talking about there being too many guns out there?"

As we had done the first time we met, we spoke for hours about a range of subjects and then ended with plans for a subsequent meeting. I let time pass so as not to become too much of a burden. Maybe I was dragging things out from her perspective, because the interview never took place.

I tried calling, but she no longer had a telephone. I dropped her a note and asked her to get in touch with me. I heard nothing. I considered ringing her buzzer, but I remembered her description of her bad days. An unannounced visit, I decided, would be too much of an intrusion. I passed messages through family members and wrote her another note, but I guess our sessions together had proved too painful. I never again heard from Annette Reed.

25

JOHN JONES

From the perspective of the Bay Area, Stockton is little more than a place between here and there. This city of 215,000 sits between the coastal mountain ranges to the west and the mighty Sierra Nevadas to the east. The land between is part of a vast farming region that Californians refer to simply as "the valley." During the summer months, Stockton is unbearably hot, and a dirty haze hangs over the valley more often than not. Sandwiched between two major freeways, Stockton is the town people in that part of the state flock to in search of department stores, farm equipment, and a night out on the town. Increasingly it's also become a source of jobs for those wanting employment in the correction industry.

No fewer than four Youth Authority facilities have been built in Stockton since the 1960s. All were built on fallow farm fields at the edge of an industrial park, just east of California Highway 99. Surrounded by a perimeter fence topped with razor wire, the four facilities are collectively called the Northern California Youth Center. The DeWitt Nelson Training Center is home to more than four hundred youthful offenders whom officials have judged trustworthy and mature enough to be housed in open barracks rather than cells, as they are at other Youth Authority facilities.

DeWitt was where Junebug was jailed in September 1993, the first time I traveled to Stockton to interview him. Eventually he would be transferred to a far more grim facility, but at that time it was assumed that DeWitt would be Junebug's home until his release sometime around the turn of the century.

Throughout the summer of 1993, I rushed to my mailbox like a father whose son was stationed overseas. "I feel compelled . . . to contribute to your work," Junebug had written to me in response to a letter proposing this book, "for moral reasons and also for my sense of 'guilt.' I have realized that no power on earth can bring that young man back, but at least I can provide assistance for others to somehow curb what's happening nationwide." His subsequent letters were like pages torn out of a private journal—intense, intimate, and painful.

In a four-page letter penned in late August, he wrote, "My only emotion has been anger lately, no tears, no nothing. I abstain from food a lot, like a small amount of self-inflicted torture. I realize that I often feel guilt when I'm hurt, like it's my fault even when it's not."

In another letter he wrote, "I never outwardly blamed my dad. I suppressed a lot of anger and refused to believe that I somehow subconsciously hated him. I reject all male figures, even today to a certain extent. . . .

"I accept full responsibility for *my* actions, but if I had had a father figure in my life, one who was attentive to my needs and gave me a stable presence, I can safely say that my life would have definitely turned out different. I will freely say that my dad has partial responsibility as well, for neglecting and abandoning me, even when I lived with him.

"I must stop here because the hurt and pain is returning, along with my anger at his neglect towards me. Hopefully we can continue this avenue of communication."

Increasingly I found Junebug bailing out of a topic ("to be more specific would require a face-to-face meeting," he would write). His time wasn't as obligation-free as one might suspect, and putting one's innermost thoughts on paper can prove frustrating, especially over time. So, two months after Junebug's first letter, I made my first of several trips to Stockton.

Our initial few minutes together were awkward, of course. Junebug would draw an analogy in a letter that would be awaiting me upon my return: "It's like writing a girl you've never seen before from the East Coast, then the next thing you know, she just flew in town yesterday and wants to see you.

"Probably a bad comparison, but at least I tried."

We were permitted to sit by ourselves in a locked conference room in the main administration building. I was asked to wear a shriek alarm around my belt—a button that, if pressed, would cause the entire facility to wail with alarms—but that was the only condition placed on our interview.

Junebug was six feet one, with a round, cheery face and almond eyes. He wore his hair in a Louisville cut, closely cropped to the scalp. He was remarkably skinny around the waist but had a bit of beef on his arms. He had delicate hands and slender fingers, which he kept politely folded on his lap.

He wore a pair of ill-fitting blue jeans and a state-issued work shirt, light blue with metal snaps, over a white T-shirt. His black shoes were rounded and plain. The green cloth belt he wore looked like it had been lifted from a stockpile of Boy Scout uniforms. To keep his pants up, he fastened the belt so tightly that it flapped when he walked.

Shortly into our first day together, he told me that he no longer wanted to be called Junebug. He would use his given name. John Jones, he said, was a name more suitable for a young man.

John was nineteen at the time of our first meeting. He still possessed that teen penchant for answering complex questions with "yups," "nopes," and "nuthin's." At other times, though, he came across as a mature young man, especially when he was dissecting his internal makeup. He laughed easily (like his mom) and often, but he also could sit and talk seriously about himself for long stretches at a time.

The wounded boy he had described in his letters often revealed himself. I heard it when he spoke of every slight, real or imagined, like his feeling of "betrayal" when his friend Aaron once failed to note his spiffy new wardrobe—a Derby jacket, voguish K. Swiss athletic shoes, a fashionable pair of overalls. Junebug would characterize his friend as jealous, but the truth was that Aaron was as clueless as a doltish husband who fails to note his wife's new hairdo.

The pain was apparent in his voice and bearing when he spoke of the duplicitousness of some adults. That the world was unfair was something he understood in his head but had not yet reconciled within his heart. He had written in one of his early letters, "My mom worked all day, my father was a nobody, and the neighbors hated us." In person he told me about a woman who had lived a few doors down and the angry lecture she had given him about his mother. In this woman's view, John's mother thought she was better than everyone else because she had a job.

"Why was she talking to me like this?" John asked, a wrenching look on his face. "I was just this little kid and she was a grown woman."

John took great pleasure in my ignorance of street slang and also the relative tameness of the life I had lived. At one point I mentioned that I hadn't started driving until I was seventeen because that was the law where I grew up. He, in contrast, had taught himself to drive when he was fourteen (he learned on a beat-up two-door Datsun he rented from a crackhead for twenty bucks' worth of rock). He had owned his own car when he was fifteen. I confessed that had I been driving under age in an unregistered car, I probably would have fainted dead away, that's how fast my heart would have been beating every time I saw a cop car. He laughed at my cowardice.

In a follow-up letter, he wrote that until meeting with me, he had never realized how distinct his world was from the one most of the rest of us inhabit.

When John spoke of the murder, he tended to use euphemisms, such as "my case," or "when what happened happened." Yet at the same time, he recognized that he tended to sugarcoat his deed through vagueness. In one letter, for instance, he wrote, "I made the mistake of choosing street justice to solve my problem." Then he clarified himself, stating

that by "street justice" he really meant that he had murdered an innocent boy.

John swore he had intended to have a fistfight that night. He said he
had been leaning into the door to muscle it open—the only way to open
the passenger-side door in Aaron's wreck of a car—when suddenly he
heard a gun going off. His first thought, he claimed, was that the kids on
the corner were shooting at *them*. Then he looked behind him and saw
the muzzle flash. He remembered looking over at Aaron and wondering
what was going through his friend's head. Aaron looked exactly how he
felt: shocked.

John was inclined to see a bright side in his incarceration, albeit at
a horrific cost. "I'm sorry Kevin Reed had to die when he was, in fact,
an innocent, but I believe this all happened for a reason," he said. "If I
wasn't here, I'd be dead or I'd have another murder hanging over my
head. It was like the only way for me to get out of that life was to end
up here."

Before his arrest, John blamed everyone but himself for Kevin's
death. 'Tone had pulled the trigger, so it was 'Tone's fault. Aaron had
known there was a gun in the car, and he had heard Junebug's angry out-
burst before they drove back to Auseon and Dowling that final time.
Why hadn't he stopped him? And then there was John Banks. Hadn't he
lit the fire that destroyed so many lives?

"I felt on the defensive because everyone was laying this on me," he
said. "I didn't feel I deserved all the blame by myself."

With time, however, he would accept most of the blame for the murder. "I don't blame Tony for anything," he said. "I take responsibility for
what I did. I was in the center of it all, not him. What happened, it can't
be changed. What we all have to do now is move on."

John, however, wanted London and Shannon to share at least some
of the blame. Early on he wrote, "With all due respect to the victims, it
seems to me as if no one took the time to analyze the fact that I was alone
when I was attacked by six people armed with metal pipes. I took on the
form of street justice, which was wrong, I admit. But had I not been a fast
runner and thinker, I would have been a sure homicide victim."

An overstatement, perhaps, yet it is instructive that just as John exag-
gerated when he spoke of six boys with pipes when it was just one, Thiem

underplayed the initial attack by referring in his log to the "stick" with which London hit Junebug, as if it was a mere twig snapped from a tree.

John anticipated every court date like someone looking forward to the holidays or a birthday. He'd be so nervous the entire day, he'd find himself shivering. He'd have to calm himself down so that he wouldn't sit there shaking in court. He paid rapt attention to every word that was said. He knew who Annette Reed was without being told. He could tell by the way she looked at him.

He'd go to and from court in vans, shackled around his ankles and his wrists. One guard explained to him why they chained him so tightly: "It's because you jackrabbits run too fast." By "jackrabbits" he assumed that the guard meant black kids.

John remembered being excited when he learned that he had been assigned a lawyer. He would finally get his chance to tell someone how Brian Thiem had denied him a lawyer when he asked for one. He started to tell Bill Daley his story, but he said Daley cut him off. "I already know what happened," he quoted Daley as saying.

"He'd ask me, 'How you doing, you want a phone call?' " John said. "That was it. He seemed to be in a hurry to get to his next case, like this wasn't very important work he was doing.

"The only reason I didn't see about how you could change lawyers is my mom was telling me to have faith in God. He'll make everything all right, she'd tell me."

He cringed when Daley told him he would have to cop to first-degree murder in exchange for a Youth Authority commitment. To John, first-degree murder was cold-blooded and calculating, while the crime they had committed was ill-conceived and slipshod. When he resisted, he said, Daley lost his patience. What difference does it make, so long as you don't end up in the state penitentiary? he supposedly demanded.

John remembered the day he entered his plea—April 8, 1992. That October he learned that he had been accepted by the Youth Authority, but until his hearing before a Youth Authority sentencing board, in early January 1993, he fought off the worry that Youth Authority would only be a first stop before being transferred to corrections to serve the rest of a twenty-eight-to-life term. The hearing wasn't much to talk about—it lasted maybe fifteen minutes—but it allowed him a huge sigh of relief. His release date was set for January 1999, two months before his twenty-fifth birthday.

DeWitt is considered "soft" compared to other prisons within the Youth Authority system. The facility built next door, the N. A. Chaderjian School—"Chad," to inmates and staff alike—is a gladiators' school by comparison. Chad was designed to house those juveniles the system has deemed incorrigible.

Chad's stated capacity was six hundred inmates when it opened in mid-1991, but by 1993 its census exceeded eight hundred. Inmates are locked in cells like at high-security adult facilities. Educational programs and vocational training are offered, but where at DeWitt they push a kid to get his high school diploma and learn a trade, at Chad their preoccupation is with avoiding bloodshed between warring gangs. Anything can spark factional warfare at Chad, according to Eddie Jeffs, the facility's gang coordinator: the flashing of a gang signal, a perceived slight, a hostile stare. Rioting is commonplace, as are "shankings"—stabbings with makeshift knives. According to Jeffs, there's nothing those in charge can do to stop the gang violence inside Chad, so they do what they can and hope things don't get too out of hand.

Chad isn't considered the roughest facility within the Youth Authority system. The Youth Training School in Chino, home to some sixteen hundred inmates, wins that dubious distinction. The trend within youth corrections circles nationwide has been a move to smaller facilities with no more than a few dozen inmates. The juvenile justice system in Massachusetts, considered a shining light by more liberal-minded reform advocates, offers a diverse range of programs and facilities operated by private providers under state contract. Studies show that Massachusetts spends no more per inmate than California does, yet where Massachusetts can boast a recidivism rate of less than 25 percent, California's rate ranges somewhere between 60 and 90 percent, depending on whose numbers one believes.

Chad is the threat counselors hold over your head at DeWitt. A single fight won't land you there—unless you use a weapon such as a "slung-shot" (a sock stuffed with a lock, batteries, or other heavy objects). Numerous fistfights, though, would earn you a spot at Chad, as would repeated thefts or too many consecutive months as a "program failure," meaning you've flunked your high school course work or you've proven yourself unable or unwilling to learn a trade.

The gangs long ago declared DeWitt neutral turf. The kind of thing that would incite a brawl at Chad—say, greeting a Blood with "Hey cuz," when that's the salutation of their sworn enemy, the Crips—would probably prompt nothing more than harsh words at DeWitt. At Chad, you'd never see a Fresno Bulldog (a Latino gang that sides with the Nortenos) socializing with someone who rides with the Mexican Mafia, which sides with the Surenos. Yet at DeWitt, it's not uncommon for kids who would be archrivals on the outside to fraternize with one another. The unwritten rules at DeWitt dictate that blacks, whites, and Latinos can socialize with one another, yet these same codes forbid you from eating with someone outside your race.

Like the majority of inmates at DeWitt, John belongs to a prison gang. He claims "415" (until recently the area code for the entire Bay Area), but he endured no initiation or any hardship to earn his way in. He was a black kid from Oakland, so his affiliation with 415 was assumed.

At DeWitt, those not affiliated with a gang are picked on, but the harassment one must endure doesn't compare to surviving Chad without the protection of a gang. At Chad you'd be beaten and preyed upon, forced to pay in goods and canteen chits for basics like using the shower. Lacking an affiliation at DeWitt would make you more vulnerable to an attack, but your main worry would be the people of your own race treating you as an outcast. Supreme White Power is the worst about harassing the white kids who refuse to join its ranks. John figured that's because the whites, accustomed to being in the majority, are outnumbered by the blacks and the Latinos, so every potential member counts that much more.

There are plenty of potential land mines even at a facility like DeWitt, but John said there was nothing he couldn't handle. The secret, he said, was to maintain your emotional distance. You could goof around with people, but you didn't reveal too much of yourself. When in doubt, a standoffish and aloof pose was your safest bet. The bottom line was you trusted no one.

A far more difficult universe to negotiate, John said, was the relationship between the inmates and the staff. One year into serving his sentence at DeWitt, he said, he still didn't know what to expect of these people whom the bureaucracy called "counselors" rather than guards. They invited you to confide in them, he said, but when you shared some grievance with them, they'd tell you, "What do you expect, you're in jail." He didn't help himself when he developed a crush on the female counselor to whom he was assigned.

John had been at DeWitt a little under a year when he got his first two write-ups within one week of each other. Both centered around this counselor, who by then had become an object of complaint whenever John spoke with his mother. The second write-up was the far more serious one. John had exceeded the time limit on the phone (an inmate in good standing is permitted four ten-minute collect calls per month). His counselor instructed him to wind it down, but John kept on talking anyway, so she cut the phone dead. He called her a "bitch" and violated a cardinal rule when he walked into the small security booth where she sat. That area is strictly off-limits to an inmate.

His punishment was a night in the "wet room." As is procedure, he stripped down to his underwear and spent the night under constant video surveillance.

Those in charge diagnosed John as having a problem dealing with authority, among other problems. In his six-month evaluation, the head counselor in his barracks had written, "John has few life skills and needs to deal with daily stress better." He complained that John was "a real leg clinger," by which he meant he was overly needy.

Ironically, John had sought guidance to help him better cope with his incarceration. DeWitt offers anger management classes, but even though John signed up for them, his request was rejected because those who are closer to their release date get first priority. He sought individual counseling, with little luck. DeWitt has a staff psychologist, but he doesn't have the time for much one-on-one therapy. Mainly he spends his day keeping up with the crush of paperwork required by the state.

The therapist's job falls on the counselors, who are required to run weekly, one-hour group therapy sessions for the ten to twelve wards under their charge. The problem, according to Carolyn Horn, the top parole agent at DeWitt, is that the skill level among the individual counselors varies widely. Some are adept at fostering meaningful dialogue while others stick to teaching practical skills like filling out a job application. Apparently, John's counselor fell into this second category; the discussion never delved deep enough for his taste. Usually they'd talk about general topics, such as racial tensions and how to get along better with your fellow inmates. Moreover, he figured that his counselor had held only about five sessions in the previous six months, despite the requirement that they be held weekly.

John had already earned his high school diploma by the time of my first visit, and his academic potential had made quite an impression on the staff. During a tour of the school facilities, several teachers and administrators remembered him without having to look up his record. They praised him as an able student who had earned good grades.

In the mid-1980s, administrators at DeWitt invested the money to create a college-prep curriculum that would offer inmates the equivalent of a community college degree. The program was started for promising young men like John, one of its architects told me. But by the late 1980s the demands for newer and more secure institutions crowded out this and other programs that only "coddled" violent offenders.

Those in charge in Sacramento feared that a great many people would want to know why their tax dollars were being spent allowing murderers and other violent offenders to earn college credits. Not surprisingly, the college-prep curriculum was one of the first casualties of the budget woes that would dominate Sacramento politics in the late 1980s. High school teaching slots were eventually cut as well. According to John, by the time he began the high school program in 1992, the staff was spread so thin that teachers rarely if ever lectured in class or led discussions. Instead they sat at their desks grading papers while the students filled out assignments, like learning through a correspondence course. John received good grades, but he didn't think he had learned much.

Of the Youth Authority's eleven facilities, three were offering college-prep course work at the time of John's graduation. Two were off-limits to him because they were solely for those who were tried as juveniles, and John's case had been remanded to the superior court. The third was the Youth Training School in Chino, the facility that stood out as the roughest in the system.

John was also barred from the federal prison system's college-prep program that was a refuge for a small number of DeWitt inmates each year. He had been convicted of murder and his jacket indicated a gang affiliation, either of which would disqualify him from participating.

Instead of college-prep work, John was spending his mornings making sandwiches in the kitchen and his afternoons cleaning the day room. The rest of his day was spent watching television, playing dominoes, reading books, or listening to music. John signed up for an Apple computer repair program, but there were no available slots. He was instead assigned to the welding vocational training program, which at least meant that he no longer had to make bologna sandwiches or push a broom. He jumped at the chance.

When an inmate is approximately six months from his release date, he's eligible to work off-site, Carolyn Horn told me, "in the culinary arts, on mobile home repairs, and with other private corporations we've made arrangements with in the community." Horn was particularly proud of this work furlough program. Its strength, she said, was that it eased a ward back into the real world. However, a counselor I chatted with described the program in a far more cynical tone. He said he wasn't sure whether "washing dishes at a Denny's or other crap jobs" would help a kid make the transition back into the world or just piss him off about the lack of opportunities available to him once he had served his time.

Our letter writing—or, more accurately, John's letter writing and then mine by default—fell off after my initial visit. For a while I wrote to him two or three times for each of his letters, but after I slowed my pace, he surprised me one Saturday evening with one of his precious collect calls. He hadn't heard from me in a few weeks, he explained, and he was worried that maybe something was up.

Our final session, which fell on John's twentieth birthday, in March 1994, was our only bad meeting of the four. Part of the problem was that Carolyn Horn, who had been away from the office during my earlier visits, sat with us "for safety reasons," and we both resented the intrusion.

Despite her concern for my safety, Horn left the room at least ten times, including the thirty minutes she was gone for what I presumed to be her lunch break. I was left without my shriek button, which by then had become something of a joke between us. You come at me with one of these pens, I would warn him, and I'm pushing the button for sure.

Another problem was that I made the mistake of telling John too much about the harsh light in which 'Tone had characterized him. I wanted his version of some stories Tony had told me, but by the time I left, John was plainly agitated. He put up a brave front—"That boy needs *serious* help if he really believes this"—but it was obvious that I had churned up feelings for which he'd have no outlet except in a brief conversation with his mother.

The previous month, John had gone before the parole board for his annual review. Except for his two write-ups near the end of the summer, his record was clean. The juvenile parole board will slice a maximum of ninety days off your sentence in any given year; John was granted a two-month reprieve, making his new release date November 1998. Yet there was no guarantee that he'd benefit from this decision. Junebug had pleaded guilty to first degree, and a premeditated murder conviction meant that his was a "governor's review case." The governor's office would have to approve his release even if only one day before January 1999.

Things seemed to be going OK for John that spring. He transferred to a new unit, which meant that he could start fresh with a new counselor. He would finally be getting the group therapy he sought, because this barracks offered what the institution called its "Wounded Child" program. Then I heard from Ann that John had been transferred to Chad. There had been no hearing, she said, but instead his transfer was declared an emergency. While at DeWitt in March, people in charge had told me how well John was doing, yet now he was deemed so dangerous as to merit an immediate transfer to Chad?

What exactly occurred is difficult to say. Officials at DeWitt declined comment—Carolyn Horn would only confirm that there had been no hearing—so there is only John's word and the story as another counselor at DeWitt told it to Ann. She was told, Ann said, that John had again threatened his former counselor, and that he was moved because John was causing her tremendous stress. John said nothing could be further from the truth: "I tried to leave the hall for over a year, but she refused to transfer me, saying—and I quote—'don't leave, we can work this out.'

"If I was so much of a threat, then how come she continually took it upon herself to keep me in the hall?" Months later he was still so frustrated that he never granted a hearing to tell his side of things. He lost the good time he had earned and, he said, felt scarred by the false accusation. He felt that because he was black, those in authority assumed the worst about him without so much as asking him for his version of events.

Yet six months into his time at Chad, Junebug's transfer seemed to have been for the best. "I'm surrounded by supportive staff, and the dorm [a cell block, actually] in general is very sociable," John wrote. He joined a murder support group—finally participating in the group sessions he had coveted. ("It has helped me realize the seriousness and tragedy of Kevin's death," he wrote. "The group is VERY POWERFUL.") He earned his certificate in Chad's warehousing program, including a forklift operator's license ("I am so proud of myself!"). He was getting paid five dollars an hour by a private firm to stitch logos onto clothing—though more than one third of the money he earns is taken by the state to defray incarceration costs and for a victim restitution fund.

"Don't worry about me," John wrote in his first letter to me following his transfer, "I tend to be persistent and persevering."

26

AARON

Aaron was found guilty of first degree murder in juvenile court two months after his arrest. There was no hearing to see whether he should be tried as an adult. He was sixteen when he was arrested but fifteen when Kevin was killed. Under California law at the time, kids fifteen or younger when they commit an offense cannot be tried in superior court no matter how grievous the crime.

There's no plea bargaining over charges within the juvenile system, nor are there any jury trials. It used to be that there were no DAs or defense attorneys, either, only probation officers and a judge, but in the mid-1970s, state lawmakers redesigned the juvenile justice system so that it more closely resembled the adult courts. Aaron was represented by a private attorney named Dan Horowitz, a loose cannon but a real comer within the criminal defense bar.

"I knew all I had to do," Horowitz said, "is ask Aaron what happened, and he'd show all this emotion and pain and gain the judge's sympathy. He truly was a remorseful kid, a good kid." In court Aaron told the judge, "I guess there are people who are like used to this. Go and shoot at somebody. But I was like—I kept it. It stuck with me. Like I felt all guilty inside. It gave me nightmares."

Horowitz told Aaron to cry when he was on the witness stand, but Aaron couldn't do it. Even when he attended the funerals of several friends in the past he never shed a tear. "I'm just not an emotional person in that way," he told his lawyer. He worked hard at not slouching his way through the hearing because he didn't want to come off as looking indifferent. He was a fidgety teenager who had to constantly remind himself to sit erect in his chair.

Aaron seemingly caught a break from the judge on the case, Saundra Armstrong. Armstrong found him guilty of first-degree murder, but she recommended that he be committed to VisionQuest for two years. VisionQuest is an innovative wilderness program founded on the traditions of the American Indians. It's more like Outward Bound than the boot camp–type programs in vogue. Kids split their time between a base camp in a remote region of Arizona and riding a wagon train through various parts of the Southwest. The idea is that this radically different environment that demands self-sufficiency will help build a kid's self-esteem.

VisionQuest, however, rejected Aaron. The program keeps no records spelling out their reasons why, but rarely do they accept kids who've been found guilty of premeditated murder. By the time the case was kicked back to Armstrong, then-president George Bush had elevated her to the federal bench. The case fell to Judge Wilmont Sweeney, head of the juvenile court system. Sweeney is renowned throughout the flatlands as a tough and unyielding judge who might have given Aaron a break on a drug charge, but never a violent offense. Sweeney sent Aaron to the California Youth Authority's northern California reception center, where he appeared before the juvenile parole board that determines a kid's target release date.

Aaron again paid a price for his lack of tears. You didn't show the proper remorse, one of the hearing officers said. "I told them what happened, but they said they didn't believe me," Aaron said. "They started talking among themselves, like psssst—psssst—psssst—and then used these big old words I didn't understand. And then they said, 'We'll give you a release date of '98,' which is seven years. And I was like, 'Damn.' "

Aaron didn't know what to expect at the Youth Authority but he was frightened just the same. He had heard his share of stories and seen

enough television to have nightmares about everything from gang war-
fare to rape. But Aaron found that it wasn't that bad. He was sent to the
O. H. Close School, another of the four institutions that are part of the
Northern California Youth Center in Stockton.

A man named Hal Baker greeted me when I arrived at O. H. Close to
meet with Aaron. Baker described himself as a former military man who
had dreamed of teaching history but somehow ended up as the top parole
agent at a Youth Authority facility designed for juveniles seventeen years
old or younger. The kids locked up inside O. H. treat him with respect
and fear, he said, because they recognize the "juice"—the power—of his
position. He was a smallish, balding white man in his fifties, but he threw
around terms like "homeboy," "the 'hood," and "dissing" (disrespecting).
I imagined the rolling eyes of the black and Latino kids under his charge.

In the old days, Baker said, he would sit down with every newcomer
to his facility and explain that one's stay at O.H. didn't need to be wasted
time—you can earn your high school diploma and work on personal
issues in the various programs the institution offers. But those sessions
were from a time long past, before lawmakers in Sacramento decided to
put less into programs so they could spend more on expansion and security. The job below Baker's was cut, as were any number of positions
throughout the facility. Baker no longer gives his pep talk, he said,
because he no longer has the time. Besides, he can no longer boast
about that same range of programs, because many no longer exist.

The only other facility in the California juvenile system that accepts
wards seventeen or younger is the Fred C. Nelles School, in southern
California. "No place you'd want to be" is all Baker would say about
Nelles. The worst that happens at O.H., he said, is a kid hits another
ward with a slung-shot. In contrast, Nelles is known for its gang rum-
blings, its shankings, and other problems endemic to Chad.

Aaron was much stockier than I had pictured him to be. He was
small—five feet five—but he was solidly built. He seemed to have
beefed up considerably since he was first incarcerated. He wore a blue
nylon jacket over a white T-shirt, and prison-issued jeans that fit only if
he cuffed the pant legs several times. We sat in a small office down the
hall from Baker's, where we were permitted to sit by ourselves so long as
the door remained open.

Aaron had responded to my initial letter with a brief missive written memo style—From: Aaron Estill—saying he was too busy to write but invited me to come out anytime I'd like. He greeted me with his eyes averted and a limp shake of the hand. Yet within minutes of our sitting together by ourselves, he was a chatty and likable young man, buoyant, excitable, and full of energy. He smiled often, a crooked, toothy smile with dimpled cheeks. He mimed out the more dramatic moments in his life, like the story of his getting kicked out of Elmhurst Middle School for pushing the vice principal's arm away when she grabbed him. He put his best what-you-messing-with-me-for look on his face as he pretended to push her arm away. He grabbed his own shoulder—as the vice principal had apparently done—and screwed up his face into a scowl that was a mix of surprise, anger, and hurt.

"Why was she putting her hands on me?" he asked. "I just had to pee real bad. Did she expect me to pee in my pants?"

Aaron would drop his brow when he told a story that made him angry. A scowl—a look of utter and complete distaste—would appear on his face when he was indignant. His feelings were equally transparent when speaking about painful issues, such as his father's absence through most of his life. He often slumped in his chair as we spoke, and he too showed a penchant for "nopes" and "yups," but he maintained eye contact throughout and spoke candidly about his life prior to the murder and the circumstances that landed him inside.

"Me and Junebug, we were like the squares on the block," he told me at one point. As incredible a statement as that may seem, compared to the rest of Fat 'Tone's crew, he was probably right.

"Maybe it's best that I'm in here," he said. "Maybe if I had been smarter, I could have beat it, but I don't regret getting caught or telling what happened. It was like getting it off my shoulders. I might be dead now, you never know."

Aaron said he had believed that they were driving over to Auseon and Dowling the night of the murder to have a fistfight. He had known there was a gun in the car, but he hadn't figured that they'd be shooting at anybody. As John had said, he had looked on the gun as insurance, a hedge against one of their foes pulling a piece.

"It was so stupid," he said. "It was never thought out. Nobody ever thought about it. It just went so fast."

I asked Aaron why he hadn't asked something like, "Hey, what's the plan? What are we fixing to do here?"

"That's what I *shoulda* said," he replied. "But remember what you were saying about Junebug saying he didn't want me to think of him as being a coward? That was like me. When we drove past the first time, I shouldn't have even said I would go over there again. But it was my friend, so I felt I had to ask, 'What you want to do?' You care when your best, best friend tells you he was beat up and some guy [almost] hit him in the head with a pipe.

"I can't say I wasn't thinking," he said. "I was thinking. But nothing was clear in my head. It was poor decision making. I didn't talk when I should have said something. That's what I can say."

After a lunch break, Aaron handed me a sheet of paper ripped from a bound notebook. "Rest in Peace My Folks" he had written in a loopy, neat script across the top of the page. It was his running list of the people he knew who had been murdered. He had twelve names on his list.

His latest addition was his friend Chris Tolliver, who had been shot to death a few months earlier. I knew of that murder; it had made the papers because Chris was killed after he and his friends drenched a girl in a passing car with a Super Soaker squirt gun. She fetched her boyfriend, who later that night shot Chris dead. He was a twenty-one-year-old who had become a father only a few weeks earlier. He worked at an office machine company and dreamed of becoming an aircraft mechanic.

According to his list, Aaron knew no fewer than six people killed in 1992. Chris Leggins, nineteen, sold crack on Eighty-ninth Avenue. A little kid was riding his bike up and down Eighty-ninth on an evening Chris's crew was expecting trouble, so they chased him off the block. One of the kid's uncles retaliated by spraying the corner with gunfire. A bullet struck Chris in the head.

Two weeks later, Douglas Sneed, twenty, was accidentally shot by another friend of Aaron's, age sixteen, while they were driving around Oakland. The sixteen-year-old was messing with a .38 in the backseat, the gun went off, and Douglas was dead, a bullet wound in the chest.

Jermaine Brown, sixteen, was killed while arguing with two men. Eugene LeBranch, eighteen, was killed when he was struck by a bullet meant for a friend. Thadius Glover, nineteen, was gunned down at three in the morning while working a corner known to the cops as a drug hot spot. He was killed despite the bulletproof vest he was wearing, so Thadius represented one of the rare instances in which an anonymous black kid's death merited mention in the area's largest newspaper, the San Francisco *Chronicle*.

A couple of times Aaron used one of his allotted collect calls to talk with his father. His father had served hard time, so Aaron figured he might get something out of it. Every time they spoke, though, Aaron ended up regretting the call.

"He doesn't talk to me like he's trying to help me," Aaron said. "It's like he knows I'm mad at him, he knows I have anger against him, so he tries to sum it up: 'You're my only son, why you trying to be this way toward me?' But that just stresses me out more.

"It'd probably be easier if I just didn't talk with him no more."

Hal Baker figured that at any given time there were at least forty kids under his charge whom he wished he could transfer to one of the system's college credit programs. In the fall of 1994, Aaron was one of them. Baker described him as bright and likable with a potentially promising future. He even violated the rules on Aaron's behalf, permitting him to stay until after his nineteenth birthday, even though technically Aaron should have been transferred once he was no longer seventeen.

"He's doing well in the program here, and he's close to finishing [high school]," Baker said. "We see a risk in transferring him out."

Baker had filled out the requisite paperwork for Aaron's transfer to a college-prep program, but that only meant that his name was added to a long waiting list. Baker had resigned himself to transferring Aaron to DeWitt, upon completion of his high school program, when he learned that the Ventura School had an opening.

Ventura might be the jewel of the Youth Authority system. Its program is tied to Ventura Community College, allowing inmates to earn an associate's degree, but it's also six or seven hours from Oakland by car. His mother and his brothers, who between them would visit Aaron several times a month while he was in Stockton, couldn't make it down nearly as often. When I spoke to Doreatha Estill more than two months after Aaron's transfer, she still hadn't made her first trip to Ventura. She had planned on going down a few weeks earlier, but a big quake hit the Los Angeles area. She finally made it down in March 1994, three months after he had been transferred.

Doreatha told me that Aaron regularly spoke of withdrawing from Ventura. It was a strict and demanding program that was a long way from home. If he quit, though, he'd be labeled a "program failure," which might mean his transfer would be to Chad rather than DeWitt. I wrote him a letter arguing that he was trapped in the Youth Authority for five more years anyway, so he may as well use the time as productively as possible, but of course that was easy to say in the relative comfort of my life. I never heard directly from Aaron, but through Doreatha I learned that he was sticking it out, although he was making no promises.

27

(CDC#) H38804

There was a time when I could feel nothing but antipathy toward 'Tone. What was he thinking, shooting out the window of a moving car? He didn't mean to hit anyone, he had told the cops, but what did he think would happen when he shot six times into a group of teens? He was drunk, he had said, he was stoned. Yet those were reasons for *not* handling a gun, especially if his aim was to shoot above the kids' heads. He had killed a thirteen-year-old and injured two fourteen-year-olds. There was also the fate of Junebug and Aaron, and also what could have been. The case was a multiple tragedy, and he had been the one to pull the trigger.

Yet eventually I came to do any number of small favors for Tony. I bought him a new tape player when his broke. I got in touch with family members on his behalf. I would cajole his mother to drop a line. I called the prison in search of "lost" packages (inmates are permitted four packages per year plus one around Christmastime) that I suspected Tony's family had claimed to have sent but never did.

My first letter from 'Tone arrived two weeks after John's. Vera had just died. "yes i would like to help you as much as i can But i need you to help me cus you see my grandmom just past away on the 15th and my family is going through alot so all i need you to do is send my forthey dollars in a money order cus times is hard real hard."

I sent him the money. A couple of months later, I sent him three tapes as a goodwill gift just before I was to interview him. I sent him two more upon my return home because he had told me he loved music, and though he was permitted twelve tapes in all, he had only six, including the three I had just sent to him. In truth, I had spent something like ten hours listening to the intimate details of his life, and he had gotten under my skin.

His letters were never intimate glimpses into the soul like Junebug's, but I came to look forward to them no less. He'd call me collect every few weeks. I was always happy to hear his voice. When more than a month would pass between letters or calls, I found myself feeling anxious. He had killed a boy. He had destroyed any number of lives. He deserved to be punished, but despite everything, I felt sympathy for this oversize kid born with the odds stacked against him, trying to survive in circumstances that were the closest thing to hell on earth that my mind could possibly imagine.

The "gulag California," the San Francisco–based Center on Juvenile and Criminal Justice has called the state's ever-burgeoning prison system. If California were a country unto itself, it would lead the world in imprisonment as a percentage of the general population, the center found. As is, the incarceration rate throughout the United States rose so dramatically during the 1980s that it surpassed even that of South Africa and the former Soviet Union (though the Russian republic would regain that top spot in the early 1990s).

California spending on prisons grew tenfold between 1980 and 1994—from $300 million to $3 billion. During that same period, the Department of Corrections' share of the state's general budget grew from 4 percent to 8 percent, while higher education's share declined from 14 percent to 9 percent. Job-training programs for teens, school-based after-hours programs that might provide an alternative to life on the streets, and other initiatives that might help prevent crime have been similarly crowded out by what the center calls the "rogue elephant" of state politics. By 1994 California would rank last among the fifty states in student access to computers and other technologies (even though it is the home of Silicon Valley) and would have the dubious distinction of being first among the states in class size. The irony—the tragedy—is that while the state's inmate population increased more than sixfold in the sixteen years prior to 1994, the crime rate continued to follow its usual pattern of rises and dips.

Tony had been sent to the Calipatria State Prison, a brand new facility in the tiny town of Calipatria, two and a half hours east of San Diego and eleven hours from Oakland by car. The penitentiary was built on three hundred acres of fallow lettuce fields in a part of the state that had rival communities fighting each other for the right to have a prison (and its jobs) in their backyard. Designed to house two thousand prisoners, it was home to thirty-nine hundred before it was a year old. Prisoners were doubled up in cells measuring seven feet by ten feet, including the space taken up by two steel slabs that serve as beds, two more slabs that serve as desks, two metal stools, a toilet, and a sink.

In 1994 Calipatria was one of the state's newest maximum-security prisons, and arguably its most secure. That year it became the first prison in the nation to be surrounded by an electrified fence—the "death fence," according to newspaper accounts appearing around the country. It's not a fence, really, so much as strands of wire in a cat's cradle pattern, sandwiched between a pair of twelve-foot-tall perimeter fences topped with razor wire. You touch one of the electrified strands, you die. It's that simple.

Between 50 percent and 70 percent of the inmates imprisoned at Calipatria are there on a murder conviction. Despite a prevailing sense that as a country we are soft on crime, the average inmate is serving a fifteen-year-to-life sentence, according to a prison spokesperson. More than two hundred convicts are there on a "life without" sentence—life without the possibility of parole. The LWOPPS (pronounced "el-wops") are the worst kind of trouble, because they alone among the inmates have no reason to feel beholden to a biennial parole board hearing.

Guards with semiautomatic rifles stand perched above the inmates, either in the loftlike command area inside each cell block or on the rooftops outside. "There are no warning shots fired in the housing units," according to the orientation guide that the prison provides each inmate. "The first round will be for effect" (i.e., the sharpshooters will be aiming to hit you). If there's trouble outside during yard time, a warning shot is fired. Within moments, virtually every inmate is on the ground. That's because anyone still standing after the warning shot is considered a provocateur and thus needs to be "disabled."

At Calipatria Tony walked into the middle of a bloody and merciless war for preeminence between the Crips—a black gang—and the Mexican Mafia. Tony claims to have witnessed at least one bloody salvo in this ongoing war. He was hanging out in the yard when several members of the Mexican Mafia attacked with knives a lone Crip. The Crip failed to heed the warning shot—he was preoccupied with saving his life—but he was still standing and thus was shot by a guard standing on a parapet.

The stabbing was the third involving these two gangs, so the authorities placed the entire cell block of one thousand inmates on lockdown for nearly three months. Yard time—three hours per prisoner—was canceled indefinitely, as were Tony's GED classes, the prison's vocational-training classes, and other activities prison officials consider a privilege. Even meals were served inside an inmate's cell to reduce the potential for further retaliations. Every inmate was confined to his cell around the clock, except for showers.

Tony was transferred to Calipatria from Old Folsom, a penitentiary a couple of hours east of Oakland, when that facility was ratcheted down from a maximum- to a medium-security facility. He arrived at Calipatria three years to the day after killing Kevin Reed. It was July when he arrived, in a part of the state where the afternoon highs during the summer months routinely topped 115 degrees.

He hadn't been at Calipatria one week when he learned that Vera had died. He felt overwhelmed by grief and memories, but there was no one for him to confide in. He was still in orientation and his temporary cell mate was a Crip. By conventions determined long before either had arrived at Calipatria, they were natural enemies. He described the days following Vera's death as one of the worst two periods of his life. The other was the time he lived in the San Antonia Villa housing project with his mother and her abusive boyfriend.

In one of Tony's early letters, he wrote, "I relly want to talk to you. I have alot of true stuff to tell you that would be relly good for the Book, I know it will cus its true. I been wanting to talk to some one for a long time Because i don't want another person going through the same thing im going through so i willing to work with you."

His letters had the same slant-lettered, hurried look of a preteen writing home from camp, except that the outside of the envelope would always be stamped, "This mail generated from Calipatria State Prison." My name and address would be scrunched into the lower-right corner rather than centered. "G, How our you doing fine I hope as for me hanging in there," he'd almost always begin. For a time he would close with something written in block letters: "WRITE BACK" or "TAKE CARE AND GOD BLESS YOU" (after I'd sent him the forty-dollar money order). Messages would be scrawled in the top margin, or they'd cascade down into the free space at the bottom of a short letter.

Over the phone he sounded more mature and thoughtful than I had imagined, based on his letters. He had a man's voice, full but sad. Every time we spoke, at least in those initial few months, he embraced the reckless stupidity of his actions on the night of July 9. He seemed incapable of mentioning the murder without tacking on a heartfelt mea culpa. Alone among the principal characters with whom I had spoken, he didn't employ euphemisms when talking of the murder. He would refer to Kevin Reed by name. When once he referred to the murder as an "incident," he interrupted his thought to correct himself. "The night I killed that young man," he said more carefully.

"I know I did a murder," he continued. "It wasn't an incident. I killed a boy. I know that. Kevin Reed. I'm not going to try and hide it by calling it an incident because it was a murder and someone—Kevin—lost his life.

"There's no excuse for what I did. I'm really sorry, but I know sorry won't change that the boy died."

As a visitor, you enter the prison with nothing but your driver's license, a single key, and no more than thirty dollars in one-dollar bills. You're allowed ten photographs, a comb or brush ("non-metallic, no pointed ends, and no detachable parts"), baby items (two jars of unopened baby food, diapers, two bottles, and wipes), but no bandannas and no food.

The rules delineating what people are permitted to wear is strictly enforced. NO DENIM MATERIAL, said the sign announcing Calipatria's dress code, but when you arrive at the desk, you learn that the prison doesn't allow dark blue pants of any kind. Another rule states that you can wear "no clothing similar to that of the inmates and/or officers." At Calipatria, at least, the sergeant in charge of visiting interprets this to mean that because inmates wear blue jeans, dark blue slacks are forbidden.

On my first morning waiting in line to enter the visitors' room at Calipatria, a man appearing to be in his fifties stood a few spots in front of me. "No blue pants allowed," the guard told him nonchalantly.

"Now, do these look like blue jeans to you?" he asked. We had chatted in the parking lot while awaiting the start of visiting hours. He had left the Los Angeles basin at around one-thirty that morning with his mother and his daughter. They were visiting his son, whom he hadn't seen in more than a month. While he pleaded his case, a creeping feeling of panic seemed to be overtaking him.

"Go back to your car, sir, and—"

Hopeless. Like trying to convince an armed robber to leave without taking your wallet. The guard is an unforgiving judge, unsmiling in her khakis, unilateral in her judgment. In an exasperated voice that was both pleading and angry, the man said, "But I didn't bring no change of pants."

"Next!"

Tan and khaki green slacks are forbidden because those are the colors the guards wear. No shorts or skirts above the knee (or "high slits"); no tank tops, no halter tops, "no strapless, spaghetti straps, or bare midriff clothing"; no camouflage material, no transparent clothing; no "offensive writing or drawing on clothing."

Visitors are told none of this in advance. The rules are posted on the wall in the visitors' waiting area, but of course by then it's too late.

At least thirty minutes, but often more like an hour or more, passes between the time you arrive at the visitors' center and when your man is finally escorted in. Meantime, you stare into space because you're forbidden from bringing with you reading materials of any kind.

Tony had lost something like fifty pounds in the two and a half years since he had been locked up. He was a burly young man with rounded shoulders and a barrel chest. He had a full face with sad eyes behind a pair of steel-framed glasses he had picked since his incarceration. He wore a blue work shirt and a white T-shirt and prison-issued blue jeans. We sat at a small round table in a room that could accommodate forty or so inmates and their families. His nickname was no longer Fat 'Tone, he told me. He was now "Potbelly."

Tony's eyes blinked in wonder as he scanned the visitors' room. I was Tony's first visitor in the sixteen months since his transfer from the county jail to the state prison system. The children everywhere around the room drew his attention as much as a twenty-something woman wearing a leopard skin bodysuit and spike heels. Sitting there, he said, was disorienting, simultaneously awkward and exhilarating. The visitors' room is a small dose of the outside, and he seemed not there with me but instead remembering his former life outside the prison gates.

There was an overbearing sadness to Tony. Much of the time he sat slumped forward, as if the weight of his deeds caused his entire body to sag. He was forever shaking his head and harshly rebuking himself over the mistakes he'd made in his life.

"I was always so jealous of Junebug 'cause he was so smart," Tony said. "I was always wishing I could be smart like him."

He blamed no one but himself for his fate, although he does harbor considerable resentment that Junebug and Aaron will be released when they are twenty-five, yet he faces an indefinite sentence that might keep him locked up for life. "It'd be easy for me to blame my mother for everything, or to blame Aaron or Junebug," he said. "But I held the gun that night. I pulled the trigger." His mother, he said, tried to do the best she could. She was a woman whom he couldn't recall ever being happy.

Because he is locked away in a state penitentiary, Tony can neither receive mail from nor send mail to others behind bars, including those locked in a juvenile facility. So he asked me to send along a message to

Junebug: "Tell him I still love him. I'm not mad at him, I don't carry no grudge, I know he didn't make me get in the car." He also asked me to pass along a message to his mother after I told him I had finally tracked her down. He wrote, "Please let her know that I'm praying for her and I love her and I think about her all the time. I worry about my mother so much. I know she need help and I know if I was out I could help her. My mother mean so much to me."

On his arm he wore a tattoo with Vera's and Paula's names written inside a heart. To Tony, Paula was the hero of his life's tale. Toward Vera he seemed to feel a genuine fondness, although the sentiment seemed rooted more in gratitude than anything else.

He had several other tattoos as well, all of which he had done while still on the streets. One was of a bulldog wearing a cap with the number ninety-two written on it. Another depicted a Tec-9, smoke wafting from its barrel, with "Fat 'Tone" above it.

Despite the horror stories one hears about maximum-security prisons, Tony claimed that he'd had few troubles inside the pen. Rule number one of survival, he said, is mind your own business. The second is to confront every challenge as it comes.

Shortly after his arrival at Old Folsom, a Crip cut the line when he was next for a shower. Tony protested and the Crip upped the ante, calling him a "broken-assed nigger." Tony reacted without allowing himself time to think. "I hauled off and hit him as hard as I could right in the face," Tony said. He risked a write-up, which hurts when you go before the parole board, but he instantly calculated that a write-up is preferable to a reputation as a punk who buckles under when challenged. That's the one thing you can't afford to obtain in prison—a reputation as someone who can be taken advantage of.

"Anyone tries to rape me, man, I end up at Quentin," Tony said. That's a common expression within the California prison system. San Quentin is where death row inmates await their fate, including those sentenced to death for killing a fellow prisoner.

Tony was wishing he was still at Old Folsom, because of its proximity to Oakland and because it's a slightly more liberal facility. In Folsom he got six hours in the yard compared to three at Calipatria. There's also the quality of that yard time. There might be nothing a prisoner appre-

:iates more than yard time, but in Calipatria it's time under a brutal midday sun located in one of the hottest spots on earth.

Tony witnessed four stabbings in his first year at Calipatria, but he still feared the guards far more than his fellow inmates. Wherever you are, he said, whether outside in the yard or inside your cell, you notice the armed sentries patrolling above you. His one recurring fear, he said, is that he'll end up shot because he happens to be near two guys in a fight. Which of course is ironic, for it was a random shot that befell Kevin Reed, the innocent bystander Tony killed.

Despite what Junebug and Aaron claimed, 'Tone swore that their plan had been to shoot over the heads of the kids on the corner that night. When we met, he stuck to the story pretty much as he had told it to the police. He had handed the gun to Junebug, he said, but Junebug handed it back to him when they were parked a few blocks away from Auseon and Dowling. "I ain't fixed to kill nobody," he quotes himself as saying. The gun just got away from him, he said. In the hands of an inexperienced shooter, especially someone holding it one-handed as Tony was, a .45 would jump around wildly. Yet the bottom line was that he stuck a gun out of a car window and started firing on a group of thirteen- and fourteen-year-olds innocently flirting on a street corner. For that, there's no possible explanation.

"I can't tell you how many times I've asked myself how I could have been so dumb," Tony said. "Like every day. It's like I was always asking myself that question growing up. I was always getting into trouble by doing stupid shit."

His attitude when he first met Al Hymer was something akin to denial. He was anxious to get back to his life on the streets, and he expected the world from Hymer despite the position in which his taped confession had put his lawyer. He figured he should do no more than ten years, out in five with good behavior. It had been an accident, so he figured he was guilty of nothing worse than manslaughter.

As Hymer had predicted, something happened to Tony a short time into his incarceration. Between the breakup with his girlfriend and the preliminary hearing, he adopted a new outlook on life. He felt relieved to be done with the dope-selling life he had been leading. He had smoked so much pot that he had become crazy with paranoia. He'd felt sick from all of the alcohol he was drinking. It was as if he needed to dry out to see the world clearly.

He readily agreed to second-degree murder, but he came to regret taking the deal. More than guards armed with rifles or the brutal Imperial Valley sun, the affliction that eats away most at Tony is his indefinite sentence. His first appearance before a parole board will come twelve years into his sentence — in the year 2003. If past practices are any guide, he'll get out sometime around the year 2010. But there's a chance he'll be in for a lot longer. Who knows how a parole board will be thinking ten years hence?

Tony is young, which may help, but he killed a thirteen-year-old, which will hurt. Another factor is family ties — tenuous at best since Vera's death. The parole board will view this negatively. Tony's sister Angela has been the best about keeping in touch with him, but she's now in Hawaii with two small kids and their father. Studies show that a prisoner who receives regular visits is far less likely to end up back in the pen after his release as an inmate who receives no regular visitors. The eleven hours separating Tony from Oakland has thus far proven insurmountable.

Friends from the outside have disappointed him. His friend Fig, for instance, swore he'd send him a tape, but it never got there, and that was the last he heard from Fig. Even Paula has let him down. She's living in Hawaii working a full-time job and raising two kids, so he understands why she can't come to visit him, but he still wonders why she at least doesn't write more often.

"In my cell, I'll be thinking about people on the TV talking about someone doing a murder and how they should never get out," Tony said. "I understand that. There's no excuse for what I did. I'm really sorry, but I know that sorry doesn't help because it won't change the fact that that boy died. I know I deserve to spend time here. But don't some people deserve a second chance?"

Tony would call me collect every few weeks. His voice always resounded with a timbre so sad and lonely that, no matter what my mood when I picked up the phone, I was glum by the time I hung up. It always sounded like he was phoning from a crowded bus station, voices echoing in high-ceilinged cell blocks constructed from concrete. He mainly talked about his life inside jail. Often I didn't know quite what to say. He was upset that I hadn't told him that my father had died, even though we had spoken around that time. "I thought we was friends," he said, obviously hurt. Yet do you share your own burdens—or, worse yet, your joys—with someone who's been on lockdown for going on three months straight?

Tony attended school as often as he could. He liked his teacher at Old Folsom, but he got caught smoking a cigarette in the bathroom between classes and he was kicked out indefinitely. He started taking GED classes at Calipatria, even though it meant that he would miss out on yard time during the week. "My first teacher here was cool, he made you use your mind," Tony said. "But then he left when we's on that long lockdown. The guy we have now, he's awright, but he's been on vacation fo' the past two months and he still ain't coming back till next month." In the interim Tony was spending his days lifting weights in the yard, watching the small television every inmate is permitted to own, or listening to his music. In 1994 alone, his GED classes were canceled for eight of the year's twelve months.

For a time he said his dream was to earn his GED and then try to get into the prison's eyeware or car repair vocational program. But then he learned that because he has a "to life" tail on the end of his sentence, he's not eligible for any of the prison's vocational programs. The best he could hope for was a prison job that allowed him to put money on his books. He dreamed of becoming a youth counselor on the outside, despite the improbability of that goal.

With time I observed Tony growing up—or "maturing up," as he would say. In the spring of 1994, he changed cell mates because his old "cellie"—also there for murder, sentenced to twenty-five to life—sat around all day not doing anything. He was a cool guy, Tony said, but he wasn't enrolled in school and he didn't work. "He was always playin' with my head 'bout none of us there on a murder beef ever getting paroled," Tony said. "I didn't need that kind of shit going on in my home." He moved in with another guy from Oakland, also in for murder, but one who worked his job, faithfully attended church services, and generally minded his own business.

Less than six months after changing cells, Tony's new cellie would be in the prison infirmary after trying to slit his wrists.

"I've been tryin' to teach myself the difference between right and wrong," Tony said. "I'm trying to learn that I don't have to always be using my hands, because I can use my mind. It used to be like I used my hands if I wanted to get someone's attention, but now I'm trying to use my mind and my mouth."

A couple of months after my return from Calipatria, Tony sent me a letter in which he apologized for taking so long to thank me for the tapes I had sent him. "I'm truly sorry But i ran out of stamps and my mother gave my uncle some money to sent to me But he dident so i couldent go to the store.

"i can't get in touch with my aunt or my sister or my mom so i dont know what's going on, its like thay dont car about me, my uncle knew How Bad i needed that money and he still dident sent it.

"i had to borrow this stemp to write to you.

"i'm sorry for putting my problems on you.

"Gary, i hope that when you get done writeing the Book we can still be friends, thats if you want to."

28

THE GOOD SON

Demmell Reed was twenty years old in the winter of 1994, a thoughtful young man who had buckled down after his brother's death and was making something of his life. In his second year at a local community college, Demmell was bashful, sweet, awkward, and, more than anything else, diligent.

My first in-depth meeting with him came the day after I had returned from Calipatria. The confluence of these two events was sobering. I was telling people that Tony had struck me as a sincere young man, despite everything. Talking to Demmell for a few hours, however, placed my use of the word *sincere* in its proper perspective.

Demmell's future appeared bleak around the time of Kevin's death. He had never been much of a student, and he had been disqualified from participating in organized sports through the end of his senior year, after getting caught forging his teacher's signature on a change-of-grade slip. The one thing that had always spurred him to show up for his classes, high school athletics, now appeared off-limits.

Yet that summer Demmell earned all A's. He repeated the same feat again that fall. A guidance counselor had informed him that there was no way he would graduate in June, but that only served to spur him on.

He would arrive at school at 6:00 A.M. and stay after the final bell to pick up extra credits. He earned nine units that fall and then carried a full load the following spring.

"I made the honor roll that year," he said. "It's crazy that it took something like my brother getting killed to motivate me."

His sudden transformation that summer and fall won him a reprieve from the ban imposed on his participation in organized sports. Dermmell ran track that spring. He set a meet record in the three-hundred-meter intermediate hurdles at a Bay Area invitational; he took first in that same event at the city championship. That was the same tournament he had missed the two previous years because his grades were never good enough.

Teachers and school officials, Dermmell said, had always assumed the worst about him and his friend David, although to Dermmell's mind they were relative innocents. "We were going home and watching cartoons and playing with G.I. Joe, but they were treating us like we were out there grinding all night with gats in our pockets," Dermmell said.

For Dermmell, his senior year was sweet with the taste of victory over people's expectations. He graduated on time and was accepted at San Francisco State. He would attend college despite the naysayers.

His life was still anything but easy after his high school graduation. His financial aid package was less than he needed to make it through the year, and although he looked around for someone or someplace to lend him the difference, he came up empty. He dropped out only a few weeks into his first semester.

The truth was that attending San Francisco State frightened him. He felt he wasn't ready for a four-year college, but it was as if State had taken on a momentum all its own. "I didn't want to let my family down, especially right then," Dermmell said. "Everyone was real happy I got in, so I just went along with the flow."

He ended up going to Laney College, a two-year junior college in downtown Oakland. He carried a full load of classes while playing on Laney's football team. Money was tight and he thought about getting a job, but he concluded that work would be impractical.

"I really had to bust my butt as is," he said. "It's not like I'm this great student. So I knew it wouldn't be smart for me to work and go to school and play football."

He told no one at Laney about Kevin or, later, about Shannon. For a time he was without a place to stay, but he kept that a secret from everybody but the coach. He had vowed that he wouldn't use his family's tragedies as a crutch. He didn't want anyone feeling sorry for him.

After practice, he'd listen silently as his teammates bellyached about their lives and spoke about quitting the team. "Here they were, living up in the hills, driving their folks' Accord, everything going their way," he said. "You know, some of them actually ended up quitting. I'd look at them and think, You foolish, you don't know how good you got it."

During his first year at Laney, Demmmell was walking down the street when a young man sprinted across his path carrying a gun in his hand. The guy was heading for the launderette across the street. Demm-mell watched as the gunman unloaded his clip through the plate glass window. A young man—presumably the target—had walked into the launderette just before the gunman passed Demmmell but the shooter ended up hitting one lady in the back and another in the gut.

"I didn't know how to react to that," Demmmell said. "The guy didn't even see who he was shooting at. He just started shooting like he wasn't aiming at nobody. It was crazy."

The only time he contemplated giving up football, Demmmell said, was when he was between apartments and neither he nor his mother had a place to live. But his coach, Stan Peters, arranged for him to stay with another player's family until Annette could find them a more per-manent place to live. Peters looked on Demmmell as a polite young man with an excellent attitude, a very good defensive back who had speed, talent, and the proper work ethic. He was happy to lend a hand.

I first met Demmmell by the weight room at Laney College. He was a sweet-faced young man with a mustache, the hint of a beard, and closely cropped hair. He had the same gap between his two front teeth as his mother. He'd talk with me, he said, because maybe it'd be good to get everything off his chest.

"There's no one I really talk about any of this with," he said in a sad, plaintive voice. He shyly proposed one caveat. Would it be OK, he wondered, if he didn't talk about those minutes he was at Kevin's side before the ambulance arrived? He started to explain why, but of course that meant getting into the subject he didn't want to talk about. He became all tongue-tied and flustered, which made him look even sadder than when we were introduced ten minutes earlier.

When we met for lunch a couple of weeks later, I mentioned to Demmell that I had just returned from Calipatria, where I had visited Fat 'Tone. He was fascinated with my trip, if for no other reason than he had contemplated killing Tony. "That could've been me you were down there visiting," he said. Seeking revenge over his brother's death would have been foolish, Demmell allowed, but 'Tone's behavior defied words. Demmell had never gotten over, would never get over, 'Tone's readiness to shoot a gun on a friend's behalf.

"He didn't even know who he was shooting at—or thought he was shooting at," Demmell said. "He kills someone because his friend asks him to?"

The behavior of his erstwhile friend John Banks was also something that was still eating away at Demmell long after the fact. "We was close friends for a while," he said of Banks. "We were never up to much good. We'd cut school together, things like that. But I didn't think he was like that."

Demmell ran into him several times after the murder, but he said Banks ran away every time he caught sight of him. "I honestly believe my brothers would have taken his life before they took Tony's," he said.

Before meeting with Demmell, I had decided that Tony should be locked away through his twenties but should be released sometime in his thirties—with the condition that if he were ever convicted of another murder or any violent crime, he should get a life sentence without the possibility of parole. The early to middle thirties struck me as about right for a second chance, whereas incarceration into his forties seemed excessive for a mistake (albeit a fatally bad one) made at age eighteen. I broached this topic with Demmell, but he didn't want to hear any of it.

"I've lost my brother for life," he said. "He should get life."

"But that could've been you—"

He cut me off. "Ain't nobody got the right to take somebody else's life," he said. "Fifteen or twenty years just isn't enough. If you kill someone, you should be there for life." He said he's known guys who are in prison for murder, and he feels empathy for at least a couple of them, but his sympathies don't change his belief that a murderer—any murderer—should be locked away for life.

"I kind of came to grips with Kevin's death," Dermmell said. "Our family wasn't doing so hot. Our mother and father got out of the church, and God was sending us a message to get our acts together by taking the innocent one so that he don't take a life that can't be saved. I understood that one.

"But Shannon, I don't know what that one was about. I'm at school. Laney. My brothers—Curtis and Shannon—dropped me off that morning. They were supposed to pick me up, but nobody came. So I'm walking home mad, I'm walking over to my sister's house and I see a police car out front. For some reason, the worst feeling came over me. And I asked myself, Goddamn, who the fuck is it this time? I didn't ask myself what happened, I asked who is it. I walk in the house and my little sister was crying.

"I didn't know what to think. I said goddamn, I'm tired of this. I was angry at Shannon. Here was this little motherfucker who was actually telling *me* to keep my head up. He would tell me, 'Don't get down, Boo, you're in school, you're playing football, things are going good for you.' He'd be like, 'I'm out here younger than you, struggling in school, trying to get my grades together 'cause I want to wrestle.' He was a damn good wrestler, too. And smart. Him and Curt—both of them had a real head on their shoulders.

"He [Shannon] was the type who could get others to follow him. Sit down and talk to a kid and convince him of something.

"But it was like Shannon couldn't just let something go. We'd be out and there's some guy staring at us. And Shannon would be like, 'What the fuck he staring at?' I'd say never mind, what's it make a difference? I'm proud of that. I ignore that little stuff now. If we're out to have fun, let's have fun. Let's not worry about someone looking at us a little funny or bumping into us. Just walk away, just walk away from it. I was trying to teach that to Shannon.

"I tried to show him the right way to go. I thought it was working, but—

"I think about Shannon more than Kevin. I can't believe he would do something that stupid. It's just hard to believe that he's gone."

Dermmell often thinks about his two fallen brothers. He keeps a picture of each of them in his locker so he's sure to think of both of them before he takes the football field. He does that to motivate himself, but also for a dose of reality. Football is only a game, not a matter of life and death.

But unlike his mother and Curtis, Dermmell rarely spoke about either of his brothers, especially around family. Talking about them only makes everyone sad, he said, so what's the use?

"I want to move on," he said. "I get sick and tired of being sick and tired. I don't want to be sad all day. It's bad enough my mom has all the pictures up and I have to look at them all day. I don't want to hear about it all day, too."

He tries to be patient with his mother, he said, but they'll be talking about nothing in particular and suddenly she'll start crying. "I don't try and cheer her up because I don't think that's right," he said. "I don't go and pat her on the back and tell her it's OK. I figure this is her moment alone with her two sons and I leave her alone."

His way of remembering Kevin and Shannon is to stick with his plan to make something of his life. He was accepted at Brigham Young University as a junior transfer to their football program. "My family looks at me and sees hope," he said. "That's the main reason I've been working so hard. It's still one person trying, trying to get somewhere. That gives me motivation to keep on going.

"But it's a lot of pressure. If I fail, then what is there?"

ACKNOWLEDGMENTS

There would be no book without the cooperation of the people whose lives are chronicled within these pages. First and foremost, I would like to thank them for the trust they showed in me and for their remarkable candor even when discussing the most private or unflattering of events. All anyone ever asked of me was that I tell it like it is. I hope the final product justifies their faith and also their courage.

I am indebted to Lt. Mike Sims and Sgt. Brian Thiem of the Oakland Police Department for their openmindedness and also for the time and access they granted me. Special thanks to Susan Sawyer of the public defender's office, who steered me in the right direction in my search for a case that would allow me to explore the human side of this country's youth violence epidemic, and to her associate Al Hymer, for convincing me that Tony and his crew would serve me well in that endeavor. Thanks, too, to Sarah Andrade of the California Youth Authority and Danny Paramo at Calipatria State Prison for their assistance.

The work of a number of journalists helped shape parts of this book, although their work goes uncredited in the narrative. Notable among them were Mike McGrath, for his report on the crack trade in the East Bay *Express*; Bill Kisliuk, for his article on the flight of East Oakland's banks, also appearing in the *Express*; Michael Covino, for an excellent pair of articles on Felix Mitchell for *California* and his piece on the Reverend J. Alfred Smith in the San Francisco *Examiner*'s *Image* magazine; Rocky Rushing, for his report on Chad's gang problem for the Contra Costa *Times*; Jacqueline Cutler, for her articles on the city's middle schools for the Oakland *Tribune*; Alix Christie of the *Tribune*, for her column on the Buckner family; Mikki Turner of the *Trib*, for her column on Demmell when he was still a high school hurdler; Tom Goff, for his columns on the criminal justice system (and especially the coroner's office) for the Alameda Newspaper Group; and Sandy Close and

Richard Rodriguez, for their fine investigative report on East Oakland for the Pacific News Service.

Because of the nature of this story, I never had a chance to speak to a few people whose perspectives would have helped this book. Foremost among them is John Banks. A note, too, on fathers—'Tone's, Junebug's, and Kevin and Shannon's. I spoke at length with none of them. 'Tone's father was incidental to his son's life story (and no one knew how to reach him, either, except to say that he was among the sixteen million people who live in southern California); Junebug's father wouldn't consent to an interview; and Donald Reed—well, I asked every member of the Reed clan I spoke with to pass along the message that I was anxious to talk with him (no one had a number or address for him), but I never heard from him.

John Raeside, my editor at the East Bay *Express*, has been unflinching in his support of my reporting on youth violence, whether for the *Express* or this book. He also served as a second editor on this book and as my impetus for the last set of chapters. Thanks, too, to Nancy Banks, publisher of the *Express*.

I'm indebted to Al Abercrombie, Tony Thompson, Howard Pinderhughes, and Neil Henry, who provided comments and criticisms on a draft of this book. My appreciation also to Jeff Cohen, Eileen Drew, David Eifler, Mike Kelly, Tiffany Martin, Susan Matteucci, and Naomi Rivlin, maybe the greatest proofreader of them all (and definitely a great all-around mom).

I was blessed with an editor, Bill Strachan, who is all that an author could hope for: patient, critical, a Knicks fan, a friend. My agent, Elizabeth Kaplan, spurred me on from the time this book was only an amorphous notion in my head, understanding its potential as a book more clearly than I did.

And last, but certainly not least, I thank Denny Martin, for allowing this book to share our life and for putting up with my new repertoire of slang and my newfound fascination for subject matter I never mentioned in our wedding vows. She has been the best friend and wisest counselor a writer could hope for.